Novel and Society in Elizabethan England

David Margolies

CROOM HELM
London & Sydney

©1985 David Margolies
Croom Helm Ltd, Provident House,
Burrell Row, Beckenham, Kent BR3 1AT
Croom Helm Australia Pty Ltd, First Floor,
139 King Street, Sydney, NSW 2001, Australia

British Library Cataloguing in Publication Data

Margolies, David
    Novel and society in Elizabethan England.
    1. English fiction—Early modern, 1500-1700
    —History and criticism
    I. Title
    823'.3'09   PR836

ISBN 0-7099-3500-5

Printed and bound in Great Britain
by Billing & Sons Limited, Worcester.

CONTENTS

for Sandra

The view of literature as words that do something, rather than texts to be contemplated in static isolation, is uncongenial to formal literary studies, which may be why Elizabethan fiction is persistently neglected. Few of the works are in print at all and fewer still are available for general readers. It has attracted relatively little academic interest and even less serious academic attention. It does not lend itself easily to 'practical criticism' or 'great tradition' treatment, and most of it (with the usual exception of Sidney's Arcadia) cannot be absorbed into the preferred critical notions of the Elizabethan age. Although it can be studied as instances of historical consciousness, that misses its essential value: Elizabethan fiction not only reflected but helped to shape consciousness. It is for that reason I have chosen to study it, but also because it has a crude vigour and unselfconscious delight which seem to have been refined out of today's studied productions, and because no other literature in English so welcomes its readers -- in short, because I like it.

My study is based on all extant Elizabethan novels and most of the shorter fiction. I use the term 'novel' as a convenience for referring to extended works of prose fiction read for entertainment. I have invested in no particular definition of 'novel' and seek no quarrel with devotees of eighteenth-century fiction.

The order in which I discuss the main authors may be thought peculiar in departing from chronology. Because my interest is in the social role of the literature, and I have come to regard the Elizabethan novel as distinct from poetry and drama not just formally in genre but often in social orientation as well, I thought it reasonable to arrange authors with regard to the development of an oppositional culture; i.e. to discuss Nashe before Greene.

The highly individualised orthography of Elizabethan books, though it may convey vitality to those versed in the period, is likely to appear disturbingly 'quaint' to others. Thus I have modernised spelling, even of modern editions, expanded contractions and dropped typographic distinctions (e.g. italics) for proper names. But I have retained original capitalisation and punctuation because, without putting obstacles in the reader's way, they suggest the emphasis and oral style of reading of the period.

I should like to thank Sandra Margolies for both her criticism and her patience. And I am indebted to Eleanor, Harriet and Alexander whose responses to stories have reaffirmed for me that metaphor is a way of ordering existence and that fiction's importance is primarily as a model of the world we live in.

David Margolies
New Cross, London

1 INTRODUCTION

In an age of daring voyages, of the charting of distant seas and remote continents, the most important discoveries made by the Elizabethans were of themselves and society. People raised in a green world ordered by the seasons and rhythms of nature flocked to London and found a world that offered an unimagined wealth of social life, of experience, of modes of being.

Here were the palace, its law courts, Parliament, the city gilds and companies; here was diversity, a teeming thrusting population, a questing interest in novelty. Here were poets, churchmen, politicians, lawyers, pamphleteers. Here was money seeking an outlet in commerce, piracy and the gentler arts of peace. Never before in English history had there been such a concentration of wealth, talent and opportunity. (1)

They were not equipped for an intellectual understanding of that complex and changing society; yet their country background helped them to provide a feeling-coherence which no abstract thought could have created. The countrymen's sense of basic, material existence, transplanted to the fertile soil of London's social relations, blossomed into the richest metaphorical language.

The excitement of Elizabethan literature is the excitement of discovering the power of language. Through language the author can impose order on chaos. He exercises a power not himself which is yet an extension of himself -- it is magic. With a judicious turn of phrase, an incantation, a trick of words, the disparate elements of reality can be made to cohere. With words the author can re-shape the

1

world to his liking or stamp it with his own image.
Language has not yet been reduced to dried symbols
of reality; it contains the reality and words seem
real things. 'I have terms', said Thomas Nashe,
'. . . laid in steep in Aquafortis, and Gunpowder,
that shall rattle through the Skies, and make an
Earthquake in a Peasants ears'(2). Like a child
with a new Meccano set, the Elizabethans exhilarated
in their capacity for creation.

The Elizabethans' delight with language has
also a childlike unself-consciousness. Most Elizabethan fiction writers accepted the role of entertainer. Unlike Shakespeare in his sonnets or Spen-
ser in The Faerie Queene, they were not concerned to
erect timeless monuments of beauty and truth. Writers such as Greene and Nashe seem to have tossed
off a pamphlet practically at a single sitting.
Their works were not subjected to minute or careful
revision and whatever 'filed phrases' they produced
owed more to instant wit than careful filing.

The writers of Elizabethan fiction were not
constructing 'English Literature'; with few exceptions, they were producing toys to amuse an audience. When they finished a work it became the
printer's business; and when it ceased to be a
profitable business, the work was forgot. The
modern reader, accustomed to the great efforts made
to discover the picture beneath an over-painted Van
Gogh or the energy and sums expended by some Ameri-
can universities to acquire the original typescript
of a work known the world over in paperback, may be
shocked at the possibility of the pages of Nashe's
The Terrors of the Night ending up as binding material or being used to stop mustard pots; yet, however
regrettable such loss would have been, modern readers must not project their own concern for permanence onto the Elizabethan writer. Elizabethan fiction was not above life; firmly rooted in its own
time, it lost its relevance as times changed. It
was not inappropriate that a story gone stale should
serve to keep mustard fresh.

Fiction may well have been regarded by the
Elizabethans in the same way as cinema early in this
century. The hastily-produced films designed to
meet the moviegoers' endless appetite for entertainment, shot in a few days on a low budget, without the benefit of re-takes or re-editing, were
certainly not considered art -- they were vulgar
amusement. Once they had made the rounds and served
their money-making purpose, no further interest was
taken in them. They were not considered worth pre-

serving. Today, when a different generation (and class) of moviegoers recognises much of the early cinema as brilliant art and appreciates the exuberant use of a new medium, many films have already been lost or destroyed -- this in a century concerned with the preservation of works of art and redressing the carelessness other ages.

Elizabethan fiction is above all public. Of course it is not public in the same way as theatre, but the spirit is the same -- fiction was designed for an audience rather than private readers, and it was often intended to be read aloud. Even though the growth of fiction as a form may reflect growing individuality and a decline of collectivity (the readership is not a single present audience as for drama), the sense of a shared world still remains in the fiction of the Elizabethan period. It has not yet become a private activity where the work removes the reader from a public world into the private world of the author, for the author is not yet a creator of a private world -- his world is the public world. Unlike many modern writers, the Elizabethan fiction writer was not primarily producing self-expression but was creating for an audience. Even Thomas Nashe, the most individualistic of Elizabethan writers, sees his fellow writer, Robert Greene, in terms of serving his readers: 'he was a dainty slave to content the tail of a Term, and stuff Serving mens pockets'(I, p. 329).

The servant image of the author, although it may reflect traditional attitudes toward patronage, is more than an echo of an earlier period or a commercial posture. The author did perform a service for the reader, something beyond the primary function of entertainment. Sir Philip Sidney, an intelligent, coherent but not an original commentator on literature (and therefore one who may be regarded in a fair degree as typical), said in his Defence of Poesy that 'the ending end of all earthly learning being virtuous action', the poet is the best instructor, the 'monarch' of all human sciences, 'For he doth not only show the way, but giveth so sweet a prospect into the way, as will entice any man to enter into it'(3). Thus Sidney sees literature as active; the poet, beyond encouraging 'virtue', leads readers to practise 'virtuous action.'

In more modern terms, Sidney is saying that literature promotes recognition of choice, decision and consequently action on the part of the readers. Elizabethan fiction, like literature generally, makes order out of a diversity of material. It

takes experience -- events, what happened to characters, their attitudes, longings, fears, etc. -- and
forms them into a coherent pattern. This coherence
is not merely an aesthetic order, an abstract pattern; it relates to the world from which it is
taken. The authors of Elizabethan fiction give an
order to their own world. Action is evaluated
through plot; for example, the princess who pursues
her own desire to marry, contrary to the wishes of
her father, is justified by success. The significance for the lives of the readers is shown through
elaboration of the conflict, its values and implica-
tions. Thus the fiction places experience in social
perspective.

What was superficially the same narrative
material could be organised from different perspectives. Sidney's Arcadia, for example, serves as a
model for Emanuel Forde's Ornatus and Artesia (and
provides matter also for his later Parismus and
Parismenos). Forde borrows situations, events and
characters from Sidney; but whereas Sidney employs
the material to validate hierarchy, Forde indicates
the injustice that common people suffer at the hands
of the gentlemen. Sidney judges the actions of his
heroes ultimately in terms of the conduct of the
state; Forde presents chivalric action from the
point of view of those beneath gentle rank as well,
such as the shepherd imposed upon by the knight.
The popularisation of the European chivalric
romance, Peter Burke remarks, was not just a
'sinking' in the class of the audience. The romances of chivalry, which he assumes were originally
created for the nobility ('they deal with the adventures of the nobility, they present events and
people from the standpoint of the nobility, and they
express aristocratic values'), were not passively
accepted by creators of popular culture: 'In fact
they are modified or transformed, in a process which
looks from above like misunderstanding or
distortion, from below like adaptation to specific
needs'(4). Thus, even though most Elizabethan
novels seem in accord with Sidney's notion that
literature promotes 'virtuous action', some of them
present an image of virtue that Sidney could not
have accepted. There arises a body of work which
could reasonably be called an alternative literature
-- fiction written from a social perspective at
variance with the dominant ideology.

As well as offering a popular perspective, an
increasing number of works addressed the interests
of a popular audience -- disguising nobles as com-

moners ('under the habit of a Merchant Gentility cannot be hid', the eponymous hero of Henry Robart's Pheander, the Mayden Knight is told when his nobility is discovered, 1595 ed., sig. F2) or directly, presenting facets of the lives of artisans and tradesmen. 'When Cox of Coventry was collecting in the 1570s, there were no books available to him that attempted to reflect his own urban or trade interests or specialities. All this changed when the works of Thomas Deloney appeared between 1597 and 1600'(5). Although I would antedate the change by a decade, Margaret Spufford is essentially correct: Elizabethan fiction increasingly dealt explicitly with the concerns of a popular audience.

Beyond a change of subject matter, the nature of fiction itself involved an alternative attitude. The concerns of fiction were different in kind from those of drama or poetry. It confirmed the importance of the ordinary because it dealt for the most part with characters whose lives were composed of commonplace occurrences and were circumscribed by concerns similar to those of the audience. Austen Saker, for example, elaborates in Narbonus the details of his hero's relations with his family and then his daily life as a conscripted soldier, his wretched diet and makeshift sleeping arrangements. The ordinary, held up for the readers' observation, as of interest in itself and not just as a function of the plot, becomes thereby something that is worthy. Its inclusion in the narrative places value on the experience of everyday life. (While jest books also deal with the lives of ordinary people, they treat only isolated incidents -- bare plot without the elaborated context or character -- and thus lack this effect of the Elizabethan novel.)

Fiction gave a new value to the concrete life of the individual. Although Marlowe's Doctor Faustus, for example, may offer a more penetrating representation of the urge of individualism than any piece of Elizabethan fiction, it remains clearly a representation; that is, the metaphor of Faustus's rise and fall is recognised as something distinctly different from actuality. It is a presentation of experience that is at a level different from the audience's own experience -- a model that, because it is generalised rather than specific, cannot be actualised in people's lives. On the other hand, the experience of Robert Greeene's characters, of Thomas Deloney's, and even of Sir Philip Sidney's, is realised at an ordinary human level. When Greene has Pandosto demand that his cup-bearer Franion

poison Egistus, Franion's agonised consideration of
his course of action is filled with the detail of
concrete experience in a specific social context.
Sidney's construction of characters according to
ideal types and rules of decorum, consistent with
his view of literature, works only for his minor
characters, Jean Robertson points out: 'the
behaviour of the two princes, perplexed by the conflict between reason and passion, falls somewhat
short of the exemplary, and in so doing makes them
that much more credible as persons'(6) -- i.e. their
realism is dependent on their specificity.
Complexity of experience (and hence 'truthfulness')
is lost in a generalised argument and Sidney has a
'commitment to the particulars that only a mimetic
fiction can convey', says Joel Altman (7). And
conversely, the fiction involves a commitment to
particulars. When authors think the details of
existence, the stuff of every day, of sufficient
importance to embody them in literature, the lives
of ordinary individuals are validated.

Freed from the demands of large-scale heroic
action, from requiring a Tamburlaine or a Titus
Andronicus or a Falstaff, it was possible for Elizabethan fiction to organise its world on different
principles and give a different priority to concerns
of its characters. Emanuel Forde's reduction of
Sidney's eloquent exposition of courtly and humanist
virtues to an artisan perspective makes the concerns
of the petty bourgeoisie more important than those
of state or status quo. An alternative principle of
being was advanced.

Even though most of the novels of the period
lacked depth in their social analysis and subtlety
in their aesthetic organisation, yet, like the
trivial use of the medium of television in our own
day, they could still alter the way in which people
perceived the activities of their world. In making
sense of reality, the Elizabethan novel made possible new judgements and even a different kind of
'evidence' from that already embodied in dramatic
and poetic literature. They were capable of re-
making the world along new lines; and they offered a
shared image of reality, one that acquired from the
fact of print an objective quality. Elizabeth
Eisenstein, speaking of Renaissance anti-clerical
themes in print, says:

> It is one thing to laugh with some friends in a
> tavern over the latest misdemeanor of a local
> monk or to feel uncharitable when approached by

a begging friar. It is another to find openly
proclaimed in printed literature all one's
secret antipathies to the tonsured and cowled
figures who wandered in the streets, requesting
alms as if it were their right. The impersonal
medium of the printed page seemed to offer
group support for antipathies that had hitherto
been kept to oneself -- if indeed one had not
repressed forbidden thoughts entirely. (8)

Through the tremendous increase of print as the
medium of public communication, the novel acquired a
wide social force. Elizabethan fiction not only
reflected but helped to shape the consciousness of
the age. If culture is considered to be not collected artefacts and texts, but conventionalised
ways of dealing with reality, and if literature is
viewed as an imaginative organisation of values in
relation to reality, then Elizabethan fiction,
however primitive its narrative techniques, is of
considerable importance as literature.

Because literature is a social relation, to
understand it requires more than the study of texts
in isolation. In this instance, to understand
adequately the peculiarities of Elizabethan fiction
it is necessary to consider the social position of
the author in the late sixteenth century, the
context in which literary activity took place
(Chapter II). The expectations of the audience must
also be considered -- the conventions they were
accustomed to and the way fiction was accommodated
within the peculiar qualities of the medium of print
(Chapter III). Then it will be possible to see in
specific cases how the relation between author and
audience -- the literature -- is actually carried
out: first in Lyly and Sidney, the two most important bearers of 'official' ideology; then in Thomas
Nashe, whose ideological ambiguity encourages his
experimentation with the possibilities of printed
communication; and finally in Robert Greene and
Thomas Deloney, the two most important creators of
an alternative literature in the sixteenth century.

NOTES

1.   Joel Hurstfield, 'The Historical and Social
      Background' in A New Companion to Shakespeare
      Studies, ed. Kenneth Muir and S. Schoenbaum
      (Cambridge, 1971), pp. 178-79.

2. *The Works of Thomas Nashe*, ed. R. B. McKerrow,
    with corrections and supplementary notes ed.
    F.P. Wilson (Oxford, 1966), vol. I, p. 195.

3. In *Miscellaneous Prose of Sir Philip Sidney*,
    ed. Katherine Duncan-Jones and Jan van Dorsten
    (Oxford, 1973), pp. 83 and 91-92.

4. Peter Burke, *Popular Culture in Early Modern
    Europe* (London, 1978), pp. 59-60.

5. Margaret Spufford, *Small Books and Pleasant
    Histories: Popular Fiction and Its Readership
    in Seventeenth-Century England* (London, 1981),
    p. 238.

6. Jean Robertson, introduction to *The Countess of
    Pembroke's Arcadia (The Old Arcadia)* (Oxford,
    1973), p. xxxvi.

7. Joel B. Altman, *The Tudor Play of Mind:
    Rhetorical Inquiry and the Development of
    Elizabethan Drama* (Berkeley, 1978), p. 95.

8. Elizabeth L. Eisenstein, *The Printing Press as
    an Agent of Change: Communications and Cultural
    Transformations in Early-modern Europe*, 2 vols.
    (Cambridge, 1979), p. 394.

2 THE SOCIAL POSITION OF THE WRITER

The Elizabethan literary world was both feudal and bourgeois. Inasmuch as an author who was not himself wealthy or socially important required a patron to ensure his livelihood and his status,

> the economy of Letters as a profession in Elizabethan-Jacobean times might still be said to be late-feudal. But this is not the full picture. In another respect we are at the beginning of the modern age. New economic relations are developing within the field of literature. Elizabeth's reign launched the modern entertainment business. (1)

The problem for the writer at the beginning of the last quarter of the sixteenth century was that he was caught between the two worlds. The growth of individualism in the sixteenth century was accompanied by a destruction of community, and the nouveaux riches who supplanted the old gentry and some of the aristocracy enjoyed the power of wealth and position without undertaking the social responsibility that had once accompanied it. With the centralisation of government in London and the movement of the aristocracy and gentry away from their estates to the Court, there was a decline of ancient hospitality and extended households in which the patronage of writers suffered. The survival of feudal forms may have stirred writers' expectations of patronage but, for fiction writers at least, the reality did not fulfil these hopes. The great variety of patrons for many individual writers indicates the insecurity of patronage (2). There was not yet a literary market (such as was highly developed by the last decade of the century) in which the writer could find a place. Like the peasant victims of enclo-

9

sure, evicted as superfluous by a new economic organisation not yet ready to receive them as proletariat, authors were being dislodged from their traditional position before a new one had been prepared for them. They could no longer rely on the support of a patronage system and only gradually did they realise the commercial possibilities of literature.

The difficulties of the writer in securing a patron were exacerbated by Humanism and the new learning, which indirectly swelled the numbers of writers. The new learning was a preparation for public office and was often pursued as the way to power by the sons of the gentry and bourgeoisie -- Phialo, hero of Stephen Gosson's The Ephemerides of Phialo, a gentle younger son, attends university 'to win that by learning, which he wanted in living' (1579 ed., sig. A3). However, in the last quarter of the century there were enough educated members of the aristocracy to fill the state offices which had earlier been occupied by non-aristocratic Humanists. In the 1570s and '80s the universities and Inns of Court had their greatest aristocratic attendance (3) and these educated aristocrats filled the places their social inferiors had hoped to gain through education. Whereas clerics, who had been the intellectuals of the feudal classes, were part of a system that could absorb in other activities an intellectual over-production, the Humanists had no such organisation behind them. Thus they turned to literature, which seemed a natural outlet for educated men denied public service. The frustrated university wits, having no broad avenues open to them, were reduced to entertaining and forced to 'contain their sense of divine mission within the bounds of a poor pamphlet'(4). Yet, rather than a substitute for position, for many writing appeared as a means to the preferment education alone could no longer secure. Even without formal patronage, a literary work could initiate an acquaintance or a discourse that might lead to preferment (5). George Gascoigne, for example, is contented to see his poems published 'that thereby the virtuous might be encouraged to employ my pen in some exercise which might tend both to my preferment, and to the profit of my country' (The Whole woorkes of George Gascoigne Esquyre, 1587 ed., sig.*3). Until the 1580s, when they began to expect money for dedications, writers seeking patronage were usually more concerned with obtaining a position or preferment than a cash reward (6). The problem, in short, was that too many writers were chasing too few patrons.

The social changes that caused the problem of declining patronage also produced the elements of a solution in the vastly expanded middle strata of the society. Merchants, tradesmen, artisans and apprentices had cultural needs which could not be served adequately by literature for the Court or traditional oral culture. They needed something that recognised their lack of accommodation in the inherited feudal ideology, that reflected the concerns of their own lives and embodied their own attitudes. Drama certainly went some way toward meeting this need, as the extraordinarily high level of attendance at the public theatres suggests, but did not meet it entirely.

The growth and increasing complexity of commercial and manufacturing life made education necessary and, as Louis B. Wright in his classic <u>Middle-class Culture in Elizabethan England</u> so enthusiastically demonstrates, the middle classes believed passionately in education. Although this education was largely concerned with practical matters rather than high culture, and encouraged a taste for utilitarian or at least useful-sounding literature, such as herbals, astrology, medicine, geography, agriculture books, and so on, it still depended on reading. There was a 'shift from "learning by doing" to "learning by reading"', Elizabeth Eisenstein pointed out: 'Possibly no social revolution in European history is as fundamental as that which saw book learning (previously assigned to old men and monks) gradually become the focus of daily life during childhood, adolescence and early manhood'(7). Reading extended to works of self-professed but less obvious practicality: moralised histories and fictions 'no less profitable than pleasant', where readers of all conditions of life are promised benefit, even if only learning what enticing dangers to avoid ('the discreet reader may take a happy example by the most lascivious histories'), and at last to works that give healthful pleasure, where readers 'may find pleasant conceits to purge Melancholy'. The burgeoning, literate middle classes became the largest consumers of fiction.

Whether Elizabethan literacy was of sufficient extent to provide a 'reading public' may perhaps be questioned (especially by those who would date the first flowering of English fiction and the novel from the eighteenth century). Margaret Spufford's <u>Small Books and Pleasant Histories</u> demonstrates at

length that literacy, although not the ability to
write, was widespread in the seventeenth century,
and that the flourishing market in chapbooks and the
huge stocks of successful chapbook publishers
depended on a public a substantial part of which was
literate. Although she focuses her study on the
seventeenth century, her evidence and anecdotes of
Elizabethan literacy suggest that the late sixteenth
century was not appreciably different and that
Elizabethan London had a sizeable literate population. That is not to say that learned culture,
classics-based literacy, was generalised in the
reading public. While the university-trained
authors like Nashe and Greene included Latin tags in
their work, sometimes with and sometimes without
glosses, many such as Henry Robarts and Richard
Johnson used neither Latin nor 'inkhorn terms'
(Latin only slightly Englished). Peter Burke,
referring primarily to the eighteenth century,
suggests: 'Between learned culture and traditional
oral culture came what might be called "chap-book
culture", the culture of the semi-literate, who had
gone to school but not for long'(8). Certainly the
reading public must have included a fair proportion
of such unskilled readers. But the extent of everyday written information, such as the written notices
pinned to pilloried offenders and specifically
literate joking like that in Twelfth Night (Malvolio
finding the letter and recognising Olivia's 'very
Cs, her Us, her Ts' -- Act II, sc. 5), suggests that
literacy was common rather than exceptional.

This literacy depended on print. Whether it
was consumed through the eye in private or the ear
in reading aloud, most Elizabethan novels reached
their audience through print (manuscript circulation
was a possible mode of publication, as with the Old
Arcadia, but only for a compact audience such as the
Court and its dependents, and for the novel is
exceptional). Print, however, sometimes posed an
identity problem for writers. Like aspiring members
of the merchant class, many writers desired to
achieve (or maintain) gentle status. Humanism had
given them the position of gentlemen of letters:
anyone who was a student of the laws of the realm,
or in the University, or professed 'Phisicke' and
the 'liberal Sciences', or was a military captain
could 'be called Master (which is the title that men
give to Esquires and Gentlemen) and reputed for a
Gentleman', Harrison informs us in An Historicall
Description of the Islande of Britayne (1577,
sig. Ol). As a servant to a lord, his patron, the

writer could certainly be a gentleman, but he was not a gentleman if he was a servant to the public. To write for the press thus jeopardised his position, since the press made his work common and the appearance of personal service rendered for a patron was destroyed in something offered promiscuously to the public through print. 'In the Elizabethan period it was considered beneath the dignity of a gentleman to have any dealings with a publisher; it was therefore customary for courtiers to circulate manuscript copies of their works among their friends'(9). The gentlemen of letters shunned print (10).

Furthermore, the printed work smacks of considered effort and may thus make doubtful the author's pretensions to extemporal grace, his sprezzatura, that was so important to the aristocratic ideal. Writing for the press suggests professionalism, which conflicts with the writers's gentle image. The professional is different from the amateur not so much in degree of skill as in the qualitative difference of exercising his talents for gain. Sidney casts scorn on 'base men with servile wits . . . who think it enough if they can be rewarded of the printer'(Defence, p. 111). Even though patronage in the Elizabethan period was often reduced to infrequent gifts of money, 'the writer still tended to look towards a patron rather than to a publisher for maintenance, feeling it less of an indignity to be provided with an annuity by some noble family than to become the employee of a bookseller'(11). To be a gentleman (Harrison qualifies his definition) a man must be able to 'live idly and without manual labour, and thereto is able and will bear the port, charge and countenance of a gentleman'(sig. O1). While the professional writer may live without manual labour, in that he is a professional, he cannot live idly. Therefore the author could not be both professional and gentleman.

The press presented no problem for Sidney and Lyly: they were both born gentlemen, Sidney did not write for the press, and Lyly was professional only in so far as writing was a secondary means of advancement (12). It was writers such as Greene and Nashe who were caught in the dilemma: they could not afford to live idly as gentlemen but, aspiring to gentility and aristocratic patronage, they could not afford not to be gentlemen. (Nashe was caught on the horns until the end but Greene relinquished by the middle of his career the idea of gentility.)

The author preserved gentle appearances to some extent by accommodating the new reality to old forms. He could attempt to avoid the 'stigma of print' by denying that it was his intention to publish. He might claim that, contrary to his instructions, a friend gave the manuscript to the printer, or that it had been so long in circulation that imperfect copies threatened his reputation, or that one of the copies would be published without his consent anyway, or (the most common excuse) he had been urged to it by friends whom he did not want to offend. Whatever the excuse, the author who wanted to maintain a gentle posture seldom admitted publishing on his own initiative; and some writers seeking no more than respectability, rather than gentility, also followed the convention. Henry Robarts, in A Defiance to Fortune, addressing the 'courteous' not the 'gentle' reader, asks pardon for the 'fault' of publishing; and even Emanuel Forde, with no social pretension, tells the reader of Ornatus and Artesia, 'Gentlemen, I have published this History, at the entreaty of some of my familiar friends, being at the first collected with no intent to have it printed'(1634 ed., sig. A4). If he admitted choosing the press he might qualify that choice by making clear that his concern was for the opinion of the patron and the educated reader only, not for that of the general reader, as does Gascoigne, who says, 'I esteem more the praise of one learned reader, than I regard the curious carping of ten thousand unlettered tatlers', and strenuously denies the charge of a commercial motive:

> For answer hereof it is most true (and I call heaven and earth to witness) that I never received of Printer, or of any other, one groat or penny for the first copies of these Posies. True it is that I was not unwilling the same should be imprinted. (The Whole woorkes, sigs. *4, *2v).

Likewise Brian Melbancke in the dedication of Philotimus (1583), while angling for reward, denies any commercial intent: 'I am not so base minded to merchandize books, although my want may stand in need to your Lordship'(1583 ed., sig. *2v).

By the mid-1580s an author could hope to succeed without the appearance of gentility. With the growth of a middle-class audience, the reading public unconcerned with the dubious connotations of

14

print and eager or at least willing to accept printed literature had grown to sufficient size for the author to abandon a gentle posture and yet hope to survive. A readership that had no scorn for professionals provided a market large enough for booksellers to pay authors and give them a chance of earning a living through the press. Yet writing for the press, as much as genteel amateurism, made demands (though different) of appearance on the writer. These demands, if we can judge them from the most popularly successful works, were somewhat contradictory in character: aristocratic flavour, 'practicality' and a subject matter accessible to middle-class experience.

The genteel aspect of the bourgeois spirit remained stronger than the popular in the literature of the Elizabethan period. The aristocracy was still the criterion for middle-class fashion, in literature as in other things, and the professional writers (J. W. Saunders stresses) had to imitate courtiers as much as possible; and most writers, even if they consciously wrote for the middle classes, attempted to make everything to do with their works appear genteel -- by, for, and about gentlemen (13). Writers generally addressed them-selves to 'the gentleman reader', whether or not the pretension to such an address had any basis. The reader may have been flattered by a sense of tempor-arily raised status in reading a work addressed to gentlemen, and the associations gained by such an address suggested the superior quality of the work to the non-gentle reader, in the same way that many people with no social pretension today hold that a biscuit or shoe polish sold to the royal household must be superior to others on the market. The 'gentleman reader' can be seen as mere convention rather than an indication of intended audience when writers begin to toy with it and a writer for artisans such as Richard Johnson could address The Nine Worthies of London to gentlemen readers 'as well Prentices as others'.

The middle class placed great value on gentility for its own sake. John Buxton's remark that Sidney's Arcadia, as 'the most successful work of fiction of the English Renaissance, reveals the taste of the age more vividly than any other'(14) may be true in a sense different from that which he intends. Whatever the aristocracy's reasons for admiring the Arcadia, the bourgeoisie's admiration may well have been based largely on the fact that it was aristocratic. The subtle, refined intricacy of the Arcadia, or of Euphues, could be appreciated only by an audience accustomed to literary (not just story-telling) conventions, i.e., in the main readers versed in learned culture (and therefore usually of higher social status). While other sections of the society may have enjoyed the works, it was probably neither the courtly subtlety nor the literary refinement that they valued. The appreciation of different classes may have been directed to essentially different things found in the same work. The popularity of Forde's reductions of the Arcadia suggests that it was not Sidney's outlook that was of particular interest to tradesmen and artisans. The middle class imitated the aristocracy simply because it was aristocratic; the ruling culture was that of the ruling class.

The character of the middle class's imitation of the aristocracy is mirrored in the way they themselves influenced the taste of the aristocracy; the aristocracy rejected what the middle classes 'defiled' by imitating. Thus when Euphues gained popularity with a common audience, it became an object of mockery among the aristocracy. Romance was rejected by the 'literary' class, R. S. Crane points out, not only for its immorality, lack of verisimilitude, and crudeness of form, but also because of its popularity with the uncultured (15). Such a negative influence on taste is merely the inversion of bourgeois imitation of the aristocracy. Similarly, the aristocratic emphasis on pure aesthetic value may be a rejection of the practical orientation of middle-class culture. Thus Nicholas Hilliard stressed the superiority of limning (miniature) to all other kinds of painting because it was not for common men's use nor for public decoration; it was not purposeful but purely aesthetic (16). Nashe's traditional Humanist exercise of praising something trivial or outlandish in Nashes Lenten Stuffe may also be in part a rejection (in what is otherwise his most popularly-orientated work) of bourgeois practicality.

The demand of the middle class for practical works has long been recognised. In addition to the wealth of instructional manuals, guides, handbooks, etc., they demanded at least an ostensible practical orientation in their literature. Though perhaps only puritanical preachers condemned as idle and lewd all books without moral instruction, authors were usually careful to promise profit as well as delight, and stories were usually presented as 'history', a confusion which gave tales connotations

of usefulness and moral soundness. Few works of
Elizabethan fiction (until the end of the sixteenth
century) fail to have some suggestion of practical
value in their full titles and the suggestion is
often given further support in the epistle to the
reader.

The demand for works relevant to the experience
of the middle class posed a more complex problem
than practicality, for the middle class was not a
social unity; the professional author had to choose
a social orientation (it was hardly possible for a
writer to bridge the social divisions of the middle
classes except on the broadest issues, as in
Greene's The Spanish Masquerado, 1589, an anti-
Spanish work, cashing in on the defeat of the
Armada). He could direct himself to the genteel or
to the popular middle class: to the upper bourgeoisie, the academics, and the gentlemen of the Inns of
Court; or to the petty bourgeoisie, the journeymen,
and the apprentices. Thomas Wilson, in The Arte of
Rhetorique (1553), offered as a justification of
rhetoric that it kept the lower orders in their
place: 'Who would dig and delve from morn till
evening', if he had not been persuaded by wit that
that was his duty? (1553 ed., sig. A4, as preceding
leaf signed A3). The commercial writer could now
present an alternative consciousness, one that,
without being directly revolutionary, saw the world
from the standpoint, if not actually of diggers and
delvers, yet of artisans and apprentices. He could
direct his writing to an outlook different from that
of the traditional patron class. The demand for
such work is clearly shown by the success of Robert
Greene's A Quip for an Upstart Courtier, three
editions of which are recorded by the STC for 1592
and Sandra Clark speaks of six editions in six
months (17), which has little story and a more
explicit social attitude than any other of Greene's
works.

In writing for an audience reached through a
literary market and personally unknown to him, the
professional writer had to shape his work to an
average or norm, and the readers, it seems, demanded
a norm that could include their own experience, an
orientation which reflected their self-image. Thus
Robert Greene, for example, appealing to genteel
readers in his early works, makes situations of
emotion the occasion for euphuistic speeches and
uses metaphors of falconry; whereas Henry Robarts,
addressing more popular elements, fills his adventures with heroes distinguished from the petty

bourgeoisie only in their armour and Richard Johnson
often relies on flat metaphors of everyday objects:
'the bigness of the Dragon was fearful to behold
. . . his belly of the colour of gold, but more
bigger than a Tun' (The Seven Champions of
Christendom, 1596, 1608 ed., sig. C2). The extent
to which a writer had consciously to adjust his work
to the level of his audience should not be exagger-
ated, for the writer himself was moulded by the same
social forces that shaped his audience. What makes
them the representatives of a class, says Marx in
The Eighteenth Brumaire, is not that they are
members of that class but 'that in their minds they
do not get beyond the limits which the latter do not
get beyond in life, that they are consequently
driven theoretically to the same problems and
solutions to which material interest and social
position drive the latter practically'(18). And
because the authors reflect the position of the
class they represent, they often display conflicting
orientations. Thus Thomas Deloney in The Gentle
Craft, Part I, asserts the worth of shoemaking
through its aristocratic practitioners; while in
Part II (probably no more than a year later) and in
Jack of Newbury (no more than a year earlier) he
mocks gentility. Similarly, in The Nine Worthies of
London the conduct of gentlemen is the general
standard Johnson offers but his point of view is
clearly that of trade. In any case, those authors
who had no marked social orientation, who were
neither clearly genteel nor popular (such as Saker
or Lodge), though they may have been as skilled in
narrative as their more successful contemporaries,
seem to have been much less successful, by and
large, than those with a strong orientation (such as
Deloney or Johnson or Sidney).

The middle classes in the Elizabethan period
were just beginning to become important in an
aristocratic world. However much their outlook in
practice may have been contrary to aristocratic
notions, they did not yet have their own developed
ideology. It was thus inevitable that to some
extent their literary representatives should turn to
the Court for a model -- the model, for the Court
was in one sense the centre of the literary world.
If we take the Renaissance as the period between
1520 and 1650, says Saunders,

it can fairly be said that half the writers of
the age earned their living wholly at Court,
that most of the others were dependent for a

major part of their income, in various ways, upon courtly patronage, and that nearly all the great important writers were either courtiers in their own right or satellites utterly dependent upon the courtly system. (Profession, pp. 34-35).

Even though fiction reached its readers mostly through commercial presses and was seldom dependent on the Court, imitation of the ways of the Court might confer respectability on the 'blushing' writer 'who ventured into print, with the stigma of social impropriety on one cheek, and the stigma of moral folly on the other' (Ibid., pp. 66-67). Yet, for the professional fiction writer addressing a middle-class audience, the Court could be little more than an ideal and a formal model, because the demands of fiction for the middle class were hardly reconcilable with literature as 'an instrument of courtly converse and entertainment'(Ibid., p. 36). Although many critics of the period have tended to regard writers for the press basically as those who failed to attain the standards of courtly literature, such a view places them in the wrong context; printed fiction generally served different ends and most of its authors addressed a new audience with new demands and outlook. Certainly the works of Sir Philip Sidney and John Lyly display a greater formal coherence than those of Robert Greene and Thomas Deloney, but discussion limited to aesthetic qualities in isolation, or which sees Greene and Deloney primarily as writers who failed to reach the Court, misses the distinctive value of the latter. It is their interpretation of Elizabehan society, which 'notable images of virtues, vices, or what else' (which Sidney called 'the right describing note to know a poet by' -- Defence, pp. 81-82) they choose to present, that gives many Elizabethan novels their value and interest.

'The great difference between the medieval and Renaissance writers', J. W. Saunders comments, 'was a difference of social security'; that whereas the medieval writer belonged very firmly to a local community, the Renaissance writer had to 'earn a place in society' (Ibid., pp. 29-30). The Elizabethan novelist had to find or make a place for himself in a society that did not naturally provide him with one. Even though some authors had a clear position in society and were part of a group to whom they could address their writings (such as the Inns of Court for Austen Saker or the young Thomas

Lodge), most fiction writers in the last quarter of the sixteenth century had to create community through their writing; they had to choose an audience and build a relationship with them. As the composition of the readership altered, so did the author's perception of that potential community. By the end of the century, authors addressing different class interests created novels based on values opposed to those of the Court and the upper bourgeoisie and created an alternative literature.

NOTES

1.   John F. Danby, Elizabethan and Jacobean Poets: Studies in Sidney, Shakespeare, Beaumont & Fletcher (London, 1964; first published 1952 as Poets on Fortune's Hill), p. 16.

2.   Phoebe Sheavyn, The Literary Profession in the Elizabethan Age, 2nd ed., revised by J. W. Saunders (Manchester, 1967), p. 23. Jan van Dorsten, confirms Sheavyn's view in 'Literary Patronage in Elizabethan England: The Early Phase' in Patronage in the Renaissance, ed. Guy Fitch Lytle and Stephen Orgel (Princeton, 1981), p. 191. Eleanor Rosenberg, in Leicester, Patron of Letters (New York, 1955), attempts to prove that Elizabethan patronage was not decadent and remarks that the usual modern concern with patronage is limited to that of belles lettres, which was perhaps the least important literature (p. 16). H. S. Bennett, in English Books & Readers 1558 to 1603: Being a Study in the History of the Book Trade in the Reign of Elizabeth I (Cambridge, 1965), takes a similar view (p. 31) and points out that only twenty-five per cent of the titles published between 1558 and 1603 are classed as 'literature' (p. 269). Whatever the qualifications, Sheavyn's main point stands: a shortage of patrons developed as the number of writers rose (p. 21).

3.   Lawrence Stone, The Crisis of the Aristocracy: 1558-1641 (Oxford, 1965), pp. 688, 691.

4.   G. K. Hunter, John Lyly: The Humanist as Courtier (London, 1962), p. 34.

5.   Jan van Dorsten, op. cit., p. 197.

6.   Bennett, op. cit., p. 45; Rosenberg, op. cit., p. xviii.

7. Elizabeth L. Eisenstein, The Printing Press as an Agent of Change (Cambridge, 1979), p. 432.

8. Peter Burke, Popular Culture in Early Modern Europe (London, 1978), p. 63.

9. Marjorie Plant, The English Book Trade: An Economic History of the Making and Sale of Books, 2nd ed. (London, 1965), p. 23.

10. J. W. Saunders, 'The Stigma of Print. A Note on the Social Bases of Tudor Poetry', Essays in Criticism, Vol. I (1951), p. 140.

11. Plant, op. cit., p. 73.

12. L. G. Salingar, 'The Social Setting' in The Age of Shakespeare, The Pelican Guide to English Literature, Vol. II (Harmondsworth, 1964), p. 42.

13. J. W. Saunders, 'The Stigma of Print', pp. 154-56.

14. John Buxton, Elizabethan Taste (London, 1966), p. 268.

15. Ronald S. Crane, The Vogue of Medieval Chivalric Romance During the English Renaissance (Menasha, Wisconsin, 1919), p. 18.

16. Buxton, Elizabethan Taste, p. 123.

17. Sandra Clark, The Elizabethan Pamphleteers: Popular Moralistic Pamphlets 1580-1640 (London, 1983), p. 127.

18. Karl Marx, The Eighteenth Brumaire of Louis Bonaparte (Moscow, n.d.), p. 51.

In 1573, when George Gascoigne wrote The Adventures of Master F. J., the earliest candidate for the distinction of first English novel, there was no work he could use as a model for his effort. A person motivated toward producing extended narrative prose fiction had few examples to follow, and there was, obviously, no tradition of the novel. Elizabethan novelists had to discover exactly what it was they were trying to achieve and, through often clumsy experimentation, had to build their own conventions. Just as early Chinese cinema in the People's Republic, I am told, had to abandon for a few years Western cinema's convention of having a person enter a room in one frame and be across it in the next, because the audiences would not accept the elision of the intervening steps and required that the complete action be shown, so with the novel, narrative organisation that we take for granted today, and which anyone setting out to write a novel would assume almost without thinking, posed problems for the Elizabethans. Anthony Munday in Zelauto (1580), for example, is unable to avoid presenting the same material three times to the reader (the author's narration of the hero robbed by bandits and the hero's twice re-telling the event) and John Lyly in Euphues and his England (1580) creates an anticlimax where a character receives an important letter which we had already read when the hero composed it.

A more fundamental problem for Elizabethan novelists was transmission through print -- how to address readers rather than a present audience. Print posed difficulties far beyond the threat to gentle status; it mediated the relationship the author had with an audience, making it indirect. 'The oral song (or oral narrative) is the result of

interaction between the singer, the present audience, and the singer's memories of songs sung',
says Walter J. Ong (1). Print, because it is fixed,
allows of no such interaction. In chronicles and
herbals, where the matter seems objective, this was
perhaps unimportant, but the personal and immediate
quality was vital to imaginative literature -- 'In
the Renaissance the author continues to speak as
though real people, not hypotheses, were listening
to him'(2).

Print seemed in its very nature opposed to
literature, giving the work an apparently
independent existence. Sidney's sonnet 15 of
<u>Astrophel and Stella</u>,

> You that do search for every purling spring,
> Which from the ribs of old Parnassus flows

has a generalised, abstract quality which sits
comfortably in print; but his sonnet 41,

> Having this day, my horse, my hand, my lance
> Guided so well, that I obtained the prize

is so specifically personal that print seems
strange. Similarly, the tone of direct address to
'Fayre Ladyes' is appropriate to a privately circulated manuscript, passed from the author or his
friends to other friends, because there is still the
character of personal relation; in a printed work,
which has passed from author to printer to bookseller, it may seem strange, like an echo that
remains when the original voice has departed.

The social conception of author Elizabethan
novelists inherited had been conditioned by writing
for manuscript circulation; i.e., literary creation
(if J. W. Saunders is correct) was regarded as a
personal activity and the work created as an extension of the author, something that could be exposed
to friends and equals or superiors but was unsuit-
able for a general public (3). Manuscript circulation was in character somewhere between the oral and
print, at one remove from personal presentation
rather than something of a different kind, and it
provided a model for the literary relationships of
the early novelists. 'In manuscript culture and
hence in early print culture, reading had tended to
be a social activity, one person reading to others
in a group'(Ong, p. 131).

The Elizabethans, conditioned by oral culture,
wrote for the ear. 'All text involves sight and

sound. But whereas we feel reading as a visual
activity cueing in sounds for us, the early age of
print still felt it as primarily a listening
process, simply set in motion by sight'(Ong,
p. 121). For Philip Sidney fiction as well as
poetry was 'heard': 'with a tale forsooth he cometh
unto you, with a tale which holdeth children from
play, and old men from the chimney corner'(Defence,
p. 92). Even Robert Greene, the writer eventually
most fully accommodated to print, envisages a
'heard' literature: in Mamillia (1583), his first
novel, he interjects an apology to the reader for
his 'slender skill': 'although between your learned
ears and my rude tongue there will be great discord'
(Grosart ed., vol. II, p. 78). Thus an intimate
tone would not really be inappropriate to the
printed work. Even if authors felt that the press
distanced them from their audience, it was natural
that a new relationship should be presented in terms
of an old, in the same way that fifteenth-century
continental printers tried to copy manuscript, in
style, ornament, margins, column width, etc., and
early printed books are almost indistinguishable
from the manuscripts they were copied from (Eisenstein, p. 51). Only gradually did the authors'
conception of their role come to include an
impersonal literary market.

The most immediate problem of writers for the
press was the anonymity of the readers, as Austen
Saker states clearly in Narbonus (1580):

> and he must write well that shall please all
> minds: but he that planteth trees in a Forest,
> knoweth not how many shall taste the Fruit, and
> he that soweth in his garden divers Seeds,
> knoweth not who shall eat of his Sallets. He
> that planteth a Vine, knoweth not who shall
> taste his Wine: and he that putteth any thing
> in Print, must think that all will peruse it:
> If then amongst many blossoms, some prove
> blasts, no marvel if amongst many Readers, some
> prove Riders. (1580 ed., vol. I, sig. A3)

Later in the century writers accommodated to the
anonymity of the readership and even played with the
idea. Thomas Nashe in The Unfortunate Traveller
(1594) says, 'Gentle Readers (look you be gentle now
since I have called you so)'(McKerrow ed., vol. II,
217), and Nicholas Breton in The Strange Fortunes of
Two Excellent Princes (1600) addresses the reader:
'Courteous Reader, for so I hope to find you, or

else shall I be sorry, to have bestowed so good a term upon you'(1600 ed., sig. A4).

The first accommodation to the anonymity of the readership of print was by the translators of novelle. The translators served as intermediaries between the readers and a story that existed 'objectively'; i.e., they did not create the story -- it existed independently -- but they performed the service of transmitting it and pointing out to readers what was relevant. They thus provided a way for novelists to deal with the objectivity of print, at once stressing the independence of their material and guiding the responses of readers in an awkwardly personal way that, despite the mediation of print, gave their writing a direct and vital quality.

The prose translations of Italian novelle by Painter, Fenton, and Pettie, although only trans- lations, are important in establishing a number of literary attitudes and conventions that prevailed until well into the 1590s; they display the basic techniques which authors during the remaining years of the century used to establish a relationship with readers through print (4).

William Painter, Clerk of the Ordinance and Armory, was not a professional man of letters. He published his The Palace of Pleasure (1566) to offer the reader 'delight and profit', as the title page of The Second Tome of the Palace of Pleasure (1567) has it. This purpose is made clear in the epistle to the reader of the first book:

> Nothing in mine opinion can be more acceptable unto thee (friendly Reader) than oft reading and perusing of variety of Histories, which as they be for diversity of matter pleasant and plausible, even so for example and imitation good and commendable. (5)

He offers to the public some of the fruits of his private reading in order that it may delight not him alone (II, pp. 150-51).

Painter regards the audience with whom he shares his delight as a collection of individuals, although personally unknown to him: 'I beseech you Gentlewomen (if there be any in the place where this novel is read)' to take the moral (II, p. 138), and 'I would wish all my friends that be widows, to follow the noble Roman matron and widow called Annia'(I, p. 115). The readers are anonymous but not abstract. He coaxes them to take the profit with the pleasure: 'Wherefore proceed (good Reader)

to continue the pains upon the reading of these, so
well as thou hast vouchsafed to employ thy time
before'(II, p. 278). Painter is aware of his audience, sensing their reactions and explaining his
own purpose:

> Pardon me, good Ladies, if I speak so largely
> . . . I am very loath to take upon me the
> office of a slanderer, and no less do mean to
> flatter those, whom I see to their great shame,
> offend openly in the sight of the world: but
> why should I dissemble that which I know your
> selves would not conceal, if in conscience ye
> were required? (III, pp. 54-55)

Painter leads his readers through a series of moral
experiences where profit and pleasure are intermixed
but not unified. To reward their attention to the
profitable matter, he offers delight in closing the
first book:

> To conclude our number of Novels, I have
> thought good (gentle reader) to bring in place
> a Doctor and his wife, to give thee a merry
> farewell: because thou hast hitherto so
> friendly and patiently suffered thyself to be
> stayed in reading of the rest: wherefore with a
> pleasant Adieu in a short and merry tale . . .
> I mean to end. (II, p. 142)

The role Painter assumes goes beyond the translation of the tales he presents; like Virgil leading
Dante, he accompanies the reader throughout both
volumes, openly displaying his own attitudes, and
speaking familiarly. He takes no credit for
originality and confesses his doubts in translating
certain passages (I, p. 115). His concern is to be
morally effective, and he regards his translations
as a public service, not to art but to morality.
Thus the tales are presented in a moral context and
the statement of the moral may exceed in length the
story that illustrates it or may even be tangential.
In the thirty-first tale of the first tome, for
example, the word 'courtier' sends him off on a
moral attack on present-day courtiers:

> (nothing like the Courtiers in these days that
> to their great shame, for their corrupt and
> rude manners would be called and reputed
> gentlemen, which indeed may be counted Asses,
> brought up and nuzzled rather in the filthy

conditions of the vilest men, than in Courts.)
In those days Courtiers occupied themselves, in
treating of peace and ending of quarrels that
bred strife. (I, p. 119)

Style is important to Painter, but as the opposite of a moral outlook; it is show instead of substance: he trusts 'the indifferent Reader' will
accept the work in good part, 'although perchance
not so set forth or decked with eloquent style, as
this age more brave in tongue than manners doth
require' (I, p. 13). In his epistle to the reader
in Tome II he says that the work was done for those
who like a plain style, 'those that more delight in
wholesome viands (void of variety) than in the
confused mixture of foreign drugs fetched far off'
(II, p. 154). It is clear that his interest
(despite the alliteration) is in moral content.

Geoffrey Fenton, in his <u>Certaine Tragicall
Discourses</u> (1567), is also concerned with morality,
but his moral view is integrated into, rather than
tacked onto, the tale and it often appears through
the tone in which the tale is related rather than
being spelled out:

Certainly good Ladies my heart abhorring no
less the remembrance of this bitchfox, than my
spirit troubled with trembling fear at the
countenance of her cruelty, gives such impedi-
ment to my pen, that it is scarce able to
describe unto you, the last act of her rage,
wherein . . . (1567 ed., sig. K5v)

There is no need to state the moral; the tone is
sufficient indication. When Fenton speaks of a
'true' picture of wickedness -- 'whereof th'italian
bandell, hath drawn a most true and lively pattern
in the person of a neapolitan Abbott' (sig. Q4) --
the 'truth' lies not in historical accuracy but in
moral correctness. Fenton confuses objective with
subjective truth in the same way that he and his
contemporaries confused story with history.

Not all Fenton's moral lessons are integrated
into the stories; he, too, makes moral interjec-
tions: women should observe 'the policy of the
serpent, who useth to stop her ears with her tail,
to th'end she be not infected with the noise of the
charmer. But now to our Blanche Maria'(sig. S5v).
He offers asides to mothers on how to treat their
daughters: 'I wish the mothers and governors of
little girls in our country, would respect chiefly

ii. most necessary rules in th'education of their tender imps', which rules he then spells out (sig. S5).

Fenton, although he does not know his audience, can like Painter avoid seeing them as abstract: he says he could adduce many examples to prove that Italy is a bad moral influence on the world,

> saving that the discourse would seem more tedious than necessary, and keep me too long from the principal points of my history, which calls me now to perform my promise, and satisfy the expectation of the reader. (sig. A3v)

and

> I am loath good Ladies to pass any further in the pursuit of this dolorous tragedy, because your eyes (already wearied with weeping,) methink I see also your ears offer to close themselves against the report of this Pandora. (sig. K6)

Fenton assumes that author and readers are sharing experience. Where Belleforest (from whom he translates) speaks of 'le pauvre gentilhomme'(6), Fenton personalises the matter and refers to 'our unhappy Philiberto'(sig. FF5v). He gives the tales a strong subjective colouring, stamping them with his own personality, and sometimes his creation swamps the translation: Bandello's novella viii has 2,300 words while Fenton's translation extends to 13,000 words (7).

The strong prejudice in Fenton's writing may offer another bond between the author and his audience. Fenton does not attempt to convince the reader of the justice of his views; rather he assumes that his audience shares them. Religion, as might be expected, is one area in which he shows marked prejudice; national pride, another: the Greeks were excellent but are over-rated, he says, because we know them only from their own writers, who would lead us to believe that they had a monopoly of excellence, and he protests that the English are as virtuous as Greeks or Romans, except in the recording of their virtue (sig. X7v). Fenton himself is zealous in praise of his countrymen: whereas Painter says that Philiberto defeated the valiant Englishman Talbot, Fenton will not endure the affront to national pride and makes the outcome

28

of the encounter that Talbot and Philiberto unhorsed each other (sig. HH5). Though Painter too displays national prejudice, he does it in asides. Thus describing Belleforest's treatment of Charles VII of France driving the English out of his lands, the matter he translates, Painter says parenthetically, 'But give the Frenchman leave to flatter, and speak well of his own Country, according to the flattering, and vaunting Nature of that Nation' (III, pp. 183-84).

Most important in Fenton's relating to his audience is the strong sense of community he felt -- not literary but social community. He does not refine life into art, and it is perhaps his vigorous attitudes coupled with attention to concrete detail that enable the reader to move in the same world as the author: a gallant enamoured of a lady is inflamed by the tenderness of her hand;

> which albeit was every day dipped in divers unwholesome confections, and always bare, t'abide the violence of the weather, not refraining the hardness or hard labour of any toil, retained such a delicate softness and natural hue of itself, that it seemed equal (for the fineness and smoothness of skin) to some Ladies which I know are assisted with the help of waters and lee made for the nonce, and other legerdemains devised by the poticary, to preserve their hands, in a continual moisture with a fine white and pleasant show. (sigs. Y4v-Y5).

George Pettie's A petite Pallace of Pettie his pleasure (1576), another collection of translations, has no moral purpose (and pretends to none), yet a relationship with the audience is created by the continued sense of the author's presence. The tales, Pettie claims in 'The Letter of G. P. to R. B. Concerning this Woorke', were written down as he first told them, at the request of R. B. who then, contrary to Pettie's instructions, took the work to the printer (8). Although the style suggests that the printed tales are rather more polished than what might at one time have been spoken, even the pretence of recorded speech creates a sense of the immediate presence of the author. Pettie's intended audience is almost exclusively women (he addresses gentlemen readers at only one point -- p. 270), whom he flatters throughout the work. Disclaiming the misogyny of one of his characters, he says:

> You must not (Gentlewomen) take these words to come from me, who dare not so much as think so much, much less say so much, for that truth getteth hatred, I mean such as tell not the truth, as he in no wise should not do, which should blow forth any such blast of the most faithful and constant feminine kind. (pp. 231-32)

His own person in very much in evidence in the flattery: he is made so sorrowful by man's estate

> that if your presence did not sprinkle me with some dew of delight, I should hardly frame my wits to procure you pleasure by any pleasant history, but rather continue a dolorous discourse of our calamity. (p. 42)

Consideration of audience reaction also becomes personal, involving the acceptance of the author as much as of his tale:

> I know not what effect my words will take, for that I know not how you courtly dames account of my cunning: but before mine own face I am able to assure you this, that the girls of our parish think that welch Sir Richard himself cannot make a better preach than I can: but it may be you will think me over saucy with my lisping lips to prefer persuasions to them, who are as void of folly every way as myself of wit any way. Yet considering how quietly you took the rude railing of Amphiaraus [one of the two eponymous characters of the tale] against you, I need not doubt but that you will take in good part words which are well meant towards you, and if not follow them, yet not mislike them, and rather weigh the will of the speaker, than the worth of the words. (p. 102)

Pettie assumes audience response and pretends that interaction between author and audience is taking place.

Painter, in performing a conscious service, Fenton, in articulating a community of assumptions, and Pettie, in feigning an interaction with his readers, provide techniques of forming a relationship with an audience. The Elizabethan novelists inevitably make use of the same techniques and employ many of the mannerisms of the translators of novelle to create a relationship, but the relationship becomes a less obvious one, perhaps because the authors of original fiction had to create the relationship within the work rather than imposing it on given (and only slightly alterable) material. The translators dealt with tales that were already made and had thus an independent existence, whereas the novelists had to create a mock reality which seemed to be more than a projection of their own feelings and attitudes and to exist independently of the author.

The early Elizabethan novelists continued the practice and oral-influenced style of the translators, most obviously in their frequent explicit guidance to the reader. George Gascoigne directs interpretation of characters' actions: 'Now to make my talk good, and lest the Reader might be drawn in a jealous suppose of this Lady Frances, I must let you understand that . . . '(9) and he remains a conscious intermediary between events and reader. John Grange, in The Golden Aphroditis (1577), more in the manner of Pettie, focuses meaning through an ironic parenthesis that follows a witty reference to a character's pregnancy: 'but what she meant thereby I refer to you Madames, whose wits herein do pass my foolish skill'(1577 ed., sig. C3). William Warner, in Pan his Syrinx, Or Pipe, Compact of seven Reedes (1584), offers simply narrative guidance that is without moral import though it personalises his relation to the characters: 'To shorten therefore their sailing, in Lydia I now land them'(1584 ed., sig. O2). Barnaby Rich, in The straunge and wonderfull adventures of Don Simonides (part I, 1581), in clarifying action similarly personalises his relation to the characters and also responds to his readers as a group. The hero and a lady hermit are preparing a meal:

> I esteem my Pilgrim to be Turnbroach, for fair
> Porcia . . . In brief, all things were in a
> readiness, our Lady Huntress returned . . .
> what Table talk they had, if you demand, it was
> none. (my emphasis, 1581 ed., sig. F3)

Anthony Munday takes unusual care in rendering realistic detail in Zelauto (1580). For example, Zelauto must find a common language -- Latin, of course -- to converse with English merchants and refers to English as 'their language'. The national specificity of languages and customs is ignored by most other authors (<u>Tarltons newes out of Purgatorie</u>, 1590, an extreme example, relates that Stephano, the cook of Signor Bartolo of Venice, 'was the chief gallant of all the parish for dancing of a Lincolnshire hornpipe in the Churchyard on sundays' -- 1590 ed., sig. E1). Yet Munday also provides a more personal guidance to what is happening in the narrative than does Warner:

> Courteous Gentlemen, in the mean time as Astraepho is providing his Dinner, and hath left Zelauto at home to peruse at his pleasure on an Amorous discourse: I will seem so saucy as to molest his studies, and desire him to let you be partakers of this Delicate discourse. (10)

The sense of community of author, characters, readers developed through the guidance provided by some authors is perhaps made clearer by the opposed quality of Stephen Gosson's direction to his readers. Gosson's <u>The Ephemerides of Phialo</u> (1579) is probably the earliest fiction seen by its author as a printed work (even if he has not fully accommodated himself to the medium); refusing demands by his friends for a longer work, he says:

> But sith they had rather see their hands full of Paper, than their heads full of knowledge, I let them go. And trusting to the courtesy of you that are skilful Gentlemen, I have performed my promise . . . (1579 ed., sig. *8)

The burden of the work is the hero's speech against courtesans (sigs. H5v to K5v) and Gosson emphasises moral purpose to the frustration of the reader's interest in the story:

> What either Jeraldi did in their absence or they when they were returned to their lodging, is the least part of my meaning to touch, because I have taken this only upon me, to show the fruit of Phialo's conference among his friends. (sig. G3v-G4)

* * *

The quality of recorded speech to an audience that is so striking in early Elizabethan fiction yields gradually to objectification. The 'fayre Ladyes' or the 'gentlemen' addressed by Sidney, Warner, Rich, or Munday occur much less frequently toward the end of the sixteenth century. The novels become de-personalised. This can in part be seen as a commercialisation of writing, the production of literature primarily for sale without regard for any particular audience. 'Typography had made the word into a commodity'(Ong, p. 131). Unlike Painter's or Fenton's public service, some authors sought immediate financial reward from the growing publishing industry. 'It is certain that the boom in low-life pamphlets in the late 1590s attracted such writers ['repertory playwrights who made a living -- rarely a good one -- from their pens'] because of the financial rewards'(11). Thomas Lodge, for example, a follower of fashion rather than an innovator, was sometimes able to produce fiction of aesthetic consistency, such as Rosalynde, Euphues Golden Legacie (1590), but also published works such as The Life and Death of william Long beard (1593) where he cannot sustain his own interest in the story and pads out the volume with short lists of different kinds of people (e.g. pirates) or exempla and traditional tales. His relation to publishing is perhaps best summed up in his imitation of Nashe's Pierce Penilesse, Wits Miserie, and the Worlds Madnesse (1596):

> for books crave labour, and labour deserves money, pay therefore the Printer for his pains . . . You run sweating to a play though there want a spirit of wit, I mean merriment in it, then stick not to give freely for this. (12)

But commercialisation was important more in terms of the whole industry than in individual authors' attempts at gain. E. H. Miller, though over-simplifying, offers a useful characterisation:

> After the printing press inaugurated mechanical reproduction of books, scribes gave way to printers, and printers eventually to publishers who organized and financed a rapidly expanding business. The growth of this new industry paralleled a similar expansion in trade and commerce. In fact, emergent capitalism produced a literate populace and thereby contributed the customers the printing trade

required for its growth. This growth, in turn, depended upon human mechanics willing to grind out the fare businessmen needed for profit and readers for entertainment and information. Thus, Grub Street was born -- born of the dreams of middle-class young men desirous of fame and position but born also of economic forces destined to wipe out feudal paternalism.

Authors who had nothing particular to offer, neither art nor strong moral sense nor relevance to a particular readership, were able to find publishers.

This commercial fiction, taken work by work, is not noticeably different from writing that is merely careless or unimaginative. What differentiates it as a body of literature is that it has no particularity. This can be seen most clearly in terms of Marx's idea of 'commodity', a product whose specific qualities are of no concern but only its exchange value. As a commodity literature has a value to the bookseller as quantity -- so many pounds worth of fiction -- not as individualised worth that distinguishes one work from another. In terms of Elizabethan novels this can be seen as the writer's failure to address the fiction to any specific readership, to be effectively indifferent to both material and audience.

Emanuel Forde, in The Most Pleasant History of Ornatus and Artesia (?1595), gives detailed attention to the reality he is presenting and displays an interest in individual motivation. He explores, though without great depth, the values of the action that occurs in the novel. Even though he modelled Ornatus and Artesia on Sidney's Arcadia (which provided him with plot incident and some names) and incorporated traditional, hierarchical views (such as the sinfulness of ingratitude -- the servant who aids Ornatus by slaying his master is condemned by Ornatus to be torn in pieces by horses for betraying someone who has 'cared' for him), he exhibits a sympathetic attitude toward humble people ill-treated by the gentry. In his next works, Parismus, The Renoumed Prince of Bohemia (1598), Parismenos: The Second Part of the most famous, delectable, and pleasant Historie of Parismus, the renowned Prince of Bohemia (1599), and The Famous History of Montelion Knight of the Oracle (shortly after Parismenos), Forde loses interest in individualising detail. He begins instead to give a generalised experience, like modern day advertising which locates complex, socially-constructed qualities (e.g., sexual attraction in advertising, chivalry in Forde) in a single product or action. The title page of Parismenos promises 'noble chivalry' in the same way that kitchen furniture may be marketed as 'sophisticated elegance'. Thus, in Parismus:

> The black knight casting his eyes towards the Tower, where his beloved Laurana stood beholding the combat, and waving his sword most courageously about his head, answered: No dastard Phrygian, (quoth he,) I scorn thy proffer: with which words he so freshly assaulted the Phrygian, that . . . (1598 ed., sig. Nlv)

'Most courageously', though it embodies the 'noble chivalry' for which the book is consumed, is here so generalised that it means practically nothing.

Similarly, Henry Robarts, in A Defiance to Fortune (1590), Pheander, The Mayden Knight (1595) and Honours Conquest (1598), writes with a lack of particularity. He offers exotic adventure, bour-geoisified knights ('Pheander, well dost thou show thyself a Gentleman, for under the habit of a Merchant Gentility cannot be hid, no poor estate can blemish the Noble', Pheander, 1595 ed., sigs. Flv-F2) and a touch of romance, all in a generalised way and without a structure that connects the separate pieces meaningfully:

> This adieu taken, we leave the knight to his adventures, the Merchants to finish their journey, until fit time serve to recount such other adventures as he enterprised, to show you further of the Lady Valia, Alynde and their honest company, left in the unfrequented Isle. (Honours Conquest, 1598 ed., sig. C3v)

Richard Johnson, the most enduringly successful of the commercial writers of the century (his Seven Champions of Christendom was still current as a children's book in the nineteenth century), had a literary career similar to Forde's. His first work, The nine Worthies of London (1592), has a vigour and clarity of values that is lacking in his subsequent publications. He offers to 'the Gentlemen Readers, as well Prentices as others' a heroic view of the bourgeoisie:

> It is not of Kings and mighty Potentates, but such whose virtues made them great, and whose

35

> renown sprung not of the nobleness of their
> birth, but of the notable towardness of their
> well qualified minds, advanced not with lofty
> titles, but praised for the trial of their
> heroical truths . . . who though their states
> were but mean, yet doth their worthy prowess
> match superiors, and therefore have I named
> them Worthies. (1592 ed., sig. B2)

And he defends his artisan literary efforts:

> let the envious fret, and the captious malice
> melt themselves, neither the objection of
> Mechanical, by such as are themselves
> diabolical, whose vicious baseness in a self
> conceit presuming above the best, is indeed but
> the dregs and refuse of the worst, nor the
> reproach of proverbial scoffs as (Ne sutor
> ultra crepidam) shall discourage me from
> proceeding to invent how further to content
> you. (sig. A3v)

The subsequent, commercially successful The Most
Famous History of the seven Champions of Christendome (1596) and The second Part of the famous
History of the seaven Champions of Christendome
(1597) and The Most Pleasant History of Tom a
Lincoln (1599) provide a mix of heroic fighting with
romance and nationalism, a well-proven commercial
formula that Johnson exercises without reflection.
His 'noble chivalry' is reduced to winning.   St.
Anthony defeats the giant Blanderon but will not
heed his pleas for mercy and slays him (1608 ed., I,
sigs. G4v-H1), displaying a lack of graciousness, of
chivalric behaviour, that we would never encounter
in the heroes of, say, Sir Philip Sidney (who may
have treated peasants that way, but not giants).
St. George at the age of fourteen cruelly disposes
of the witch Kalyb who had brought him up, keeping
her virginity for the knight she had abducted as a
child (I, sig. B2v). Sabra (later the wife of St.
George) has her companion devoured by two lions who
then lay their heads in her lap, which incident
draws no emotional response from characters or
author, but is used only to establish to Saint
George that, since lions will not eat virgins, Sabra
is a virgin (I, sigs. Plv-P2).   Emotion may be
mentioned but it is never particularised, and
therefore remains, like 'noble chivalry', a value
but not an experience for the reader. The wicked
Leoger, who has just mortally stabbed himself,

realises that the heroine Rosana is his daughter by
the unfortunate Queen of Armenia:

> and they joined their faces the one with the
> other, distilling betwixt them many salt and
> bitter tears, in such sort that it would have
> moved the wild beasts unto compassion. (1597
> ed., II, sig. T2v)

The same Rosana is attacked by a knight with two
heads, 'who was a ravisher of virgins, an oppressor
of infants, and an utter enemy to vertuous Ladies,
and strange travelling Knights'(II, sig. Z4). This
is completely generalised, in keeping with the
unimportance to Johnson of the specificity of the
evil knight (in fact he gives him a third head
sixteen lines later on the same page).
   Certainly commercial intention did not ensure
commercial success. The STC lists four editions of
Forde's Ornatus and Artesia and five of his Parismus
(including those of the second part, Parismenos) of
which the third, that of 1615, is described as
'fourth time imprinted'. Robarts's Pheander has two
editions listed, the second of which is described as
the fourth edition. For Johnson's The Seven
Champions of Christendom seven editions are listed;
and two of Tom a Lincoln, of which the first is
described as the sixth impression. On the other
hand, Robert Parry's Moderatus, or the Adventures of
the Black Knight (1595) and Christopher Middleton's
The Famous Historie of Chinon of England, with his
strange adventures for the love of Celestina
daughter to Lewis King of France (1597), which rely
on material similar to that of Forde, Robarts and
Johnson, have no editions beyond the first recorded
by the STC. John Dickenson's Arisbas, Euphues
amidst his slumbers: Or Cupids Journey to Hell
(1594), like much of Forde's work, relies heavily on
Sidney's Arcadia and presents a democratised picture
of relations between Arisbas the prince and Damon
the shepherd (which is possible because Dickenson
simply labels his petty-bouregois hero a prince
rather than preserving a distinct character for
different classes). Yet the work has only one
edition listed by the STC. Dickenson's uncertainty
about what posture to take may have undermined his
appeal for a popular audience. Although the work
has material for a popular adventure, Dickenson may
be attempting fashionable work, which is suggested
by his genteel denial of having laboured on the work
and the invocation of Euphues in the title (although

euphusim was at that date no longer admired at Court and perhaps not even among the middle classes, for The Cobler of Caunterburie, 1590, mocks euphuistic style -- 1590 ed., sigs. E4-Flv).

* * *

Objectification of the text was broader than commercialisation; it involved an acceptance of print as a medium and an accommodation of conventions to print. The readers are addressed differently from those of the oral-influenced manuscript, in a manner that suggests an audience that is not just 'temporarily' absent (as with earlier print), but was clearly never present yet is not necessarily seen as abstract. The readership is assumed to be of a certain character, although unknown and anonymous, and the personality of the author tends to be diffused in the work rather than appear embodied in a person. Sidney, for example, moves from addressing 'Fayre Ladyes' in the Old Arcadia to impersonality in the New Arcadia; the novel becomes objectified. In print, the novel did in fact exist independently of the author and generally by the end of the sixteenth century it also appeared to be independent. The product comes to fit the mode of consumption.

After the novelle translations and earliest novels, authors do not talk about themselves in the manner of Pettie's digression on the high regard in which his verbal skills are held, and they appear 'in person' with decreasing frequency. (Greene appears in his conny-catching pamphlets, but assumes a dramatic role; i.e., he is transformed into a character.) Henry Chettle also moves from entering the work as a character to objectification in a first-person narrator different from himself. Whereas in Kind-Harts Dreame (1592) he explains his connection with the late Greene's Groatsworth of Wit (his innocence in Greene's calling Shakespeare 'an upstart crow') and achieves a literary-personal quality through being himself the central character, Kind-hart, in Piers Plainnes seaven yeres Prentiship (1595) the eponymous hero narrates most of the work. Chettle's Piers, like Nashe's hero (Jack Wilton rather than Pierce Penilesse), addresses an internal audience, Menalcas and Coridon, who react to his tale and criticise him when they think he is digressing. They stop him early in his tale, for example, to remind him that he promised to tell about his apprenticeship, not the elaborate tale of Aeliana

(1595 ed., sig. D2v), which is, of course, the story of his apprenticeship in a roundabout, witty fashion.

Piers Plainnes offers both earthy verbal agility (Piers talks like Hamlet's grave-diggers) and a more refined style (Aeliana and Aemilius talk in a courtly fashion), within an elaborate integration of several tales in a single story that preserves the unities. (Warner's Pan his Syrinx was a primitive effort in that direction and Sidney's New Arcadia displays it brilliantly, but as only one facet among the many of Sidney's diamond.) Chettle's control of his material is a virtuoso performance, done for its own sake rather than because the material demands such an arrangement. The work shows character without the intrusion of an author's personality.

Austen Saker more clearly makes a realism which is independent of the author. Narbonus: The Laberynth of Libertie (1580) exists objectively aside from very occasional first-person remarks (e.g., 'Now Gentlemen, you must imagine', 'You shall therefore understand', and 'Behold here gentlemen, the libidinous lust of licentious liberty' -- 1580 ed., vol. I, sigs. Ll, D4). The work is tailored to a middle-class orientation and Saker is more concerned with character than with the exercise of social forms. This can be seen from the way he uses such literary conventions as following a dinner with tales told by the guests. After the first post-prandial tale (which Saker says the company liked, but would have liked better had it been less long -- I, sig. O2v), Narbonus begins his tale only to stop abruptly in the middle, disturbed, as he later explains privately to her, by his passion for Fidelia (I, sig. O3v). Saker creates a clear sense of distinction here between private and public worlds, without making the private world simply a place to which one's thoughts retire in order to consider how better to effect desires in the public world (as it often is in Euphues). Saker's private world seems free from dissimulation, a realm where individuality and character are more important than public image.

Consistent with an interest in individuality, Saker does more to create personality than his predecessors. Despite Lyly's much greater skill, Euphues is a less distinct personality and more of an abstraction of certain qualities than Narbonus (though Philautus has a more developed character in Euphues and His England). Part of Narbonus's individuality is his lack of heroic qualities. It is not necessary that he exemplify any ideal, such as wit or honour. Mediocre, outstanding at nothing, Narbonus has a freedom simply to be on the homely scale of bourgeois thinking and stardards, without having to live up to aristocratic ideals of conduct.

Saker's sense of humanity and of human needs free from demands of honour is evident in his presentation of military life. Narbonus did not enlist to seek fortune and glory; he became a soldier only because he could not escape conscription even with his uncle's influence. His life as a soldier is miserable. When he describes his misery and poverty to an old friend, the friend, without ulterior motive, divides his purse with him (II, sigs. C4v-D1). Such homely, uncalculated generosity is not often found among the Elizabethans. Certainly Sidney's Pyrocles and Musidorus are generous, but theirs is a heroic, not a simple, generosity. Saker presents evil as well as good on a humble level. Thus when some of Narbonus's fellow soldiers torture the local gentry to get their money, the soldiers are not portrayed as wicked creatures (in contrast to, say, Sidney's Cecropia) so much as men brutalised by war (II, sig. D1v).

Saker's middle-class humanity is best illustrated by Narbonus's uncle, Henricus, a minor figure who receives considerable attention unwarranted by his role in the plot. His character, although not fully drawn, is consistent and is held together by his concern for and warmth toward Narbonus. Welcoming him home from soldiering in Spain, he says, believably, that he wishes he could have shared the burden of Narbonus's trials (II, sigs. E3v-E4). The childless uncle unselfishly devotes himself to fostering his nephew, for Narbonus's sake rather than from concern for family honour or continuity of the name. This warmth of family relationships and the conception of the family as a human unit rather than a necesary means of perpetuating wealth and title suggest that Saker was relating to a bourgeois audience, shaping a fiction that, without his own appearance in the work, has a bond of moral outlook.

The most striking bond of moral perspective in the novels of the period is in The Adventures of Ladie Egeria by W. C., Master of Art (entered in the Stationers' Register in 1580 but issued, the STC surmises, about 1585). There is no pretence of the author's service of entertaining the reader; the bond is exclusively moral. The tone of the dedication (unique for Elizabethan fiction) is one

almost of equality, which was possible perhaps only
in the work of a Puritan (the book was printed by
Waldegrave, later the Martinist printer), who held
that morality was the area of greatest importance
and was not dependent on rank. Although W. C.
points out his literary shortcomings, he is firm
about the value of the work:

> yet presuming your Honourable goodness, more
> than my own worthiness, do Dedicate this famous
> and excellent history of Lady Egerias
> adventures to your acceptation. No doubt, a
> princely and tragical discourse. Although
> through mine own unmeetness, the outward phrase
> as growing upon harsh, heathy, rough and
> unsavory ground, yet digging more deeper,
> inestimable treasures are discovered. Now
> lastly, assuring your excellent courtesy, with
> perfect judgement of a direct plain meaning, to
> lenify my boldness, as persuaded to show some
> spark of humble gratitude. Although my
> unskilfulness therein, unable to reach and
> attain the heighth of my duty. (?1585 ed.,
> sig. A3v)

The moral seriousness shines through the awkward
prose. In attacking the arrogant persons who
censure everything, in his address to the reader,
W. C. is not offering the conventional charm agains
the taunts of the Momi and Zoili, the carping
critics, to which publication exposes an author, but
pointing out the unnatural and immoral quality of
those who will malign his work. The reader for whom
he designs the work is, however, a moral creature:
'To the good honest discreet Reader therefore, I
commit this worthy history'(sig. A4v).

Unlike Stephen Gosson, W. C. is not providing
merely a clothed discourse; he manages a gripping
story and The Adventures of Ladie Egeria is a poetic
construction unified by moral purpose. The unity of
the invention and the morality in the work make its
many fantastic elements acceptable. They are not
made credible in themselves, but they become
completely acceptable because they have a poetic
appropriateness. Thus the devouring of Andromus the
flatterer by ravens and the transmogrification of
Duke Lampanus into a snake after he has raped his
daughter are totally incredible in abstraction, yet
the effect is not more disturbing to the reader than
the equally incredible punishment of Paolo and
Francesca in Dante's Inferno. Both succeed because

they are entirely consistent on an emotional and moral level with the rest of the work. Needless to say, Master W. C. achieves neither the insight nor integration of Dante and he cannot always sustain his own poetic imagination (when Duke Lampanus encounters a peasant who speaks frankly of the Duke's moral lapse, W. C. weakens the imaginative unity by making the peasant an obvious abstraction, 'Truthtelall' -- sig. K3v).

Master W. C. need not make an explicit moral statement; the material and the way it is organised often provide the moral without further comment. This can be seen clearly in the behaviour in exile of Duke Lampanus. Reduced to begging, he exchanges his costly garments with an experienced beggar to obtain the assistance of the beggar's daughter, but then leaves her with a lecherous friar who takes the child into the bushes to 'shrive' her (sig. L4v). The context of the incident informs the reader's reaction; W. C. need not comment. If the incident were abstact, then the moral might require elucidation, but the homely quality of the events gives the incident a particular horror unmitigated by a romantic conception of evil (such as occurs in Lodge's Robin the Devil). W. C. portrays simply the detestable abuse of humanity. The same sense of evil as immediate, concrete and individually felt is evident elsewhere in the work. Civil strife is not seen by W. C. in broad political patterns (as in the Arcadia) or in a generalised recognition of human disaster (as Nashe sees the destruction of the Anabaptists at Muenster), but in terms of its effect on people; he is concerned, not with the political chaos among the aristocracy wrought by civil disorder, but with depopulation, lack of tillage, and destitution (sig. M2v). Eldorna, who supplants Egeria in the affections of the duke Lampanus, is as beautiful as Venus, but 'her body, an unchaste sink, vomiting out the ruin of this commonwealth' (sig. N1). The problem that attracts W. C.'s attention, rather than the individuality of Eldorna's wickedness, is the ruin of countless other individuals. He does not focus on casual violation of moral codes or nominal vice in attacking the life of the Court (as do Lyly and Rich); he attacks vicious behaviour among rulers at a level of significance -- its socially disastrous consequences.

W. C. offers his readers no stylistic attraction. Morality is his content and, in showing that retribution strikes down evil, his assumption is that the justice is self-evident -- perhaps a Puri-

tan over-simplification. Yet he must have offered
considerable comfort to those who can look only for
a future justice in the present harsh world, and
although such a view would inevitably be simplistic
in serious moral discussion, here it provides a bond
of feeling with the audience. W. C.'s personality
is not revealed and is of no importance; the
strongly felt, common moral view is what links
author and audience.

Once the conventions of print in the novel were
sufficiently established, authors began to play with
them. Nashe is the most adept but John Harington,
godson of Queen Elizabeth, in A New Discourse of a
Stale Subject, called the Metamorphosis of Ajax
(1596) delights in playing with literary
impersonality:

> Now (gentle Reader) you have taken much pain,
> and perhaps some pleasure, in reading our
> Metamorphosis of Ajax: and you supposed by this
> time to have done with me: but now with your
> favour I have not done with you . . . First
> you thought me fantastical . . . I would but
> ask you this question, and even truly between
> God and your conscience, do but answer it. If
> I had entitled the book, A Sermon showing a
> sovereigne salve for the sores of the soul. Or
> a wholesome haven of health to harbour the
> heart in. Or A marvellous medicine for the
> maladies of the mind, would you ever have asked
> after such a book? (1596 ed., sigs. H7-H7v)

Nicholas Breton's The Strange Fortunes of Two Excellent Princes (1600), as well as teasing the readers
about the way they are addressed ('Courteous Reader,
for so I hope to find you, or else shall I be sorry,
to have bestowed so good a term on you'), plays with
the conventional divisions of the book, presenting
metaphorically the relation between the address to
the reader and the text proper: 'and therefore
leaving you, through a little Door, to go into a
great House . . .'(1600 ed., sig. A4v).

The objectification of the novel increased the
importance of the story itself. Without the interpretation or guidance of the author, the reader had
to find the meaning in the story alone. But it was
clearly not an uninterpreted slice of life, and the
familiarity of readers with the moral quality of
early fiction had prepared them for story as something that commented on the world they lived in;
they were competent to make moral (or social)

evaluation of a novel even if the point was left unstated. And thus all literature could be seen as having moral potential (as Sidney himself says it in the Defence -- the poet is a maker of notable images of virtue and vice). The novel could present not only what Sidney understood as virtue; it became a perfect vehicle for presenting a view of the world that differed from or even attacked official ideology, and for embodying in a seemingly objective tale that which a prudent author would not say in his own voice.

NOTES

1. Walter J. Ong, Orality and Literacy: The Technologizing of the Word (London, 1982), p. 146.

2. William Nelson, 'From "Listen Lordings" to "Dear Reader"', University of Toronto Quarterly, Vol. 46, no. 2 (1976-77), p. 117.

3. J. W. Saunders, The Profession of English Letters (London, 1964), p. 36.

4. See Rene Pruvost, Matteo Bandello and Elizabethan Fiction (Paris, 1937), p. 6.

5. William Painter, The Palace of Pleasure, ed. Joseph Jacobs, 3 vols. (London, 1890), vol. I, p. 10.

6. The French Bandello, A Selection: The Original Text of Four of Belleforest's Histoires Tragiques translated by Geoffrey Fenton and William Painter Anno 1567, ed. Frank S. Hook (Columbia, Missouri, 1948), p. 57.

7. Hamish Miles, introduction to Painter's The Palace of Pleasure (London, 1929), vol. I, p. xiv.

8. George Pettie, A petite Pallace of Pettie his Pleasure, ed. Herbert Hartman (London, 1938), p. 5.

9. A Discourse of the Adventures passed by Master F. J. in George Gascoigne's A Hundreth Sundrie Flowres, ed. C. T. Prouty (Columbia, Missouri, 1942), pp. 66-67.

10. Anthony Munday, Zelauto: The Fountaine of Fame, ed. Jack Stillinger (Carbondale, Illinois, 1963),, p. 107.

11. Brian Gibbons, Jacobean City Comedy, 2nd ed. (London, 1980), p. 161.

12. The Complete Works of Thomas Lodge, ed. Edmund W. Gosse, 4 vols. (Glasgow, 1883), vol. IV, p. 5.

13. E. H. Miller, The Professional Writer in Elizabethan England: A Study of Nondramatic Literature (Cambridge, Mass., 1959), p. 204.

4 JOHN LYLY

John Lyly's famous style, more than the mere decoration it became for many of his imitators, is the artistic embodiment of a world view. Euphues: The Anatomy of Wyt (1578) and Euphues and his England (1580) perfected the style that dominated genteel fiction during the following decade. Any writer unable to offer Lyly's elaborate aural patterns and pseudo-learned analogies -- and the courtly appeal associated with them -- was liable to be considered inferior. But to understand the style we cannot divorce it from the life situation in which it arose; Lyly's style is determined by his relationship with his audience and is the product of the rhetorical situation in which it had to function.

Writing was not a self-justifying activity for Lyly; it was one of the few avenues by which he could prove his wit and demonstrate his suitability for position, and he used it as an entree into Court society. The situation was a characteristically rhetorical one where, in Aristotellian terms, Lyly had to make his address 'ethical'; i.e., he had to demonstrate his personal qualities without talking about them directly. Unlike Nashe, say, who entertains by talking about himself and often becomes, in effect, his main character, Lyly's purpose was indirectly to reveal through writing his suitability for power. Thus the character of his relationship with his audience, and even his choice of writing as the means to create a relationship, is determined by his aspirations and social position. It depends on the fact that Lyly is a gentleman (a real, not a nominal, but still only a gentleman) at Court, trying to gain social advancement among an aristocratic audience. His position in his prose is that of a suitor.

JOHN LYLY

The particular problem of Lyly's suit is that, while discretion should prevent his making it publicly, the work is printed and is, therefore, public. In the dedications and addresses to the reader of Euphues he attempts to resolve this contradiction by immediately making clear that he regards his aristocratic readership as the audience of importance and yet recognises the common, non-Court, reader. In the dedication of Euphues and his England he says he is presenting the Earl of Oxford with the second face of Euphues, 'the picture whereof I yield as common all to view, but the patronage only to your Lordship, as able to defend' (Bond ed., vol. II, p. 4). Oxford, and the rest of his class by implication, are to be the sole judges; the opinions of the general reader are not of concern to Lyly: 'In that I have written, I desire no praise of others but patience'(II, p. 5). He recognises the existence of a wider audience for Euphues but they are not important and he dismisses them:

> I submit myself to the judgement of the wise, and I little esteem the censure of fools. The one will be satisfied with reason, the other are to be answered with silence. I know gentlemen will find no fault without cause, and bear with those that deserve blame, as for others I care not for their jests, for I never meant to make them my Judges. (I, p. 183)

Those who are not gentlemen may buy and read Euphues but it is the aristocratic audience that interests Lyly; and, conventionally, he asks pardon for his offence in publishing, having set the work in print only because of the duty he owes to his patron, Lord Delaware (I, p. 182). In Euphues and his England, perhaps in recognition of the popular success of The Anatomy of Wyt, Lyly's dismissal of the common reader is less harsh and perhaps somewhat ironic: 'not meaning thereby to be careless what others think, but knowing that if your Lordship allow it, there is none but will like it'(II, p. 6).

As a gentleman addressing aristocrats, Lyly is someone of the same basic kind as his audience (the first of Harrison's four divisions of the population includes gentlemen and above) but of a slightly, though significantly, different degree. He can talk to his audience almost as an equal, but not quite, and he maintains deference in his tone:

I go not about (gentlemen) to inveigh against
wit, for then I were witless, but frankly to
confess mine own little wit, I have ever
thought so superstitiously of wit, that I fear
I have committed Idolatry against wisdom, and
if Nature had dealt so beneficially with me to
have given me any wit, I should have been
readier in the defence of it to have made an
Apology, than any way to turn to Apostacy. (I,
p. 196)

Lyly here goes beyond the demands of the conventional apology; for a recognised wit to belittle his
ability at such length sounds a note of obsequious-
ness. The Anatomy of Wyt was already running into
its fourth edition when Euphues and his England
appeared, yet in the dedication of the sequel he
says he wished he had kept quiet and runs down the
first book far more than traditional modesty would
require:

What I have done, was only to keep myself from
sleep, as the Crane doth the stone in her foot,
and I would also with the same Crane, I had
been silent holding a stone in my mouth.
But it falleth out with me, as with the
young wrestler, that came to the games of
Olympia, who having taken a foil, thought scorn
to leave, till he had received a fall . . . and
being with my first book stricken into
disgrace, could not cease until I was brought
into contempt by the second. (II, pp. 5-6)

The tone is not that of the mortal writer addressing
a patron among the gods, but of a gentleman defer-
ring to an aristocrat -- of a shared hierarchical
world rather than two separate worlds. The popular
success of the printed first volume is no reason for
Lyly to assume the posture of success with the
aristocracy; he still requires their favours and is
still in the position of pleading his case before
them. This is in marked contrast to his address to
the gentlemen scholars of Oxford that appeared in
the second edition of The Anatomy of Wyt where
Lyly's tone is haughty:

Thus loath to incur the suspicion of unkindness
in not telling my mind, and not willing to make
any excuse where there need no amends, I can
neither crave pardon, lest I should confess a

fault, nor conceal my meaning, lest I should be thought a fool. And so I end, yours assured to use. (I, p. 326)

If Lyly here refrains from craving pardon where there is no need, he certainly craves much needless pardon in the dedication to Euphues and his England; but the Earl of Oxford is of the Court, while the gentlemen scholars of Oxford are merely gentlemen.

Once Lyly's orientation toward his audience is appreciated, the character of his suit becomes more clear. Whereas the earlier Humanists could use their wit in the service of wisdom, the proper role for the courtier described by Castiglione, Lyly had no audience for wisdom; the Humanist at Court was now a courtier in a reduced sense. The position of learned counsellor was no longer open to him and, having less and less access to the sources of power, the Humanist employed the wit and didacticism of his tradition to provide learned entertainment, pleasing both the new and old nobility with his Humanistic eloquence (1). The Anatomy of Wyt can be seen as a treatise more than a proto-novel (2), in which Lyly shows that wit without experience is not sufficient to deal with an environment of moral choice and, through the hero who has gained experience, lectures his characters and readers. But, denied a situation where it can have practical consequence, Lyly cannot be serious about his advice (in the way that Sidney can). He is only playing with a potentially serious form; his arguments are only of literary consequence.

Albert Feuillerat suggests that Euphues continued the task undertaken by Ascham in The Scholemaster, developing methodically and at length ideas that Ascham had left in disorder and the consequences of which he had not drawn out; and he says that it is most interesting for its presentation of the ideal of Protestant humanism, though he later adds that Lyly did not feel the grandeur of his mission and wanted only to be an entertainer (3). Yet to take Lyly's moral view seriously is to treat him unfairly. C. S. Lewis says:

the more seriously we take its actions and characters the more odious his book will appear. Whether Lyly's moralizing was sincere or no, we need not inquire: it is, in either case, intolerable. The book can now only be read, as it was chiefly read by Lyly's contemporaries, for the style. (4)

It is necessary to see Lyly's style and his moral purpose in relation to his audience. Morality is certainly to a large degree his subject matter, but not his purpose. Morality (a traditional fund of Humanistic argument) becomes literary; it is a vehicle for wit. As G. Wilson Knight remarks, Lyly's method is his matter (5).

There are many reasons for dismissing the idea that Lyly was seriously presenting a moral work. In the first place (and crucially in light of the demands of his rhetorical situation), he could not really undertake to lecture his superiors, even under the guise of entertainment, without undermining his position. Had he addressed himself to a Puritan audience in the manner of Master W. C.'s Adventures of Lady Egeria, an assumption of moral equality would have been possible; or had the work been an abstract moral treatise, the lecture would have been acceptable; but an author who says (even in the irony of sprezzatura) 'I am content this winter to have my doings read for a toy, that in summer they may be ready for trash'(I, p. 182) can hardly pretend to seriousness (Gosson, in contrast, stresses his fiction's moral value even though it is a much slighter work). The aristocratic ladies of the Court, although unlikely to want moral direction from a mere gentleman, would probably not mind playing morality games with him.

Aside from these reasons why Lyly would not be likely to attempt a moral work, there are also sufficient indications that he did not in fact attempt one. Compared to the other Elizabethan novelists, Lyly is a remarkably careful artist. Although he occasionally nods (Cassander carries to the grave 'more gray hairs, than years: and yet more years, than virtues' -- II, p. 18), he sometimes makes clear that an apparent nod is only a wink (as in justifying the paradoxical 'silly Wolf': 'an unapt term, for a Wolf, yet fit, being in a Lions hands' -- II, p. 43). Despite the suggestions of critics that his style contains word balances unrelated to meaning, Lyly shows more care than most authors to be consistent and appropriate within particular passages, although between passages many contradictions of sense appear and the moral attached is not infrequently irrelevant to the plot. This suggests that Lyly, otherwise completely in control of his work, is not interested in the subject of his argument for itself but in its rhetorical effect.

Lyly is quite capable of reasoned, logical argument (e.g., Psellus's dissuading Philautus from magic) but, in questions of moral reasoning, he is often satisfied with a punning-type, associative reason that serves as a stylistically more interesting substitute for logical rigour. Thus Lucilla, having read that the fig tree causes a bull tied to it to lose his strength, reasons, 'And then no marvel it is that if the fierce Bull be tamed with the Fig tree, if that women being as weak as sheep, be overcome with a Fig'(I, p. 223). Witty argument is more satisfying to Lyly and his audience than a reasoned discussion.

Lyly is unconcerned to present morality and virtue positively. The name of the hero, taken from Ascham, suggests a moral type -- an individual of good natural endowment -- but Lyly frames him according to a privative conception of virtue. Thus Euphues is free, or eventually becomes free, from various vices, and although we are told in Euphues and his England that he is highly regarded by the English courtiers, no definite character formed on positive qualities is presented to us. Neither does Lyly offer a positively constructed picture of morals gone astray -- Philautus is merely deprived of virtue (unlike Sidney's Amphialus, say, who is a fully-developed negative character).

The constant mouthing of virtue and simultaneous inability to present a rounded conception of it is not hypocritical. Like so many other Elizabethans, Lyly could probably accept that morality and virtue are necessary and desirable and yet, at the same time, not see actions immediately in terms of them. The goodness of a Christian ethic is completely accepted, but it is sufficiently in conflict with the life and views of the Court that it is accepted only at a distance. The moralising of the hero -- 'to abstain from pleasure is the chiefest piety' say good men (I, p. 320) -- is irreconcilable with the obvious and often-stated purpose of the work to create pleasure, and speaking in his own person, toward the end of Euphues and his England, Lyly says, 'they that feed only upon virtue at board, will go with an hungry belly to bed' (II, p. 160). Lyly is playing with morality.

Morality was ideally suited to the external demands made on the work, as well as to a style reliant on contraries, and it was traditional in themes and many particulars. Samuel Lee Wolff comments that someone who writes in a tradition enjoys 'an incalculable advantage in the attitude of his audience, reader, spectator, toward his work. They come to him already in possession, though they hardly know it, of that "nucleus of apperception" which ensures him a welcome'(6). When the audience recognises familiar material either their interest is aroused in a new working-out of an old theme, or they feel the vague comfort of accustomed surroundings. The reader, familiar with the subject matter, is not distracted by its novelty and can see more clearly Lyly's art. Lyly could demonstrate his cleverness through a skilful integrating of the traditional themes of wit and wisdom. Furthermore, morality provides a natural basis for the extended monologues and dialogues that are so important to the work's stylistic effect and it offers great scope for the classical allusions and comparisons from pseudo-natural history which can create the appearance of humanistic learning. Lyly's morality, then, is really only a vehicle for style -- material for witty display. The poet 'doth not learn a conceit out of a matter, but maketh matter for a conceit', Sidney stated in The Defence of Poesie (p. 99); Lyly, it might be said, of a conceit makes matter.

Although it is less true of Euphues and his England than The Anatomy of Wyt, Lyly is not really interested in narrative and he believes his audience as well to be more interested in discourse than plot action. Camilla's monologue on her love for Surius is interrupted by a knock:

> which she hearing left off that, which all you Gentlewomen would gladly hear, for no doubt she determined to make a long sermon, had not she been interrupted: But by the preamble you may guess to what purpose the drift tended. (II, p. 184)

Despite his ironic tone, Lyly appears to think his feminine readers would rather hear what was said next than done next. The suggestion is that plot exists to serve discourse, rather than the often-assumed reverse. Some elements which apparently display an interest in the details of plot development are seen on closer examination to be merely the occasions for wit. Thus Philautus, faced with the problem of how to deliver a letter to Camilla, whom he is wooing through correspondence, contrives its delivery in a hollowed-out pomegranate. But it is not a genuine problem, seeing how easily it is solved on following occasions (Camilla's first reply is delivered in a volume of Petrarch which she asks Philautus to construe and her second by a manservant). Lyly considers the device clever enough to draw the reader's attention to it directly, saying he is not going to relate the conversation between Philautus and Camilla's ladies 'which here to insert were neither convenient, seeing it doth not concern the History, nor expedient, seeing it is nothing to the delivery of Philautus Letter'(II, p. 125). The idea is probably borrowed from Whetstone's The Rocke of Regard (1576) in which Giletta makes use of a hollowed-out apple to deliver a letter to Rinaldo (1576 ed., sig. C8-C8v). The borrowing is immaterial; what is important is that it appears as clever invention. It is not an attempt at realistic detail but a narrative artifice. In both parts of Euphues content is largely a function of style.

Lyly displays a virtuosity in the integration of metaphors equalled only by Thomas Nashe and the Shakespeare of Love's Labour's Lost. When Lucilla responds to Euphues's renewed suit by telling him that he is making 'a long harvest for a little corn' and angles 'for the fish that is already caught', Euphues picks up the fishing metaphor to tell Lucilla,

> if you be a fish you are either an Eel which as soon as one hath hold of her tail, will slip out of his hand, or else a Minnow which will be nibbling at every bait but never biting: but what fish soever you be you have made both me and Philautus to swallow a Gudgen.
> (I, pp. 239-40)

Euphues, when he asks Philautus to accompany him from England to Athens, realises that 'his friend was so fast tied by the eyes, that he found thorns in his heel, which Euphues knew to be thoughts in his heart'(II, p. 185). Even with classical allusions, Lyly can switch the meanings to suit his argument. Lucilla cites Helen and other figures to justify her conduct, to which Euphues responds that on the basis of classical examples she might mate with her father or with a bull (I, p. 240).

It is sufficient to say the style has a marked brilliance, a pure enjoyment of language and words and creation of patterns that is at once childlike in its delight in sound-balance and sophisticated in its involved wit. He offers a collection of separate jewels, the taste for which is paralleled in Elizabethan painting, brilliant single items that

can be valued more for their individual richness
than for their relation to a larger context. But
the very purity of the style made it limited: it was
ruined by application to a particular matter. It is
probably this, as much as the changing taste of the
Court, that doomed euphuism. (The problems of the
style applied to story can be seen in Greene's early
works, where euphuism trammels narrative.)

* * *

Euphues says to Philautus, 'talk the more it is
seasoned with fine phrases, the less it savoureth of
true meaning'(II, p. 99), which has often been considered to apply very much to Lyly's own prose (7).
However, style is intimately connected with his
thought; it is not mere ornament unless thought,
too, is mere ornament (8). Whereas content usually
carries an author's meaning, here content is a
function of style, and thus it is to style we must
turn for meaning, as Jonas Barish suggests:

> One would scarcely need to go further for the
> moral of Euphues than the style, which offers
> for our inspection the world as antithesis.
> Contraries, potential or realized, lurk
> everywhere in nature and human nature. Right
> action consists in the power to perceive them
> and to choose the worthier alternative. (p. 25)

He says that Lyly brings a 'logic' into English that
previously had existed only in the learned languages
and, through language, makes everything logical, in
its appearance at least (p. 27).
'Logic' is, however, only one part of a broader
meaning for Lyly's style. He is not attempting to
reproduce external reality but is replacing real
chaos with the order of an artificial world. It is
not an actual order; it is the sense of order. The
nearest parallel is perhaps music which, although it
does not deal with the external world, can create a
sense of order in the listeners which they transfer
to the external world. This quality, though more
obvious in Lyly's plays, is noticeable in his prose
as well. He offers a complete world which, in its
completeness and self-enclosed quality, provides for
the audience a sense of security, of a world
completely controlled and well-ordered into which
the outside world never enters. It has also a
richness and formal beauty that someone with

courtly, refined sensibilities could only find pleasurable.

It is frequently observed that Lyly is given to employing superlatives, saying, for example, not 'snakes are found in green grass' but that 'the greatest snakes are found in the greenest grass' (Barish, p. 22). This is not mere decoration. The effect of the combination of superlatives is to make an otherwise open-ended situation finite, which is important to Lyly's creation of order through style. By using 'greatest' snakes and 'greenest' grass he seems to have combined the highest points in the range of grass and snakes, which suggests (psychologically, not grammatically) that all possibilities are covered. Of course the smallest snakes might lurk in the palest grass, but that does not seem important if the major possibilites are accounted for. He is not trying to provoke thought; he is creating an impression of order. Superlatives create the sense of the whole, of completeness, and the finite world presented seems to encompass the whole world, and thus the order is as satisfying as if the whole world had been ordered. The more comprehensive the feeling, the more aesthetically satisfying. It is in this completeness and order that Lyly is a consummate artist, and it is the product of his style alone.

Lyly's style was successful at Court because it is based on the world view of the Court, which is regarded as natural. It is a mirror for the Court, a flattering mirror. Lyly conveys the feeling (especially in the plays) that his works themselves are of no importance; the Court is the real world, the only world of true significance. In Euphues the same attitude is suggested by the quality of dramatic arrangement even of the novelistic material. Lyly brings various 'scenes' on the stage and finishes them off like dramatic scenes. After the first part of Fidus's tale, in Euphues and his England, Philautus wakes Euphues when Fidus has finished his 'chapter':

> And so waking Euphues, who had taken a nap, they all went to their lodging, where I think Philautus was musing upon the event of Fidus his love: But there I will leave them in their beds, till the next morning. (II, p. 57)

The posture here is different from that taken by Lyly at other points where he treats the material as having an independent existence with his own function being the selection and reporting to the audience; here the audience is seen as having the only real existence and it is for them that the events are arranged. Although not consistent, the attitude occurs throughout: 'But I will leave Camilla, with whose love I have nothing to meddle, for that it maketh nothing to my matter. And return we to Euphues, who must play the last part'(II, p. 184). The audience is what matters; the 'toy' of Euphues is created only for their pleasure.

Lyly's reader is flattered, as Hunter says, by being allowed to enter into such a refined world. Flattery of that sort is reinforced by his ironic wit, which involves a sense of the author sharing certain experiences and attitudes with the readers, having in common with them understanding denied to the characters. Thus Lyly says he will not appor-tion blame for the parting of Euphues and Philautus, although some of his audience might be able to decide, 'being of deeper discretion than I am'(I, p. 198). The feminine audience is given a friendly teasing in Euphues and his England, which is a pleasant evolution of the fashionable misogyny of the first part: 'so resolute was she in her opinion, I dare not say obstinate lest you gentlewomen should take pepper in the nose, when I put but salt to your mouths'(II, p. 141). To the reader denied the Court, the opportunity to partake in its gracious forms, even if only remotely as a reader, must be flattering. Thus dialogue, in which almost as much space is occupied by courtesy and gracious inter-ruption as by the substantive part of the discourse, may be regarded as normal courtesy by the members of the Court, but the non-Court audience probably is charmed by being allowed to witness it.

Besides the indirect and subtle appeal of the rhetorical posture, Lyly makes remarks that directly flatter the readers. In saying (in the epistle 'To the Ladies and Gentlewomen of England' in Euphues and his England) that 'Euphues had rather lie shut in a Ladies casket, than open in a Scholars study' (II, p. 9), he is directly appealing to his feminine audience as well as characterising the work. He offers much praise of the English Court through the mouths of Euphues and Philautus. The Queen is given considerable, but perhaps customary, praise (e.g., I, p. 323; II, pp. 38 and 203ff.); Burghley is praised (II, p. 198); and England is lauded by Euphues in a letter to Livia at the court in Naples: 'a place in my opinion (if any such may be in the earth) not inferior to a Paradise'(II, p. 189). In

'Euphues Glasse for Europe' all of England's traits are portrayed as good and those of Europe, in contrast, as bad (II, pp. 200-203). Philautus, doubting his chances of winning Camilla, flatters the entire courtly audience:

> Dost thou not see every minute the noble youth
> of England frequent the Court, with no less
> courage than thou cowardice. If Courtly
> bravery, may allure her, who more gallant, than
> they? If personage, who more valiant? If wit
> who more sharp, if birth, who more noble, if
> virtue, who more devout? (II, p. 87)

However, the most important flattery in Euphues remains, not the direct remarks, but the style which appeals to the reader's sensibility and position.

In that he writes for a courtly audience, it is natural that Lyly shows an unquestioning acceptance of a hierarchical system and, for an audience of established rather than new aristocrats, he does not need to harp on rank and status. Fidus, for example, an embodiment of generous wisdom with experience of the Court from which he has removed himself, stresses the importance of classes remaining in their places: emperors can be inquired of only by their equals; 'For this is sufficient for you to know, that there is a Lion, not where he is, or what he doth'(II, p. 43). Lyly does not labour the point; it is a view assumed without argument. He speaks of Surius as 'the best in the company, and therefore best worthy to answer, and the wisest, and therefore best able'(II, p. 163), which clearly suggests that 'best' means simply of highest birth.

More important than such obvious values are those which are definite yet less clearly articulated, such as sprezzatura. In the competitive reality of the Court, sprezzatura helped to keep competition in bounds by disguising efforts, virtues, etc. 'This combination of a reality of competitive violence and an imposed code of humble and light-hearted appearance is responsible for much of the doubleness and indirection of court art', Hunter explains (pp. 130-31). 'He that cannot dissemble in love, is not worthy to live', Euphues argues after he has betrayed Philautus's trust (I, p. 236). Wit is used, especially in the plays, 'to distance the emotions and express a remote and refined pattern of their equivalents in wit' (Hunter, p. 105). Emotion directly felt or expressed destabilises the delicate balance of the

Court situation; as in the Courtier, it must be not
so much repressed as sublimated to a socially-
acceptable form. We can see this also in a negative
example. Lucilla, having rejected both Philautus
and Euphues, marries Curio -- 'in body deformed, in
mind foolish, an innocent born, a beggar by
misfortune'(I, p. 240). Curio is not beyond the
bounds of social acceptability (as is Erona's
Antiphilus in the Arcadia) but is the worst of the
range of possible choices. The name suggests
'curious' (in the sixteenth-century sense of careful
or laboured) -- the contrary of sprezzatura. It is
this contrary that is the worst choice, because
opposed to one of the most important ideals
(functionally, even if not in the hierarchy of
professed ideals) of the Court. Sprezzatura, as
Castiglione said, is essential to achieve grace, and
grace is perhaps the most necessary quality for an
author trying to appeal to the Court.

Sprezzatura provides Lyly's lightness of touch
and makes him acceptable to the Court, but his
problem is maintaining with sprezzatura his
relationship, in print, with his audience. Some of
his techniques are simple ones which became standard
in later authors, such as drawing the moral for his
audience; 'Here Gentlemen you may see, into what
open sins the heat of Love driveth man'(II, p. 109).
But Lyly manages to make the technique his own and
adds a playful, personal quality:

> Here Gentlewomen you may see, how justly men
> seek to entrap you, when scornfully you go
> about to reject them, thinking it not unlawful
> to use Art, when they perceive you obstinate,
> their dealings I will not allow, neither can I
> excuse yours, and yet what should be the cause
> of both, I can guess. (II, pp. 120-21)

Questions to his audience, which appear in Euphues
and his England, help to make the audience conscious
of a shared experience, and thus to connect them
with Lyly. Philautus says that the end of love is
wedding, not wooing, and Lyly asks the ladies
whether they do not agree with Philautus, adding 'As
good it were to be silent and think no, as to blush
and say I' (II, p. 160). Lyly says you need not
resolve the question now, because Euphues and
Philautus did not; 'but every one as he liketh'(II,
p. 161) -- characters, author, and audience are all
woven into the same fabric. Sometimes, however,
Lyly enters the work at the expense of the fiction:

'Thus after many words, they went to their dinner, where I omit their table talk, lest I lose mine'(II, p. 130). This is fine for calling Lyly himself to the reader's mind, but the fact that the characters' and Lyly's dinners exists in two separate universes breaks whatever 'historical' reality the story has. Lyly is not being a careless artist here: he chooses strength of relationship above narrative consistency.

It is Lyly's actual relationship with his audience that in large measure determines his style and perhaps a change in that relationship can offer some explanation for the change from The Anatomy of Wyt to Euphues and his England. It is evident that he felt more secure in the writing of Euphues and his England and on that basis we can say it is likely that he no longer felt it necessary to prove himself, but merely to entertain. Lyly probably felt novelty was required for the entertainment but novelty that preserved the same old qualities, and he felt free to indulge his imagination further.

Euphues and his England is maturer as fiction; Lyly displays increased objectivity and has more development of plot and character. Characters react even to the style of other characters. But increased circumstantial detail does not necessarily mean realism; it can be traditional detail, convention rather than observation (e.g. the problem of letter delivery), and Euphues and his England is more obviously conventional than Munday's Zelauto published the same year. Lyly is preserving his role as courtly entertainer and at the same time adjusting his entertaining to the demands of print. Euphues and his England is probably the first work of English fiction designed specifically for (rather than just recognising) an audience reached through reading the printed work. The difference is not a vast or even a very marked one; it is one of balance of tendencies, like the difference between a stage play filmed for television and a television play.

Lyly, like many Elizabethan writers, was uncertain about the attitude to take toward his material and raised a number of problems which were not solved but which are of interest in showing development of a consciousness of fiction. The construction of the fiction demands a degree of objectivity -- i.e., the story must appear to have some existence independent of the author. Lyly begins to attempt it in The Anatomy of Wyt. In the dedication he says that if Euphues seems frivolous at first, it is necessitated by truth, and not caused by the lightness of the author (I, p. 180), but this excuse is perhaps conventional. The first real indication of objectivity is at the end of the volume in 'A cooling Carde for Philautus and all fond lovers', where Euphues first addresses Philautus, and then lovers, and then gentlemen (I, pp. 246-47) and finally asks Philautus 'that thou show this cooling card to none, except thou show also this my defence to them all'(I, p. 257). We can see that Lyly is attempting (though with limited success) to give Euphues an independent existence.

Objectivity leads to the problem of omni-science: if the events are to have some reality for the readers, how can the author know everything that has happened? Lyly recognises that objectivity precludes his being in more than one place at one time, and thus he says, when Euphues and Philautus part, 'Philautus to London where I leave him, Euphues to Athens where I mean to follow him, for he it is that I am to go with, not Philautus'(II, p. 188). Again, he says he will let Euphues say what he has been doing all the while because he is not of his counsel (II, p. 143). At other points he also lacks information to report: 'What cheer they had I know not, what talk they used, I heard not: but Supper being ended, they sat still, the Lady Flavia speaking as followeth'(II, p. 162). The problem is not solved, of course, because Lyly is on the scene without being an actor. At other times no objectivity is achieved because what is supposed to be objective is obviously the result of the author's intention -- it becomes mock objectivity: 'Thus letting Surius and Camilla to whisper by themselves (whose talk we will not hear) the Lady began in this manner to greet Martius'(II, p. 169).

Perhaps Lyly's posture can be seen more clearly if we characterise it as dramatic. Both Lyly and the characters appear real, but the feigned reality of the characters is not like that of char-acters of mock historical reality (Don Simonides II, for example), but like actors who are playing parts. Lyly is the manipulator of real characters, as in a play:

> But why go I about to set her in black and white, whom Philautus is now with all colours importraying in the Table of his heart. And surely I think by this he is half mad, whom long since, I left in a great maze. Philautus viewing all these things, and more than I have uttered (for that the lovers eye pierceth

deeper) withdrew himself secretly into his lodging and locking his door, began to debate with himself in this manner. (II, p. 85)

The reality of the character here is not 'historical' reality, when Lyly as a historical person also 'hears report'; Lyly is the director, dealing with semi-independent dramatic characters and himself only semi-omniscient. The question for Lyly is less one of what attitude to take toward the characters than where he should stand himself.

Other problems of fiction result from Lyly's attempts at objectivity and following a straight time-line. He offers a letter to the reader, explains how it was delivered, and then explains the reaction of the recipient. Thus the reader reacts before the recipient and the latter's reaction is an anti-climax (see II, pp. 127-30). Greene was able to solve the problem by showing the letter to the reader after it has been received, and thus character and reader share the reaction (e.g. with Publia's letter to Pharicles in Mamillia I). Lyly, although he did not solve it, was aware of the problem. Unlike Munday, whose Zelauto retells twice what Munday has already reported about his being attacked by bandits, Lyly edits the dialogue. Philautus tells Euphues of his love:

> who left out nothing that before I put in, which I must omit, lest I set before you, Coleworts twice sodden, which will both offend your ears which I seek to delight and trouble my hand which I covet to ease. (II, p. 154)

The one solution he found, though not too graceful, works. Events left hanging in the text are concluded often by letter (this technique is found in both parts). At the end of Euphues and his England Euphues, after he has been in Athens more than three months, receives a letter from Philautus in England: 'which I thought necessary also to insert, that I might give some end to the matters in England, which at Euphues departure were but rawly left'(II, p. 217). This straightforward epistolary relation of events serves his fiction much better than teasing the reader with unfinished matter as in The Anatomy of Wyt, where, refusing to relate the end of Lucilla and Curio, he says:

> but what end came of her, seeing it is nothing incident to the history of Euphues, it were

> superfluous to insert it, and so incredible
> that all women would rather wonder at it than
> believe it, which event being so strange, I had
> rather leave them in a muse what it should be,
> than in a maze in telling what it was.
> (I, p. 245)

However, this too is eventually resolved by letter.
The great fictional advance of Euphues and his
England is not in such artifices of plot relation,
but in growth of naturalness and character. The
setting is a 'real' world -- contemporary England,
not abstract Athens and Naples. Dialogue has more
the character of actual interchange than the set
speeches of The Anatomy of Wyt and takes place
sometimes in a natural setting, such as Fidus's talk
about the bees: 'who now removing himself nearer to
the Hives, began as followeth'(II, p. 44). But it
is character that shows the greatest advance -- the
character of Philautus mostly, for Euphues is not
much different from the vice-free man we were left
with at the end of The Anatomy. Philautus's character affects his actions in the sequel. On shipboard
he would rather sleep than hear Euphues's tale of a
hermit (being inclined only to subject matter of
love -- II, p. 14) and Euphues, less credibly, falls
asleep during Fidus's story of the Court (II,
pp. 49, 56-57). Philautus begins to answer back
Euphues, objecting that Euphues, in talking to him
cannot say three words without the third being
'love'(II, p. 83). Lyly has finally achieved the
use of set speeches as display of character.
Philautus tries to get his own back on Euphues when
Euphues gives up his misogynous attitude:

> Is this thy professed purity to cry peccavi?
> thinking it as great sin to be honest, as shame
> not to be amorous, thou that diddest blaspheme
> the noble sex of women without cause, dost thou
> now commit Idolatry with them without care?
> (II, p. 93)

The whole speech is constructed on attitudes that
(in the work) are peculiar to Philautus, and thus
reveals his character. Even Philautus's diction,
differing from what Lyly would consider objective,
reveals character: asked where Euphues is, he
replies that Euphues 'nowadays became so studious
(or as he termed it, superstitious) . . .'(II,
p. 127).

Brilliant as he is, Lyly is inevitably limited as a writer because he lacks a personal point of view, which gives vigour to even the slightest work of Thomas Deloney. He laboured under a world-view uncritically borrowed from the Court, to which he completely adapted himself but never made really his own -- a view never argued but present in all his writing. His dependence on the Court and desire to avoid offence show through all his work. His intimate relationship with his audience, though created through his prose, is less the result of a specifically literary intention than the product of the necessities of his personal circumstances: the artist and the courtier are in opposition. Striving to maintain a relationship with his audience through print, he so frequently throws his own person into the matter that the fiction's objectivity is shattered. In the plays the same problems of relationship with the audience do not arise and he can construct an amazingly solid structure from the frail reeds of his limited content. But in the prose, his objectivity and need for relationship were in contradiction, and the relationship was of paramount importance. Like Odysseus escaping from Polyphemus's island, Lyly cannot resist announcing whose wit performed the deed, and thereby he crazes the delicate crystal of his fiction.

NOTES

1. G. K. Hunter, John Lyly: The Humanist as Courtier (London, 1962), pp. 35, 14.

2. See Hunter, pp. 50-51, and Walter R. Davis, Idea and Act in Elizabethan Fiction (Princeton, 1969), pp. 114ff.

3. Albert Feuillerat, John Lyly (Cambridge, 1910), pp. 67-68 and 499.

4. C. S. Lewis, English Literature in the Sixteenth Century excluding Drama (Oxford, 1968), pp. 314-15.

5. G. Wilson Knight, 'Lyly', The Review of English Studies, Vol. 15 (1939), p. 147.

6. S. L. Wolff, 'The Humanist as Man of Letters: John Lyly', The Sewanee Review, Vol. 31 (1923), p. 33.

7. See Margaret Schlauch, <u>Antecedents of the English Novel 1400-1600 (from Chaucer to Deloney)</u> (Warsaw and London, 1963), p. 188.

8. Jonas Barish, 'The Prose Style of John Lyly', <u>ELH</u>, Vol. 23 (1956), p. 15.

5 PHILIP SIDNEY

Philip Sidney was the literary flower of the English aristocracy but, unlike a writer such as Thomas Nashe who exists for us almost entirely through his writing, Sidney's reputation as a man precedes that of his work. Fulke Greville felt his own primary claim to remembrance to be his friendship with Sidney, choosing as his epitaph, 'Servant to Queen Elizabeth, Counsellor to King James, and friend to Sir Philip Sidney'(1). People who can hardly name an Elizabethan non-dramatic writer (let alone having read one) have heard how the wounded Sidney gave his drink to a dying soldier. We are now accustomed to 'great men' being created by public relations officers and the mass media -- men whose 'greatness' owes more to the film editor than to their own actions -- and it is natural to be sceptical about Sidney's applauded virtues. Roger Howell, in fact, suggests that Sidney's reputation is more created image than reflection of fact: 'Although it may be true that he was not a "great" man by concrete tests of achievement, he was very plainly the beau ideal of his age'(2). But scepticism about his virtues as a man fades when one reads the Arcadia; and even if he was not one of the profound thinkers of the time, he was without doubt one of the great spirits of the age.

It is easy to regard Sidney as the representative Elizabethan, since in his life and the Arcadia he displays the great qualities of the age -- individuality, intensity, magnanimity, adventurousness, and wit -- and because our conception of the age may often be based on Sidney and a few others (as the title of Frederick S. Boas's Sir Philip Sidney, Representative Elizabethan would suggest). Sidney is, more accurately, the representative of a class; he represents the age inasmuch as his class

dominates the age. Although his literary and personal greatness may give him the appearance of a
universal Elizabethan spokesman, he serves a class
function.

More than a member of the ruling class, Sidney
is an active ruler, a conscious leader of his
society. His leadership is carried on through all
his activities, including literature where he
instructs as well as entertains. Whereas Lyly, not
himself an aristocrat, could only play at instruction, Sidney instructs with authority. The New
Arcadia is the only Elizabethan work of fiction to
present a fully conscious ideology. It provides a
model of an aristocratic world-view. Art, for
Sidney, is not a mere plaything; it has a value for
living. True poetry, as he explains in The Defence
of Poesie, feigns notable images of virtue and vice,
and Fulke Greville said it was Sidney's intention in
the Arcadia 'to turn the barren Philosophy precepts
into pregnant Images of life'(3). The Arcadia is a
serious work -- socially serious. Lyly, whose
audience was probably much the same as Sidney's, was
serious in his art rather than in his moral view;
his moralising has an abstract quality that makes it
unimportant as morality. Lyly produces a model for
style, while Sidney produces a model for life. As
G. K. Hunter pointed out in discussing Sidney's
increasing and Lyly's declining popularity at Court,
Lyly's 'wit was based on pedantry aspiring to
courtliness; Sidney's was courtly in essence'(4).

Sidney's seriousness can be seen in his revision of the Arcadia. The Old Arcadia was a 'trifle'
written about 1580 for a semi-private audience, to
be read aloud in the intimate company of his sister
and her friends. In writing the New Arcadia (about
1584) it would seem that Sidney intended to reach a
wider audience and the work has clearly a more public character. He did not reject the material of
the Old Arcadia in his revision; on the contrary, as
R. W. Zandvoort has shown, he re-used in the New
Arcadia almost all of the material of the Old (5),
but it undergoes an artistic and philosophical
refinement, and he achieves a more 'objective' work
which appears to exist independently of the author's
attitude. The tales are moralised and the whole
work made into an ethical tool, as Walter R. Davis
has shown (6).

The ethical tool that Sidney creates is designed to serve his class, particularly the new
aristocracy (7), in several ways. He provides a
sense of continuity and establishment. The new

aristocracy were still sometimes regarded as inter-
lopers and their own insecurity can be seen in such
things as Sidney's father, Sir Henry Sidney, seeking
to construct for his family a long (though dubious)
lineage. In the Arcadia Sidney serves a function
similar to Virgil's in regard to Augustus and the
Senatorial families in the construction of the
Aeneid (although Sidney plays both Virgil and
Maecenas): he offers the psychological reassurance
of continuity and distant origins. Such assurance
would have no weight before a king of arms, and is
not primarily of value to specific individuals; it
is of value to the new aristocracy as a class.
Sidney also serves his class in showing that order
is the basis of society's well-being (by the last
quarter of the sixteenth century the new aristocracy
had been long enough established that they regarded
substantial social mobility with pronounced disfav-
our) and in prescribing the virtues that will maintain his class's position. He provides, somewhat
like Castiglione's Courtier which he so much admired, a perfect code of conduct for the aristocrat.
Rather than simply an assertion of aristocratic
morals, the whole work elaborates an aristocratic
perspective: the New Arcadia is as much a guide for
comprehending the world as for acting in it.

The problem that Sidney did not face in making
a literary model for aristocratic life was relevance
to reality. The new aristocracy, no longer so
necessary as administrators or as mediators between
the monarchy and bourgeoisie, were declining in
importance. The full courtier's role of soldier-
statesman-counsellor and policy-maker was hardly
possible any longer, and the courtier was fast
becoming a 'carpet knight', a mere ornament.
Sidney's solution was romance. He recreated his
ideals in a timeless past and the Arcadia has a
large element of escapism. He creates a substitute
for the world of the present in a shimmering world
of knightly values -- a world that offers a scope
for his values that the present denies. But this
world of action, removed from the context of
sixteenth-century life, becomes pure action. As
serious as he may be about life, Sidney finally
reduces life to style and becomes a decadent.

Decadence in a writer of such power is not
immediately apparent (8). In his revision of the
Arcadia Sidney made considerable technical advances
and created a more controlled work than any other of
Elizabethan fiction; but his very virtuosity, which
became an end in itself, was eventually self-

defeating. Life and action are reduced to aspects of Sidney's wit and the work becomes a brilliant formal exercise.

* * *

One of the New Arcadia's many advances in fictional technique is increased objectivity. The Old Arcadia had already displayed a considerable fictional objectivity in that Sidney often gives the reactions of characters an existence seemingly independent of the author. Thus rather than say directly that Basilius swells when Cleophila praises him, he says, 'You might have seen Basilius humbly swell'(9). The blushing of Cleophila and Dorus, though undetected by other characters, is given a similar objective existence: 'At these words a man might easily have perceived' that they blushed (IV, p. 64). Though he trips over his pen in his eagerness to entertain his audience with verse, Sidney tries to make its inclusion seem natural and independent of his own taste. He explains how four pages of verse in the middle of the action do not actually interrupt it: 'But do not think (Fair Ladies) his thoughts had such Leisure as to run over so long a Ditty: The only general fancy of it came into his mind fixed upon the sense of the sweet Subject'(IV, p. 226). This reveals a significant sense of objectivity (however awkward) in that the actual events of the story are distinguished from Sidney's relation of them. Although he still employs the same techniques of objectivity in the New Arcadia (without, however, the clumsiness of justifying the inclusion of verses not uttered by the characters), he further removes dependence of the work on his own personality. He drops the numerous addresses and parentheses to the Fair Ladies and refrains (with one and a half exceptions -- I, pp. 168-69 and 448) from author's first-person address. Morals are drawn for the audience of the New Arcadia, not by the author, but by characters themselves. The description of characters or setting also is often artfully made indirect in the New Arcadia, characters being described by others. We learn about Basilius, for example, from Kalander: Kalander learns of the oracle and, from him, the heroes and the reader learn. Lest the reader detect the author hiding behind the character or accuse him of improbability, the source of the character's information is often made clear. When, for example, Pamela relates the adventures of Plangus, she says

she follows as closely as possible what Plangus
himself said: 'And that which seemeth most
impossible unto me, (for as near as I can I repeat
it as Plangus told it) . . .'(I, p. 244). Sidney's
sense of objective fiction has become highly
sophisticated.

Another fictional advance of the New Arcadia,
which must in part result from the simple fact of
revision, is the increased unity of character and
motivation within the plot. A simple example is the
case of Philanax. In the Old Arcadia the initial
view of Philanax as an intelligent, well-
intentioned, capable man does not prepare us for the
vengeful, irrational, and semi-competent executive
of Books IV and V. Sidney removes this difficulty
in the New Arcadia. Even though the revision was
not completed to the point where we see the final
character of Philanax, assuming that his character
has not been substantially revised, we are prepared
for such a transition. In Book III, Ch. 19,
Basilius asks Philanax how to respond to Cecropia's
threat to kill his daughters and Zelmane if the
siege is not raised. Philanax's advice, though it
is entirely rational, has an inhuman coldness (I,
pp. 467-68). No quality of evil appears in Philanax
here, but his hardness would prepare the reader for
his zealous prosecution of the heroes in their
murder trial in Book V of the Old Arcadia.

A further indication of increased unity in the
fiction of the New Arcadia is seen in its greater
concern for causation. Almost all the parts of the
story that happen in Arcadia itself are fully
motivated. Sidney takes matters out of the hands of
Fortune and makes the plot the result of the actions
of people. Wolff stresses that Sidney is free from
the Renaissance slavery to the notion of Fortune;
that, while he pays lip-service to 'Fortune' as a
word, he provides real causes (10). Certainly the
plot in its total development is fantastic, but the
events that compose it are caused rather than
accidental. The chance attack on the royal family
by a lion and a bear of the Old Arcadia, for
example, becomes in the New Arcadia part of
Cecropia's plot -- she has kept dangerous beasts for
just such a purpose. Cecropia herself is more than
a mere embodiment of evil; she is fully human and
motivated by a jealousy that Sidney explains in
terms of both character and circumstance. A
corollary of the concern for causation is attention
to the conditions that enable the event to happen;
i.e., Sidney removes from the reader's mind any

doubt about the feasibility of the event. Thus if the reader wonders how, when she has been under such close observation, Zelmane can steal away from the King's lodge to follow Pamela and Philoclea to the river Ladon, Sidney reassures him that Gynecia's injury and Basilius's birthday devotions divert attention and facilitate her escape (I, p. 216). In short, action becomes in the New Arcadia the result of character and it is set firmly enough in a detailed context that it is clear how it could come about.

A matter less of technique than of vision and understanding is Sidney's matured grasp of the complexity of life, which provides one of the most notable advances of the New Arcadia. Beyond the ability to portray individual character, Sidney shows a sense of life as an elaborate pattern of many individuals interacting -- a literary sense of society that is unique among Elizabethan writers. This may be attributable in part to his experience of the Court, a whole society of comprehensible size. His contemporaries seldom get beyond pairs of individuals interacting and no other fiction writer of the time displays a sense of mass.

This understanding of mass and individual can be seen clearly in the battle scenes of Book III, where Amphialus and his followers charge the approaching forces of Basilius. Sidney begins the battle with a single pair of combatants -- Amphialus and Agenor -- brilliantly describing in immediate close-focus their encounter: Comely, youthful Agenor,

> all armed saving that his beaver was up, to have his breath in more freedom, seeing Amphialus come a pretty way before his company, neither staying the commandment of the captain, nor recking whether his face were armed, or no, set spurs to his horse, and with youthful bravery casting his staff about his head, put it then in his rest, as careful of comely carrying it, as if the mark had been but a ring, and the lookers on Ladies. But Amphialus lance was already come to the last of his descending line, and began to make the full point of death against the head of this young Gentleman, when Amphialus perceiving his youth and beauty, Compassion so rebated the edge of Choler, that he spared that fair nakedness, and let his staff fall to Agenors vamplate: so as both with brave breaking should hurtlessly have

performed that match, but that the pitiless
lance of Amphialus (angry with being broken)
with an unlucky counterbuff full of unsparing
splinters, lighted upon that face far fitter
for the combats of Venus; giving not only a
sudden, but a foul death, leaving scarcely any
tokens of his former beauty: but his hands
abandoning the reins, and his thighs the
saddle, he fell sideward from the horse. (I,
pp. 386-87)

After describing the death of Agenor and of his
companion, as well as Amphialus's emotional response
to their deaths, Sidney returns to a larger
perspective. He has a generalised, distant focus:

But by this time there has been a furious
meeting of either side: where after the
terrible salutation of warlike noise, the
shaking of hands was with sharp weapons: some
lances according to the mettle they met, and
skill of the guider, did stain themselves in
blood; some flew up in pieces, as if they would
threaten heaven, because they failed on earth.
But their office was quickly inherited, either
by (the Prince of weapons) the sword, or by
some heavy mace, or biting axe; which hunting
still the weakest chase, sought ever to light
there, were smallest resistance might worse
prevent mischief. The clashing of armour, and
crushing of staves; the justling of bodies, the
resounding of blows, was the first part of that
ill-agreeing music, which was beautified with
the grisliness of wounds, the rising of dust,
the hideous falls, and groans of the dying. (I,
pp. 387-88)

Sidney gives a broad view of the carnage,
describing the general scene, but makes it immediate
and real with concrete illustration:

In one place lay disinherited heads,
dispossessed of their natural seignories: in
another, whole bodies to see to, but that their
hearts wont to be bound all over so close, were
now with deadly violence opened: in others,
fouler deaths had uglily displayed their
trailing guts. There lay arms, whose fingers
yet moved, as if they would feel for him that
made them feel . . . (I, p. 388)

Despite the conceits, the battle scene is so specifically depicted, that it achieves a sense of actuality. Sidney creates a sense of a vast, active, yet anonymous group -- i.e., he creates a mass. Through his very material description he establishes here an intense atmosphere° that has few, if any, rivals in Elizabethan prose. The chapter ends with individual combats again, but they are described in more distant focus and more general terms than the sharply-outlined first encounter.

The following chapter begins with a generalised account of the chaos of the battle -- 'Then those that had killed, inherited the lot of those that had been killed'(I, p. 390) -- and then moves again to particular combat. Here Sidney provides reflection, without the vividness of the first scene, and then resumes the plot, relating the capture of Philanax and a combat between Amphialus and the Black Knight (Musidorus) (I, pp. 391-93). In these two chapters a splendid balance between mass and individual has been maintained, offering context and plot and further defining character through the context. This is one of the peaks of Elizabethan prose fiction, displaying an art and flexibility of vision rarely equalled.

Sidney's sense of the complexity of interrelations is also apparent in his chains of causation, of which the death of Argalus provides a good example. Basilius calls on the unrivalled champion Argalus to fight against Amphialus; but instead of presenting this as a simple action, Sidney breaks it down into a series of smaller acts. The final action is the same -- Argalus is killed in single combat -- but it is the product of a chain of decisions, a process. Basilius, because he is aware that Argalus's relationship with Parthenia has been achieved only by their endurance of dreadful trials and is a model of elevated domestic felicity, is reluctant to summon the newly-married champion; but, as his own honour stands on overthrowing Amphialus, 'he could no longer forbear to challenge of him his faithful service'(I, p. 420). Argalus, 'like a man in whom Honour could not be rocked on sleep by Affection'(I, p. 420), must follow Basilius's messenger. Even so, his departure is not automatic; he is loath to go and Parthenia actively objects to his going:

> My Argalus, my Argalus (said she) do not thus
> forsake me. Remember, alas, Remember that I

have interest in you, which I will never yield
shall be thus adventured. Your valour is
already sufficiently known: sufficiently have
you already done for your country: enow, enow
there are besides you to lose less worthy
lives. (I, p. 421)

Argalus goes resignedly rather than willingly,
'carried away by the tyranny of Honour'(I, p. 422).
He does not go immediately to fight. First he tries
to dissuade Amphialus from his wrongful course and,
that failing, challenges him, is defeated in a
struggle of military and psychological complexity,
and dies. We can see that his death, although it is
necessary, does not result from a simple, single
cause. Sidney has developed a sense of complex
tragic necessity.

* * *

The most striking change Sidney made in his
revision of the Old Arcadia was to increase the
formal or ceremonial elements, often undermining his
advance in realism. Some of this increase, in areas
such as fashion description, is not incompatible
with the development of the fiction, although
probably motivated by the taste of a fashion-crazy
Court that delighted in gorgeousness and display for
their own sake. The element of knightly encounter,
which becomes important only in the New Arcadia,
gives him a great opportunity to deal in military
fashion. Even encounters of military consequence,
as well as ceremonial fighting such as Phalantus's
tournament to defend the beauty of Artesia, are
occasions for lengthy descriptions of armour,
emblems, horse-furniture, etc., and sometimes it
seems that Sidney brings in trials of arms for no
other purpose than to present the sumptuous
costumes. At other points, however, fashion is
significant in terms of a character's situation in
the plot. In the trial scene of the Old Arcadia and
in Amphialus's first interview with Philoclea after
she has been kidnapped by his mother, Cecropia, the
extended treatment of clothing is justified because
dress has a rhetorical value, indicating degree of
worship and frame of mind (IV, pp. 349-50; I,
p. 367). As Sir Thomas Elyot said in The Book named
the Governor, 'Apparel may be well a part of
majesty' (11).
Where the forms have increased importance, it
is often at the expense of realism. Incidents in

the Old Arcadia that have an individualised human
quality become artificial in the New Arcadia when
reorganised to fit a chivalric code. Musidorus, for
example, becomes much more a cardboard figure
through his strict adherence to a chivalric courtly
love. Pamela repulses Dorus-Musidorus when he
offers to kiss her and says, 'Let me see thee no
more, the only fall of my judgement, and stain of my
conscience'(I, p. 355). He runs into the woods,
starves himself for two days, and then decides to
keep his hated self alive only to preserve the image
of Pamela that was in him.

> Then began he only so far to wish his own good,
> as that Pamela might pardon him the fault,
> though not the punishment: and the uttermost
> height he aspired unto, was, that after his
> death, she might yet pity his error, and know
> that it proceeded of love, and not of boldness.
> (I, p. 356)

This is a far cry from the Musidorus of the Old
Arcadia who, breaking his promise to her, is only
just prevented from ravishing the sleeping Pamela
(IV, p. 190). Sidney has transformed a human,
though somewhat stiff, character into a pasteboard
courtly lover. Musidorus's social existence is not
simply formalised; it is give a different content.
Sidney removes his chivalric characters from the
realm of life and puts them clearly into the area of
ideals and artifice.

The chivalry, independent of its fictional
value, is important as a reflection of courtly taste
and the new aristocracy's desire to seem
long-established; but aesthetically it is part of
Sidney's increasing preoccupation with formality.
He does not merely present action in a formal
fashion; chivalry for him is an exercise in form.
The Old Arcadia shows a sense of ceremony and of
formal action, which is to be expected from an
aristocratic writer of the Elizabethan period, but
the sense is of natural actions formalised rather
than purely formal events. Thus Philoclea's moonlit
revision of her verses written on marble (IV,
pp. 104-5) has a ceremonial quality, an enjoyment of
scene and staging distinct from plot value. The
same appreciation of situation appears where
Cleophila watches Philoclea running from the lion
Cleophila has already slain:

her light Nymphlike apparel being carried up
with the wind, that, much of those beauties she
would at another time have willingly hidden,
were presented to the eye of the twice wounded
Cleophila: which made Cleophila not follow her
over hastily, lest she should too soon deprive
herself of that pleasure. (IV, p. 43)

The event has a patterned, ceremonial quality and
yet seems natural. Similarly, orchestration of
actions is enjoyed for its own sake in the Old
Arcadia, as in the comic return of Dametas after his
failure to find the gold for which he was digging,
when he is greeted by Mopsa, who thinks he is
Apollo, and Miso, who thinks he is embracing his
non-existent lover, Charita (IV, pp. 248-52). A
similar enjoyment of pattern on a broader scale is
to be seen in the contrary forces brought about by
Cleophila's being the object of three loves. The
eclogues contribute to the same effect; they are a
self-consciously formal presentation, a formalising,
of the actions that have preceded them.
    The New Arcadia also shows enjoyment of pattern
but increases the degree of purely formal action
within the work. While chivalry, as the exercise of
a code, is necessarily formal, Sidney makes into
formal events in the New Arcadia other things which
need not be formal in themselves. Complexity of
causation is a fictional advance of the revision,
but Sidney also plays with causation, to the detri-
ment of the fiction. If the effect is not of real
interest to Sidney as part of the plot, then to
attempt to satisfy the reader with its causes
becomes a game. Thus when Pyrocles, to fulfil
Zelmane's dying request, goes off to release
Plexirtus by killing a monster, Sidney says he takes
'sufficient security, that Plexirtus should be
delivered if I were victorious'(I, p. 301), suddenly
endowing his wandering-knight hero with an entour-
age. Or, when Pyrocles has been attacked by mighty
Otaves with the aid of two giants, the sons of
giants slain by the two heroes earlier in the same
kingdom, Sidney explains that these giant sons
avoided being killed at the time 'they having been
absent at their fathers death'(I, p. 296). The
causal explanations here do not explain anything
important in the narrative but are an intellectual
game; Sidney demonstrates his wit in finding causes
or enabling conditions, even though those conditions
are unimportant or are not essentially relevant to
what he is saying. Pyrocles proves his identity to

Philoclea with a letter from his father Euarchus
which he fortunately happens to have in his Amazon's
garb (he neither left it with his other possessions
in Mantinea nor lost it in his series of maritime
disasters). He and Musidorus need ready money when
they are with Kalander, which problem Sidney solves
by their selling some jewels. He gives realistic
recognition to the need for money (one of the things
Don Quixote discovered to be lacking in the models
of chivalric adventure he followed), but does not
bother to explain how pastoral Arcadia can so
readily provide a cash market. The effect here is
that Sidney is impressing the reader with his ready
wit, offering a clever device that makes the
situation he is dealing with possible, yet without
showing sustained attention to the reality. The
causes fail not through lack of cleverness (he has
given sufficient demonstration of intellectual
power), but because he is interested in them as wit
rather than as actual causation.

Increasing formality appears in the developing
rhetoric of the New Arcadia. In the Old Arcadia
Sidney favoured a style of rational oppositions --
statement that reflects convoluted contradictions
rather than the sound-opposition of Lyly. Thus
Musidorus gives a bribe to Dametas so that the
latter will allow him to be his servant: 'he
[Dametas] became slave to that which he that would
be his servant bestowed upon him'(IV, p. 40). When
Basilius goes off to the cave to meet, he supposes,
Cleophila, Sidney describes the situation in a pair
of neat contraries: 'Thus with a great deal of pain
did Basilius go to her, whom he fled, and with much
Cunning left the person for whom he had employed all
his Cunning'(IV, p. 213). The New Arcadia sometimes
sacrifices the strength of the rationality to a more
euphuistic construction that plays on word-repeti-
tion: 'His arm no oftener gave blows, than the blows
gave wounds, than the wounds gave deaths: so
terrible was his force, and yet was his quickness
more forcible than his force, and his judgement more
quick than his quickness'(I, p. 392). The opposition is more contrived than real and superficial
contradiction of words rather than things seems to
be the main focus of interest. Sidney engages at
times in a style very like that which drove Don
Quixote out of his mind:

> O Amphialus I would thou were not so excellent,
> or I would I thought thee not so excellent, and
> yet would I not, that I would so . . .(I, p.67)

Such convolutions of speech from Queen Helen of
Corinth do not significantly divert narrative
interest, yet there are other points where fictional
effects are lost through rhetorical excess. While
the scene of the death of Argalus is powerful
because of its tragic necessity, that of Parthenia
is rather conventional. That it is improbable is
not important, for whatever pathos it achieves is
due, not to tragic necessity, but to the fact that
someone young and beautiful dies needlessly and for
love. Whereas Argalus's dying speech is effective
and affecting because his sentiments are addressed
directly to Parthenia, her own dying words lose
their emotional impact because they are formal
rather than personal. (But is is possisble that
Sidney intends this.) Parthenia makes a
conventional 'good-night', addressing a formal
rhetoric to the world:

> I come, my Argalus, I come: And, O God hide my
> faults in thy mercies, and grant (as I feel
> thou dost grant) that in thy eternal love, we
> may love each other eternally. (I, p. 448)

The pathetic quality of the scene would be destroyed
by the formality of the rhetoric were it not for
Sidney's picturing the reactions of Parthenia's
stricken maids in the next paragraph.

The most marked indication of Sidney's turn to
formal material is the plot complexity of the
revised version, the re-weaving of the work on 'the
loom of Heliodorus' that Wolff so much admired (The
Greek Romances, pp. 352-53). Such complexity is
different from that of the motivation of characters.
Motivational complexity was an increase in realism
but plot complexity adds nothing to the fiction; it
is a delight in complexity for its own sake. Yet
pure complexity is something that Sidney strives
for, because it has the same value as a conceit. It
is a demonstration of wit on a larger scale -- of,
mental capacity, of how much interrelation of plot
can be held in the mind at once. The central
illustration of this is the connection of most
incidents with the Plangus-Erona-Antiphilus complex.
The fifteenth story of Painter's second Tome, the
Philon-Euphemia-Acharisto story, which seems to be
Sidney's immediate source, is not complicated by
far-reaching, tenuous connections, nor is the
suggestion of the Plangus-Erona story in the Old
Arcadia. In the New Arcadia the connection between
secondary tales and Plangus-Erona is seldom

essential and usually can be drawn after the secondary tale is told; that is, the secondary tales do not grow organically from the Plangus-Erona tale but are merely tied to it by Sidney. There is no necessity, for example, in the connection between the Palladius-Queen Andromena incidents (the escape of Pyrocles and Musidorus from the lust of Andromana through the aid of Palladius for the sake of Zelmane) and the Plangus-Erona situation; yet Sidney makes a connection in that Andromana is Plangus's step-mother who caused him to be disinherited; only the name of the villainess connects the two sets of incidents and there might just as well have been two different evil women. Similarly, the complication is unnecessary when Pyrocles is saved from Chremes's betrayal. He is rescued from Iberian attackers who hope to gain a reward of 100,000 crowns offered by Queen Artaxia (Erona's enemy) for Pyrocles's death in revenge for his slaying of her brother Tiridates (whom Plangus served). The rescuer of Pyrocles in this situation is the King of Iberia; he is the estranged father of Plangus who thinks that Artaxia (the king's niece) fosters Plangus against him (I, pp. 275-77). Certainly Sidney has created a most intellectually involved set of relationships here (although perhaps not much more intertwined than many Elizabethan family trees), but it is unnecessary to the plot and serves no fictional purpose. This complexity exists only to demonstrate the capacity of Sidney's wit.

The quality of much of the action itself illustrates Sidney's turn to formality in the New Arcadia. The greater part of the chivalric encounter and of the secondary tales is action for its own sake. These scenes do little to advance the plot. Moreover, some of them are now concerned with giants and monsters (see, for example, I, pp. 204, 296, and 300) whose only value is to provide more action. Rather than advancing the fiction, they tend to move it away from a recognisable reality into pure romance. They did not appear in the Old Arcadia. The action in most of the New Arcadia is static in terms of the fiction -- it is a tapestry of action that does not lead to anything and is non-developing.

The enjoyment offered here is similar to Sidney's attention to fashion -- seeing things or qualities that one likes. We are presented with a lush picture of action where the pleasure is the contemplation of the action as scene; there is no demand that we analyse events or understand them in a broader context. Uccello's San Romano battle paintings present a convenient parallel. Uccello had a full command of the techniques of scientific perspective, yet he used them not to capture reality, but as a game, depicting scenes of great action that lack an active character. He was interested, as Vasari said, in perspective for its own sake (12). The results are colourful and delightful, but the action is denied consequence and remains a formal exercise. The audience of the New Arcadia, in like manner, can enjoy action as mere pattern, without real significance in terms of the development of the story -- action as a quality. Thus it is not really important to the reader's appreciation of it that the New Arcadia is unfinished; like a sweet-box that can be dipped into whenever one pleases, and where enjoyment of the parts is sufficient, the work requires no conclusion. (For most readers of the work the need for a conclusion never arises, thanks to the industry of the Countess of Pembroke in completing the New Arcadia with the addition of an edited version of the Old.) In its treatment of action the New Arcadia loses the sense of immediate reality of the Old Arcadia, presenting instead a brilliant, static patterning.

* * *

In the New Arcadia Sidney abandons his charming relationship to the Fair Ladies and assumes instead the more serious role of moral leader. The actions in the Old Arcadia, like acts in real life, have a moral value which is not necessarily obvious. As Richard Lanham remarks, 'the moral orientation which the narrator provides is essential to the reader's evaluation of the action. The narrator performs, in fact, the function Aristotle looked for from the chorus'(13). In the New Arcadia many elements of the main plot have a clear moral construction and a moral view is made more central to the work. Separate scenes are designed to point different moral lessons; for example, the revolt of the Helots -- where Sidney gives a moral to the gentry about greed (I, p. 39) -- or Pamela's refutation of Cecropia's Lucretian view of the world (I, pp. 407-10). The directness of the relationship of the Old Arcadia is replaced by 'objective' lessons; Sidney fulfils his role as moral leader by demonstrating through the action of characters the meaning of various tenets

and ideals. Many of the incidents that already have
a moral value in the Old Arcadia have that value
emphasised in the revision. In both versions
Musidorus becomes a shepherd to win Pamela. In the
New Arcadia, however, Sidney makes more obvious the
point that Musidorus debases himself in order to
approach Pamela by having her ask how she can help
feeling love toward Prince Musidorus, who 'is
content so to abase himself, as to become Dametas
servant for my sake?'(I, p. 178). Sidney's relationship with his audience is as definite here as in
the Old Arcadia -- he is still drawing morals -- but
it is less direct and personal.

In the New Arcadia Sidney makes a stronger
connection between moral and social order, and
morality is brought into closer harmony with an
aristocratic world-view. Aside from the frequent
minor assertions of the goodness of order, such as
shepherds are 'a happy people, wanting little,
because they desire not much'(I, p. 14), he provides
new incidents based on the idea of order, such as
the Helot rebellion (the Lacedaemonians, demanding
too much, have over-stepped order). The central
theme of the main secondary tale is the trouble
caused by violation of social order when the
upstart, base Antiphilus marries Princess Erona.
The reconstruction of incidents from the Old Arcadia
shows well the increased importance of order for
Sidney. The most notable of these is the Enispian
(Phagonian in the Old Arcadia) rebellion. In both
versions, of course, the rebellion is seen by its
very nature to be a violation of order, because it
is an attempt to overthrow the properly-constituted
authority. The rebellion is caused by adventuring
to judge of the ruler's doings, itself an over-
stepping the bounds of order. (Both versions also
make clear that Basilius the ruler, in failing to
exercise his rule, is not keeping to the proper
order.) However, in the Old Arcadia there is very
little violence -- only three sentences of general
description (IV, pp. 118, 120) -- while the New
Arcadia has an extended, particularised violence and
a viciousness absent in the original. Basilius
slices off a tailor's nose. 'But as his [the
tailor's] hand was on the ground to bring his nose
to his head, Zelmane with a blow, sent his head to
his nose'(I, p. 312). A drunken miller falls
between Dorus's legs. Dorus puts his foot on the
miller's neck and, refusing the bribe offered for
his life, thrusts his sword through the man's head,
whose ears 'took it very unkindly, to feel such news

before they heard of them'(I, pp. 312-13). A painter who desires to see wounds to be able to paint them has his hands struck off by Dorus and thus returns from the battle 'well skilled in wounds, but with never a hand to perform his skill'(I, p. 313). More butchery follows before Basilius grants a general pardon. There is no other point in the New Arcadia, and none in the Old Arcadia, where the heroes act in such a totally ruthless manner, and Sidney obviously approves of their attitude for he mocks their victims (compare the deaths of the Enispian rebels with that of Agenor, for example). Even the scornful Thomas Nashe, who never squirms from unchivalrous bloodshed, in The Unfortunate Traveller expresses pity at the slaughter of the Anabaptists whom he despises (II, p. 240). There is only one justification in Sidney's terms for his heroes' total lack of chivalry and decency here: that the rebels, in moving outside and against order, have removed themselves from the bonds of society and therefore from human sympathy. But this is perhaps realistic: Sidney's Dudley grandfather -- the Earl of Warwick, later Duke of Northumberland and father-in-law of Lady Jane Grey -- displayed little more sympathy in 1549 in putting down the peasants of Ket's rebellion in Norfolk.

In a more general way, the conflict between reason and passion is also a problem of social order. Reason is objective, outside oneself, and often equivalent in the New Arcadia to social order. Pamela does not give in to her feeling for Musidorus because it conflicts (in her view, which Sidney presents as an ideal) with her social position; i.e., to yield to her feelings would be destructive of social order, as it proved to be in the Old Arcadia. Reason is important as the control of passion, and passion must be controlled because it disrupts the delicate balance of society. Amphialus is the primary example of such disturbance. A hero of outstanding chivalric virtue, charming, beautiful, and equal in valour to Musidorus, he is, however, without control of his passions. That lack makes him evil in effect, as Sidney spends so much time demonstrating.

Sidney has a problem with morality and order, as his treatment of Amphialus shows. Amphialus is so much a hero that his vice is somewhat buried beneath his shining virtues. He is not in himself wicked, which Sidney makes clear by leaving the dirty work to Cecropia; it is only in the effect that he is evil. His goodness is such that his townspeople remain loyal to him rather than to Basilius their sovereign. Since Sidney is a member of the new aristocracy, tied to centralisation of the government, I do not think that this loyalty can be attributed to any feudal hang-over on his part. The general impression of Amphialus that remains is one of goodness. Either Sidney is over-subtle here in showing the intertwining of vice and virtue, or his attitude is ambiguous. His very virtuosity may be at fault; so eager is he to exhibit his literary powers in different ways that the results sometimes cancel out each other. The effect, in any case, is to make the issues disappear and to turn civil war into a formal matter.

A similar problem occurs with Pyrocles and Musidorus. In exercising their virtue they are often a force for social order, restoring the rule of wrongfully-deposed kings, punishing villains, etc. But their individuality is unbridled. Their personal heroism is in the service of chivalry more than of the state, and serving chivalry is, Hotspur-like, in effect serving one's personal honour. In the Old Arcadia their individualistic behaviour, such as Musidorus's succumbing to his desire to ravish the sleeping Pamela, is presented as weakness (though no less enjoyed for that) but that type of weakness has largely been eliminated in the New Arcadia. Personal glory and service to a well-ruled state are both idealised, but they appear to be in conflict without Sidney's having intended it. Chivalric honour seems, in practice, to be the main criterion of action; and, on that basis, defeating the rebelling Amphialus, rescuing Erona, and saving the villainous Plexirtus because the dying Zelmane requested it as a favour, all have the same value.

The moral conflict can perhaps be related to the difficult position in which Sidney and his class found themselves. The new aristocracy's position was being eroded and they were beginning to lack a real social role when the Old Arcadia was undergoing revision in the early 1580s (14). Chivalry provides an escape, offering an absorbing role that is not a real social role. It has all the superficial qualities of a social and socially-orientated role, but it is a game played for want of a real role. I do not wish to suggest that this accommodation was conscious on Sidney's part; only that his real-life position affected the ranging of his imagination and that chivalry provides a poetic answer to a real problem.

Perhaps Sidney was forced to reduce his perspective of the actual world to individual chivalric-aristocratic virtues because his position in the real world was too much in conflict with his ideology. Although the New _Arcadia_ indirectly attacks the nouveaux riches, the spendthrift sons of the gentry, and enclosing landlords (see, for example, I, pp. 273, 393), R. H. Tawney has pointed out that, traditionally, the _Arcadia_ was composed in the park at the Herberts' country seat at Washerne, made by enclosing the land and evicting the tenants of a whole village (15). In such conflicts it is easier to turn to artificial codes and golden-age morality. It is natural for a frustrated man of action to make action into his escapism; in the New _Arcadia_ the action that grows out of character is less realistic than the actors themselves. Sidney, despite his dealing in high, serious concerns, probably took comfort in placing his characters in a context unrelated to his real world and in events of no significance shaped more into a pattern than a plot. Real problems, perhaps incapable of solution at the time, are dissolved in romance.

The distinction made between Philip Sidney and John Lyly -- that Sidney dealt with life and Lyly with style -- has only a superficial truth. Sidney, the writer of action, reaches a point where action ceases to be active, where it becomes instead ceremonial and decorative. Both Lyly and Sidney, then, arrive at a position of 'pure' art, of an aesthetic enjoyment that, instead of re-arranging or facing it, shuts out actual reality. Sidney, leader of his society, in the end leads his readers nowhere. He has nowhere to lead them to, for the code he offers has only apparent relevance to life. Like Lyly, he offers a style. The _Arcadia_ is noble and brilliant, good and beautiful, but not, finally, true.

NOTES

1. Nowell Smith, ed., Sir Fulke Greville's _Life of Sir Philip Sidney_ (Oxford, 1907), p. xii.

2. Roger Howell, _Sir Philip Sidney: The Shepherd Knight_ (London, 1968), p. 10.

3. Fulke Greville, _Life of Sir Philip Sidney_, p. 15.

4. G. K. Hunter, _John Lyly_, p. 286.

5.   R. W. Zandvoort, Sidney's Arcadia: A Comparison Between the Two Versions (Amsterdam, 1929). See pp. 71-72 for a general statement.

6.   Walter R. Davis, A Map of Arcadia: Sidney's Romance in Its Tradition (New Haven, 1965), passim., and Idea and Act in Elizabethan Fiction, p. 70.

7.   See Paul N. Siegel, 'English Humanism and the New Tudor Aristocracy', The Journal of the History of Ideas, Vol. 13 (1952), pp. 450-68.

8.   See Ernest A. Baker's discussion of romance and decadence in his introduction to the Arcadia (London, 1907).

9.   The Prose Works of Sir Philip Sidney, ed. Albert Feuillerat, vol. IV, p. 168. All page references are to Feuillerat's edition -- vol. I, the New Arcadia (Cambridge, 1912; rpt. 1969); vol. IV, the Old Arcadia (Cambridge, 1926; rpt. 1967).

10.   Samuel Lee Wolff, The Greek Romances in Elizabethan Prose Fiction (New York, 1961; 1st ed., 1912), p. 324.

11.   Sir Thomas Elyot, The Book named the Governor (London, 1962), p. 102.

12.   Giorgio Vasari, The Lives of the Artists, trans. George Bull (Harmondsworth, 1965), pp. 95-96.

13.   Richard A. Lanham, The Old Arcadia (New Haven, 1965), p. 321.

14.   See Paul N. Siegel, Shakespearean Tragedy and the Elizabethan Compromise (New York, 1957), chapter II.

15.   R. H. Tawney, The Agrarian Problem in the Sixteenth Century (London, 1912), p. 194; and Religion and the Rise of Capitalism (Harmondsworth, 1961; 1st ed., 1926), p. 145.

6 THOMAS NASHE

Thomas Nashe makes good throughout his work his boast of phrases 'that shall rattle through the Skies, and make an Earthquake in a Peasants ears' (McKerrow ed., vol. I, p. 195). His power in the medium of language is such that the medium seems superfluous and, endowing abstractions with physicality and conjuring up the solid texture of the material world, Nashe appears to present, not mere word-pictures of reality, but reality itself. Even when he turns to purely verbal wit, it is of such manic intensity that it threatens to burst the fabric of language. But the brilliance is superficial. For all his linguistic virtuosity, Nashe has very little to say and his interest, now as in the sixteenth century, lies almost entirely in his style (to which he himself directs the reader). Yet Nashe's emphasis on style is more than the simple choice of one literary strength above others. His lively depiction of material reality would suggest that he was also capable of elaborated character in the manner of Sidney or constructing plot in the manner of Greene. His choice is the product not merely of aesthetic orientation -- taste -- but of a complex social accommodation. Nashe's adherence to the hierarchical view of the world that underlies the work of Lyly and Sidney -- official ideology -- was in conflict with his own social position; his emphasis on style is largely the result of his inability to resolve that contradiction.

Nashe's relationship with his audience has an accidental character compared to the conscious construction of that of Sidney or Lyly. And whereas Greene could accommodate his writing to social change and take advantage of new situations, Nashe was a shuttlecock of fortune, tossed between the contradictory attractions of his age, and unable to

master his situation. Nevertheless his relationship
with his audience is the most obvious one in Elizabethan fiction. Unlike Greene, Deloney and Sidney
(in the New Arcadia), whose personalities are
camouflaged by an objective fiction, Nashe enters
directly into his works -- so much so that the work
frequently appears to be little more than a projection of his own personality. More than any of his
contemporaries, he displays in his writing a sense
of an audience and often takes a strikingly intimate
tone; yet that intimacy is usually no more than the
playing of a role. Nashe, as a performer, cannot
really be intimate; he is only acting the part of
Thomas Nashe for his audience.

The contradictory character of his relationship
with his audience results largely from his inability
to adjust to the changes of the last quarter of the
century. Caught between a disintegrating feudal-
aristocratic world-view and the beginning of commer-
cialised, bourgeois social relations, he writes for
a market yet tries to preserve the character of a
literary world run on patronage. Other authors
faced with the same problem were able to deal with
it usually by rejecting either the old or the new
(Sidney ignored the literary market and Greene
adapted himself to commercial relations). Nashe was
not so flexible. He at once inclined toward the old
value system and the new individualism, and he was
incapable of making a satisfactory combination of
outmoded consciousness with new social reality.
Even though he was unsuccessful in carving out a
position for himself in an aristocratic world, he
could not fully accept the idea of a literary
market. His solution (if it can be called that) was
to be an angry young man or, as he would have it, a
'biting satirist'. Invective became an end in
itself and, as long as he maintained his wit, he
could display contradictory values without being
rejected for inconsistency. Too shallow to be a
real social critic, Nashe let style replace argument
in his writing.

* * *

Early in his career Nashe had some success with
patronage. McKerrow suggests that he found a patron
to keep him, perhaps in return for secretarial work
(V, p. 16) and Pierce Penilesse (1592) indicates
that he received benefits from 'Amyntas' (on whose
virtues he digresses to 'show myself thankful (in
some part) for benefits received' -- I, p. 245), but

it was probably his relations with the Carey family that supplied the model for his conception of patronage and led him to believe in it as a system. He viewed the patronage relationship as one in which the patron protected the author from want and his work from attack, while in return the author proclaimed to the world the appropriate virtues of his patron. Nashe's sense of material benefit is made clear in Christs Teares over Jerusalem (1593) and The Terrors of the Night (1594). In dedicating Christs Teares to Lady Elizabeth Carey he says: 'Divine Lady, you I must and will memorize more especially, for you recompence learning extraordinarily'(II, p. 11). He echoes her praise in The Terrors of the Night: 'Ever honoured may she be of the royallest breed of wits, whose purse is so open to her poor beadsmens distresses' and adds that he has been the grateful recipient of her 'extraordinary liberality and bounty'(I, p. 342). In the same work, after praising the 'ancient hospitality' of the Isle of Wight and the merits of Geroge Carey, its governor, he proclaims that:

> whatsoever minutes intermission I have of calmed content, or least respite to call my wits together, principal and immediate proceedeth from him.
> Through him my tender wainscot Study door is delivered from much assault and battery: through him I look into, and am looked on in the world; from whence otherwise I were a wretched banished exile. Through him all my good (as by a conduit head) is conveyed unto me; and to him all my endeavors (like rivers) shall pay tribute as to the Ocean. (I, p. 375)

Were it not for the Careys, he concludes, 'my spirit long ere this had expired, and my pen served as a poniard to gall my own heart'(I, p. 375). The patron's assistance to the artist is repaid with his eternal glory in print: in Christs Teares he says, 'To the eternizing of the heroical family of the Careys, my choisest studies have I tasked'(II, p. 10). Nashe fulfils his duty and at the same time seems to have some genuine feeling for the family.

In the dedication of The Unfortunate Traveller (1594) to Henry Wriothsley, Earl of Southampton -- Nashe's last serious dedication -- he makes clear the notion of patronage as literary protection, seeking an aristocratic stamp of approval:

lest any man should challenge these my papers as goods uncustomed, and so extend upon them as forfeit to contempt, to the seal of your excellent censure lo here I present them to be seen and allowed. (II, p. 201)

He further expands the idea with a different simile:

This handful of leaves I offer to your view, to the leaves on trees I compare, which as they cannot grow of themselves except they have some branches or boughes to cleave to, and with whose juice and sap they be ever more recreated and nourished; so except these unpolished leaves of mine have some branch of Nobility whereon to depend and cleave, and with the vigorous nutriment of whose authorized commendation they may be continually fostered and refreshed, never will they grow to the worlds good liking, but forthwith fade and die on the first hour of their birth. Your Lordship is the large spreading branch of renown, from whence these my idle leaves seek to derive their whole nourishing. (II, p. 202)

The idea of protection of a work is certinly not a novel one in the sixteenth century, nor is that of 'authorized commendation' unusual; yet Nashe seems really to believe in the inherent value of aristocratic approval, rather than paying it the lip-service of many of his contemporaries.

Both before and after the Careys, however, Nashe had difficulty with patronage. In Pierce Penilesse he complains at length that wit and learning go unrewarded. Yet he does not seek his rewards from a general public; he still looks to the traditional forms of patronage. Gentle Sir Philip Sidney knew how to reward art and learning but, says Nashe, 'there is not that strict observation of honour, which hath been heretofore'(I, p. 159). Dedications are taken for granted:

Men of great calling take it of merit, to have their names eternized by Poets; and whatsoever pamphlet or dedication encounters them, they put it up in their sleeves, and scarce give him thanks that presents it. (I, p. 159)

The writer cannot survive without support: 'How then can we choose but be needy, when there are so many Droans amongst us? or ever prove rich, that toil a whole year for fair looks?'(I, p. 159). Not only are writers denied their partial patronage for dedications, but 'every gross brained Idiot' who should be employing writers, churns out rubbish that too often finds sale on the booksellers' stalls when better things lie unsold. In effect, Nashe complains that the old form of patronage, where the scholar was maintained for his service and art, has been supplanted by a literary market in which the artist sells his goods piecemeal and his well-being is of no interest to the buyers: 'Learning (of the ignorant) is rated after the value of the ink and paper: and a Scrivener better paid for an obligation, than a Scholar for the best Poem he can make'(I, pp. 158-59).

Nashe himself has in fact fallen victim of the commercialisation of literary relationships. In <u>Pierce Penilesse</u> he presents patronage as a mere financial arrangement:

> but this I dare presume, that, if any Maecenas bind me to him by his bounty, or extend some round liberality to me worth the speaking of, I will do him as much honour as any Poet of my beardless years shall in England. (I, p. 195)

The tone is not entirely ironical; there is some seriousness in his suggestion, which reduces the human qualities of patronage to an abstract, monetary relation. In the epistle to the readers at the end of the work he says that a good patron will pay for a witty conclusion but then asks where such a patron is:

> But cap and thanks is all our Courtiers payment: wherefore, I would counsel my friends to be more considerate in their Dedications, and not cast away so many months labour on a clown that knows not how to use a Scholar: for what reason have I to bestow any of my wit upon him, that will bestow none of his wealth upon me? (I, p. 241)

Patronage has degenerated into a commercial transaction.

In his last two works Nashe seems to have rejected the idea of patronage altogether. <u>Have with You to Saffron-Walden</u> is mockingly dedicated to Richard Lichfield, barber of Trinity College, Cambridge, and <u>Nashes Lenten Stuffe</u> to 'Lusty Humfrey' King. The latter dedication displays a considerable warmth and seems to be repaying a debt of hospitality, yet, addressed as it is to 'Most courteous unlearned lover of Poetry', cannot be seen as serious. However sincere the warmth, the character of the recipient and the comical tone make it clear that the dedication is only a formal substitute for the patronage that has abandoned Nashe and the pursuit of which he now abandons.

A corollary of his view of patronage is his self-image as a servant to, or would-be representative of, the aristocracy. This must have been partly justified by circumstances: he probably carried out various tasks for the Carey family and Bancroft or Whitgift. But the idea of Nashe as a servant must not be construed as his desiring merely to carry out the orders of the aristocracy; he wanted to be associated with them and a satellite of their glory.

Nashe sought to place himself as high as he could on the social ladder without actually appearing a climber. Thus he calls himself 'gentleman' in Pierce Penilesse and Strange Newes, a style his university education, but not his family background, entitled him to. Greene, who had as much justification but a different social outlook, did not find it necessary so to advertise his status. Although Nashe lays stress on being above the commonality, with his strong belief in hierarchy he also accepts that he must keep his place. Defending himself in Strange Newes against 'interpreters' (finders of dangerous topical allusions), he denies the least allusion in Pierce Penilesse to 'any man set above me in degree' (I, p. 320). He knows who can and who cannot be touched; he does not meddle with the aristocracy. Similarly in Pierce Penilesse when he attacks lechery he makes clear that he will leave alone those above him: 'The Court I dare not touch, but surely there (as in the Heavens) be many falling stars, and but one true Diana'(I, p. 216). He feels comfortable in making the general suggestion that there is vice at the Court, but a closer look is not in keeping with his position. Further, when he mentions the 'Gorgeous Ladies of the Court' in his attack on extravagance of dress in Christs Teares, he declines to criticise:

> I dare not meddle with ye, since the Philosopher that too intentively gazed on the stars stumbled and fell into a ditch; and many gazing too immoderately on our earthly stars,

fall in the end into the ditch of all
uncleanness. (II, p. 138)

More than any of his contemporaries, Nashe
attaches an ethical value to the distinctions of
class. It is not merely that he applauds hierarchy
and holds to the idea of the chain of being; each
link in the chain has a progressively greater value
the higher one goes. Certainly a traditional view
holds that a prince is of more worth than a peasant,
but it also entails that each degree is important by
virtue of being part of the chain. Thus the wounded
Sidney can give his drink of water to a dying common
soldier because (aside from his magnanimity) they
have equal validity, even if not worth, in the chain
of being. Nashe regards the lower links not only as
less worthy but as actually meriting scorn. There
is a viciousness and small-heartedness in his view
which does not appear in the traditional position.
He reverences those above him and disdains those
below, asserting his own worth, not through showing
how well he fills the demands of his degree (which
would be an approach more akin to Sidney's), but
merely by showing himself to be above those below
him.

We see his scorn for the lower classes from his
earliest work, The Anatomie of Absurditie (1589):

What politic Counsellor or valiant Soldier will
joy or glory of this, in that some stitcher,
Weaver, spendthrift, or Fiddler, hath shuffled
or slubbered up a few ragged Rhymes, in the
memorial of the ones prudence, or the others
prowess? (I, p. 24)

If we recollect Richard Johnson's defence of his
literary efforts as a mechanical in The Nine
Worthies of London (see above, p. 36), Nashe's view
appears more his own narrow spirit than a social
commonplace. He continues this line in resuming his
attack on Gabriel Harvey, in the second edition of
Christs Teares, where he belittles the learned
doctor by saying his work is fit to be read only by
the lower classes:

Some few crumbs of my book he hath confuted,
all the rest of his invention is nothing but an
ox with a pudding his his belly, not fit for
anything else, save only to feast the dull ears
of ironmongers, ploughmen, carpenters, and
porters. (II, p. 180)

The ears of such an audience are dull only because
they belong to workmen who as such are an unworthy
audience for literature and beneath his consideration. Nashe is not directing his attack at workmen
here but at Harvey, which indicates his unthinking
acceptance of a hierarchical ideology.

Nashe seems almost totally without sympathy for
the bourgeois as well as the mechanical. In a
passage in Pierce Penilesse he asks the devil to
take away the merchant's wife:

> In another corner, Mistress Minx, a Merchants
> wife, that will eat no Cherries, forsooth, but
> when they are at twenty shillings a pound, that
> looks as simperingly as if she were besmeared,
> and jets it as gingerly as if she were dancing
> the Canaries: she is so finical in her speech,
> as though she spake nothing but what she had
> first sewed over before in her Samplers . . .
> What should I tell how squeamish she is in her
> diet . . . and spends half a day in pranking
> herself if she be invited to any strange place?
> (I, p. 173)

His lack of sympathy is obvious, and it is even
clearer if the passage is compared to Deloney's
treatment in Thomas of Reading of the country
clothers' wives who decide to become the sartorial
equals of London merchants' wives (see Lawlis ed.,
pp. 299-303).

Indeed, anyone beneath the aristocracy Nashe
regards as fair game. In Strange Newes, mocking
Richard Harvey's use of legalistic terminology in
The Lamb of God, he says: 'You that be gentle
Readers, do you not laugh at this Lawyers english of
former premisses and future consequents?'(I,
p. 272). The laughter he expects seems to be caused
by more than the inappropriateness of legal terms in
religious matters; the lawyer, though entitled to
the style of 'gentleman', is often a stock upstart
character for Nashe and others at the end of the
sixteenth century; thus, he is asking the gentle
reader to laugh at upstarts. Greene also attacks
upstarts, most notably in A Quip for an Upstart
Courtier (1592), but more for the social evils that
accompany them than for the newness of their
gentility.

Not all Nashe's class invective can be seen as
jealous guardianship of his gentle status. Some-

times he shows genuine disturbance at the deterioration of the aristocracy:

> Scandalous and shameful is it, that not any in thee [England] (Fishermen and Husbandmen set aside) but live above their ability and birth; That the outward habit (which in other Countries is the only distinction of honour) should yield in thee no difference of persons: that all thy ancient Nobility (almost), with this gorgeous prodigality, should be devoured and eaten up, and upstarts inhabit their stately Palaces, who from far have fetched in this variety of pride to entrap and to spoil them. (II, p. 142)

It is bad enough that the aristocracy waste their substance on vanities but much worse that through their ill husbandry the class has become riddled with upstarts and the principle of blood is in decline.

The bourgeoisie 'sprung up by base Brokery', says Nashe in _Pierce Penilesse_, have no regard for honour but only for their 'execrable lucre' (I, pp. 212-13). They have taken over knightly attributes and made them hollow. Nashe would like to believe in knights as men of action, and scorns the bourgeois broker who buys his arms without performing any deeds, proposing for his arms:

> the Lion, without tongue, tail, or talons, because his master whom he must serve is a Townsman, and a man of peace, and must not keep any quarrelling beasts to annoy his honest neighbours. (I, p. 213)

This image of the fierce beast rendered harmless on the burgess's arms encapsulates Nashe's view of the deterioration of the position of the aristocracy and the rise of upstarts who avoid military honour and are intent only on their own interests.

Nashe's contempt for the lower classes and desire for status are consistent with his role as a servant of the aristocracy. He believes in the desirability of a stable hierarchy and at the same time his individualism demands his own advancement. Like the second and third generations of humanists, he is a victim of social change. Instead of his merit being rewarded, he is spurned by the unworthy elevated to positions of power and honour. But he is not patient; he cries out at once for and against social mobility. The quarrel with Gabriel Harvey seems largely motivated by Nashe's hatred of Harvey's ambition; he could not abide, McKerrow says, that such a person of ability aspired beyond success at university and failed to recognise his proper station (V, pp. 67-68). Yet Nashe feels he has himself been denied proper advancement, which he makes ringingly clear in <u>Pierce Penilesse</u>:

> I grew to consider how many base men that wanted those parts which I had, enjoyed content at will, and had wealth at command: I called to mind a Cobler, that was worth five hundred pound, an Hostler that had built a goodly Inn, and might dispend forty pound yearly by his Land, a Car-man in a leather pilch, that had whipped out a thousand pound out of his horse tail: and have I more wit than all these (thought I to myself)? am I better born? am I better brought up? yea, and better favoured? and yet am I a beggar? What is the cause? how am I crossed? or whence is this curse?
> (I, p. 158)

Although he wrote this before his patronage from the Careys, he frequently echoes the sentiment later on.

Apparently Nashe feels that one should be able to rise in wealth and position on the basis of his merits but that worship must be given only for breeding. Thus, only a few pages after he has complained about base men's success, he attacks Denmark for being a static society and praises England for its social mobility, where hope of honour makes good soldiers and, of religious offices, learned divines, and where 'the common Lawyers (suppose in the beginning they are but husbandmens sons) come in time to be chief Fathers of the land, and many of them not the meanest of the Privy Council'(I, p. 178). He expressed the same view as early as 1589 in <u>The Anatomie of Absurditie</u>:

> It is learning and knowledge which are the only ornaments of a man, which furnisheth the tongue with wisdom, and the heart with understanding, which maketh the children of the needy poor to become noble Peers, and men of obscure parentage to be equal with Princes in possessions. (I, p. 34)

He makes clear, however, that he has no respect for purchased rank. Without his elaborate rationalisation, Nashe can be seen simply to resent lack of advancement in the system to which he adheres, and envy the success of those who have risen on different principles.

Contradictory attitudes are revealed in Nashe's approach to professionalism. Concern for a gentle image makes him reluctant to accept being a professional and relying on a press that makes literature common, while poverty forces him to operate within commercial relations and drives him to the press. Yet he also takes pride in his commercial success. In the earlier writings he assumes a genteel posture: he gave The Terrors of the Night to the press, he says, only because it had so long circulated in manuscript and he would rather have the profits himself than leave them to the scrivener (I, p. 341). In the second edition of Pierce Penilesse he offers a warning against a rumoured continuation of the work, calling it 'a cosenage and plain knavery of him that sells it to get money'(I, p. 154). Neil Rhodes points out that Pierce Penilesse had at least five editions between 1592 and 95 and that, after the deaths of Green in 1592 and Marlowe in 1593, Nashe was 'the most celebrated professional writer in London'(1). Nashe certainly accepts money from the press but rejects a purely financial motivation. In Strange Newes he denies Gabriel Harvey's charge that Pierce Penilesse was born of 'ungentleman-like want', adding 'yet my muse never wept for want of maintenance as thine did'(I, p. 303). Poverty is a social embarrassment -- ungentleman-like -- and Nashe laughs at Harvey's early poverty.

Not having money is ungentlemanly, but so is making money. Without money to begin with, and constantly troubled by poverty, Nashe had to relinquish his gentle attitude toward the press. He complains in The Terrors of the Night that amateurs can spend the better part of a year to produce something worthless but such as he 'either must have our work dispatched by the weeks end, or else we may go beg'(I, pp. 343-44). Again, in Lenten Stuffe, he complains that he must write with a speed that precludes revision, causing him to 'leave some terms in suspense that my post-haste want of argent will not give me elbow room enough to explain or examine as I would'(III, p. 213). But sometimes he adopts a completely commercial posture, as in Strange Newes, where he says:

> Gentleman, I have no more to say to the Doctor, dispose of the victory as you please; shortly I will present you with something that shall be better than nothing, only give me a gentle hire for my dirty day labour, and I am your bounden Orator for ever. (I, p. 333)

This attitude occurs again in Christs Teares:

> Have at you, backbiters, with a bargain; rail upon me till your tongues rot, short cut and long tail, for groats apiece every quarter. Mince me betwixt your teeth as small as Oatmeal, I care not, so I have Crowns for your scoffs. (II, p. 186)

His ambivalence is summed up in Have with You to Saffron-Walden in his answer to Harvey's accusation that he derives his maintenance from the printing-house:

> till the Impression of this Book, I having got nothing by Printing these three years. But when I do play my Prizes in Print, I'll be paid for my pains, that's once; and not make myself a gazing stock and a public spectacle to all the world for nothing, as he does, that gives money to be seen and have his wit looked upon, never Printing book yet for whose Impression he hath not either paid or run in debt.
> (III, p. 128)

Though Nashe still regards himself as something of an amateur, pleased not to owe his living to the press, he adopts a contradictory attitude, proud that his publications are a financial success.

* * *

However ambiguous his attitude toward the commercial press, there is an immediacy in Nashe's relationship with his audience that is lacking in that of his contemporaries. Excluding base mechanicals and proper bourgeoisie from his sympathy, and relying heavily on latinate learning and urban wit, Nashe appears to address himself to young gentlemen, members of the Inns of Court, and city wits. Such an audience (men whose aspirations and lack of position must often have coincided with his own) would have been highly receptive and, as himself a frequenter of St. Pauls and a London wit,

Nashe was probably acquainted with many of his readers, which may well account for the directness (though there was unlikely to have been such a degree of mutual acquaintance in the literary world of London, with everyone known to everyone else, as Charles Nicholl postulates (2)). 'List, Pauls Churchyard (the peruser of every mans works, and Exchange of all Authors), you are a many of you honest fellows, and favour men of wit'(I, p. 278), he addresses his readers in Strange Newes. He was accustomed to interchanges of verbal wit -- his writing bears the marks of one whose literary contacts are not limited to printed works.

Nashe maintains the directness of the relationship with frequent first-person narration and commentary. Pierce Penilesse is largely personal diatribe and it makes little difference that Pierce is a constructed character, for his qualities are hardly distinguishable from Nashe's own (the identification of the two was continued by Gabriel Harvey and Nashe himself -- see, for example, III, p. 154, where Nashe refers to himself as 'Pierse Pennilesse'). Similarly, when Nashe speaks in his own voice, in the concluding epistle to the readers, the tone is not that of written discourse but of personal discussion:

> Gentle Reader, tandem aliquando I am at leisure to talk to thee . . . Whilst I am thus talking, methinks I hear one say, What a fop is this, he entitles his book A Supplication to the Divell, and doth nothing but rail on idiots, and tells a story of the nature of Spirits. Have patience, good sir, and we'll come to you by and by. (I, pp. 239-40)

Not only is Nashe himself present in most of his works, but there is also a considerable sense of an audience's presence.

The relationship with his audience is developed to the point where he demands an active response from the reader. He addresses the pages in The Unfortunate Traveller:

> Memorandum, every one of you after the perusing of this pamphlet is to provide him a case of poniards, that if you come in company with any man which shall dispraise it or speak against it, you may straight cry Sic respondeo, and give him the stockado. (II, p. 207)

In Lenten Stuffe he makes a similar demand of Yarmouth fishermen:

> No more can I do for you than I have done, were you my godchildren every one . . . One boon you must not refuse me in, (if you be boni socii and sweet Olivers,) that you let not your rusty swords sleep in their scabbards, but lash them out in my quarrel as hotly as if you were to cut cables or hew the mainmast overboard, when you hear me mangled and torn in mens mouths about this playing with a shuttlecock, or tossing empty bladders in the air.
> (III, p. 225)

Nashe is hardly serious here, but even in jest his words convey a relationship warmer and closer (though unspecific) than that created by any other Elizabethan writer.

Yet the warmth and intimacy have a certain artificiality. They often seem to be merely the projection of the writer's feelings -- projected without direction. I am reminded of an anecdote related on record by Tom Lehrer in which he received a letter to the effect, 'Darling, marry me or I will kill myself', and then discovered it was addressed to 'Occupant'. Similarly, Nashe often displays abstract good feeling, broadcast without regard to the recipients -- and it tells us more about him than about his relationship with his audience. This abstract quality is part of Nashe's role as a performer; it is his performance of an intimate role.

The sense of performance is evident in the way that he addresses his readers. Although he often speaks of 'readers' he addresses them also as 'mei Auditories' and 'Spectatores' (I, p. 199 and III, p. 139). The audience are following Nashe himself rather than observing an objective fiction. In Strange Newes he says: 'Sweet Gentlemen, be but indifferent, and you shall see me desperate' (I, p. 263). He regards the readers as observers of action of which he is the centre: 'You that be lookers on, perhaps imagine I talk like a merry man, and not in good earnest'(I, p. 280). The character of performance is extended to active audience response, 'betting' on the action, in Lenten Stuffe:

> Stay, let me look about, where am I? in my text, or out of it? not out, for a groat: out, for an angel: nay, I'll lay no wagers, for now

I perponder more sadly upon it, I think I am
out indeed. Bear with it, it was but a pretty
parenthesis of Princes and their parasites,
which shall do you no harm, for I will cloy you
with Herring before we part. (III, p. 219)

In Have with You to Saffron-Walden this posture is
developed to that of a staged play: 'Hem, clear your
throats, and spit soundly; for now the pageant
begins, and the stuff by whole Cart-loads comes in'
(III, p. 42). He achieves a music-hall tone in
Lenten Stuffe: 'Let me see, hath anybody in Yarmouth
heard of Leander and Hero, of whom divine Musaeus
sung, and a diviner Muse than him, Kit Marlowe?'
(III, p. 195).

In The Unfortunate Traveller and Have with You
to Saffron-Walden Nashe introduces something akin to
a studio audience. In the former he has 'The
Induction to the dapper Mounsier Pages of the Court'
in which Jack Wilton first passes his good wishes to
the pages through Nashe, who then makes a number of
manic remarks to that audience and draws to a
conclusion with 'Heigh pass, come aloft: every man
of you take your places, and hear Jack Wilton tell
his own Tale'(II, p. 208). When Jack begins to
address the audience of pages -- 'list, lordings, to
my proceedings'(II, p. 210) -- the readers of the
work are there and not there at the same time: they
are placed in the position, not of immediate
audience (for that role is filled by the pages), but
of observer of audience and action. As observers
they are witnesses to the intimacy but not really
partakers of it. Similarly Have with You begins
with a dialogue between several people, in which
Nashe is participant and subject (the work proper
then grows out of that dialogue), and ends with the
group going off to dinner. The performance is made
for these created audiences and it is to them that
Nashe relates. But, since they are creatures of his
own construction, his performance has only the
appearance of intimacy.

At times Nashe speaks in his own voice without
personal quality. The first-person narration in
Nashes Lenten Stuffe offers no more personality than
a modern tour guide:

The length and breadth of Yarmouth I promised
to show you; have with you, have with you: but
first look wistly upon the walls, which, if you
mark, make a stretched out quadrangle with the
haven. They are in compass . . . (III, p. 166)

Perhaps the difficulty here is the material: if the subject matter does not attract him he cannot get up steam for his rhetoric. And away from a rhetorical situation, his personality fades:

> Soft and fair, my masters, you must walk and talk before dinner an hour or two, the better to whet your appetites to taste of such a dainty dish as the red Herring; and that you may not think the time tedious, I care not if I bear you company, and lead you a sound walk round about Yarmouth, and show you the length and breadth of it. (III, p. 159)

Nashe is peculiarly brilliant in combining the sense of spoken performance and of written word. In Piers Plannes Chettle also displays both these senses but he does not fuse them so well. We see Nashe unite the two qualities in The Unfortunate Traveller:

> This tale must at one time or other give up the ghost, and as good now as stay longer . . .
> What is there more as touching this tragedy that you would be resolved of? say quickly, for now is my pen on foot again. (II, p. 241)

The work is clearly literary for Nashe -- his pen is instrumental -- but it has the active character of being 'on foot'. Have with You to Saffron-Walden combines immediacy and a sense of the literary activity: '. . . which information piping hot in the midst of this line was but brought to me'(III, p. 122). The character of the writing is conversational and at the same time clearly literary, which is true also in The Unfortunate Traveller: 'In a leaf or two before was I locked up: here in this page the foresaid good wife Countess comes to me'(II, p. 314). Nashe substitutes literary time for conversation time in which the events exist. This strongly emphasises the literary quality, and without impeding the narrative, shows that the events depend on his literary wit.

Even where the character of the writing lacks the immediacy of speech in a group, the sense of performance remains strong: 'Readers, be merry; for in me there shall want nothing I can do to make you merry'(III, pp. 79-80). Nashe has a true performer's consciousness of his audience -- of what is required to entertain them and what will be tedious:

Be of good cheer, my weary Readers, for I have espied land, as Diogenes said to his weary scholars when he had read to a waste leaf. (III, p. 223).

Whereas the dramatic character is required for intimacy, the bookish character of the works is esential for Nashe to appear as a learned wit for an audience of wits. In Pierce Penilesse he begins his supplication with a neat inversion of the usual material of dedications that preserves the standard form (I, p. 165); and in most of his works he mocks literay conventions. In Strange Newes he blows out the virtues of the dedicatee: he would speak of the hospitality of Master Apis Lapis (William Beestone) but that it is chronicled in the Archdeacon's Court (for moral offences) 'and the fruits it brought forth (as I guess) are of age to speak for themselves'(I, p. 256). His literary wit shows in the literal treatment of the convention of bidding the reader farewell at the end of the epistle to the readers in Have with You to Saffron-Walden: 'I take my leave of you all, at least of all such as here mean to leave and read no further, and haste to the launching forth of my Dialogue'(III, p. 24). In The Unfortunate Traveller he sends up the 'gentle reader' convention -- 'Gentle Readers (look you be gentle now since I have called you so)'(II, p. 217) -- and ironically plays naive with the standard excuse for presenting vicious material (relied on so heavily by writers such as Greene), that the telling will promote virtue: 'as freely as my knavery was mine own, it shall be yours to use in the way of honesty'(II, p. 217). He had already attacked directly this pretence of the virtuous use of a dubious tale in The Anatomy of Absurditie (I, p. 10); but the ironic humour here is more effective.

Nashe is one of the few sixteenth-century fiction writers who displays any open concern for posterity. More than any other novelist of his day, he stresses the 'eternizing' of patrons through works of literature and is concerned, even in his joking, that his work will endure. He received such good hospitality at Great Yarmouth, he says, that crumbs of it will remain in his papers to be seen when he is dead: 'from the bare perusing of which, infinite posterities of hungry Poets shall receive good refreshing'(III, pp. 154-55). His greatest claim to the attention of posterity, he rightly feels, is his style and he takes pride in its originality:

> This I will proudly boast . . . that the vein which I have (be it a median vein or a mad [vein]) is of my own begetting, and calls no man father in England but myself, neither Euphues, nor Tarlton, nor Greene. (I, p. 319)

With neither originality of intellect nor a critical attitude toward the assumptions of his society, style was the only area in which he could make his mark. In The Terrors of the Night he gives some indication of his practice, explaining that he takes common material and decorates it to interest the reader:

> God is my witness, in all this relation, I borrow no essential part from stretched out invention, nor have I one jot abused my informations; only for the recreation of my Readers, whom loath to tire with a coarse homespun tale, that should dull them worse than Holland cheese, here and there I welt and guard it with allusive exornations and comparisons: and yet methinks it comes off too gouty and lumbering. (I, p. 382)

Style is everything. Barnaby Rich receives one of his barbs in Have with You to Saffron-Walden because of his stylistic plainness (III, p. 16), while it is a particularly sharp style that makes Nashe admire Aretino:

> his style was the spirituality of arts, and nothing else; whereas all others of his age were but the lay temporality of inkhorn terms. For indeed they were mere temporizers, and no better. His pen was sharp pointed like a poniard; no leaf he wrote on but was like a burning glass to set on fire all his readers . . . His sight pierced like lightning into the entrails of all abuses. (II, pp. 264-65)

Nashe thinks of himself (and was so regarded by Thomas Lodge -- Gosse ed., IV, p. 63) in the same role as Aretino, the biting satirist. However, in his shallowness, Nashe had much more bark than bite; his work is brilliant but (except in regard to Gabriel Harvey) generally toothless. This can be seen in the terrible threats he makes, to the liter-

ary interpreters, for example: 'they shall know that
I live as their evil Angel, to haunt them world
without end, if they disquiet me without cause'(I,
p. 155). He promises an eternal vengeance to those
who ill-treat him:

> let him look that I will rail on him soundly:
> not for an hour or a day, whiles the injury is
> fresh in my memory, but in some elaborate,
> polished Poem, which I will leave to the world
> when I am dead, to be a living Image to all
> ages, of his beggarly parsimony and ignoble
> illiberality: and let him not (whatsoever he
> be) measure the weight of my words by this
> book, where I write Quicquid in buccam venerit,
> as fast as my hand can trot; but I have terms
> (if I be vexed) laid in steep in Aquafortis,
> and Gunpowder, that shall rattle through the
> Skies, and make an Earthquake in a Peasants
> ears. (I, p. 195)

Nashe exercises his vengeance hardly at all, save on
the Harveys, and there the effect is largely to make
us remember the ebullient Nashe rather than scorn
forever the object of his attack.

Nashe's role as stylist is essentially isolated
as well as individualistic. He has a great sense of
an audience but not necessarily of an actual one.
He creates his own audience. Unsuccessful finan-
cially, burdened with trivial literary occupations,
having found no place for himself in the obsolescent
system to which he adhered, Nashe was isolated from
a real community. Certainly he had his circle of
London literary wits, but he sees no broader community of which he is a part as did the adherents of
official ideology or the purveyors of an alternative
literature. Unlike Lyly or Sidney, his use of
official ideology is to some extent contradicted by
his accommodation to commercial, printed literature.
He can attempt to disguise but not overcome the
contradiction, and as a result his work becomes
self-referential. Instead of a community confirmed
through an objective-seeming fiction, as occurs in
the work of Greene and Deloney, Nashe gives a
fiction that substitutes its own community, at once
seeming to welcome the readers but ultimately
excluding them.

Nashe has only his individualism to offer.
Greene, who had other interests beyond his own
personality, hardly rose to defend himself against
Harvey; Nashe, with nothing but himself to concern

him, feels his essential being attacked by the doctor's taunts and serves thereafter the endless muse of revenge. He has an unsurpassed power of concrete description but he was too superficial and too alienated to put together the separate pieces of the Elizabethan world to which his prose gives enduring life.

NOTES

1. Neil Rhodes, <u>Elizabethan Grotesque</u> (London, 1980), p. 92.

2. Charles Nicholl, <u>A Cup of News: the Life of Thomas Nashe</u> (London, 1984). See, for example, p. 43.

7 ROBERT GREENE

Robert Greene was the first professional writer in England. Born in 1558, dead only thirty-four years later in 1592, Greene wrote in his last thirteen years some thirty works of fiction and six plays at the very least, aside from assorted verse and translations. He was the most prolific of Elizabethan novelists and, it would appear from the numerous sixteenth-century editions of many of his works, one of the most popular. Not a gentleman reluctant to appear in print nor a man for whom writing was merely an honourable pastime, he wrote to earn his living.

Probably Greene thought of himself as a playwright --'After I had wholly betaken me to the penning of plays (which was my continual exercise)'(Grosart ed., vol. XII, p. 177) -- which he doubtless felt was more respectable than being the author of love pamphlets, although he says his income came largely from the press: 'These vanities and other trifling Pamphlets I penned of Love, and vain fantasies, was my chiefest stay of living' (XII, p. 178). Writing fiction, unlike being a playwright, was not yet a recognised mode of economic existence (it is by turning his wits to writing plays that Francesco recoups his fortunes in Francescos Fortunes); Greene was the first man in England to gain his living by writing for the public.

Being a professional writer meant being a commercial one as well. 'Many things I have wrote to get money, which I could otherwise wish to be suppressed', he said in his death-bed epistle to the earlier Greenes Vision (XII, p. 195). Successful recipes were often served up again under different names -- as in the conny-catching series of pamphlets which grew from an original two parts (the

105

first edition of the second pamphlet of the series
is entitled The Second and Last Part of Conny-
catching) to six -- and practically all of his
writing shows an awareness of commercial possibilities. Yet Greene served an audience as well as
exploiting a market: 'Of force I must grant that
Greene came oftener in print than men of judgement
allowed of', said Thomas Nashe, 'but nevertheless he
was a dainty slave to content the tail of a Term,
and stuff Serving mens pockets' (McKerrow ed., I,
p. 329).

Greene establishes a definite relationship with
his audience but different from that of Lyly or
Nashe, an indirect relationship where he organises
in fiction a reality for his readers, independent of
the author's intrusive interpretations. He accommodated himself fully to the demands of print and
his commercial awareness of a new audience not yet
catered for determines many of the specific
qualities of the relationship.

Greene's commercial attitude is immediately
apparent in his use of dedications. Although the
traditional relations of patronage had largely
broken down in the last quarter of the sixteenth
century, most authors retained the forms and, to
judge by their dedications alone, seemed to take the
view that patronage still existed. Some of Greene's
individual dedications have that appearance when
viewed separately but, taken as a whole, a change is
clear. In twenty-six works with dedications Greene
has twenty different dedicatees (or sets of
dedicatees), ranging through Leicester, Essex,
Oxford, Cumberland and Arundel among the earls, as
well as other notable aristocrats and less notable
commoners. Even if we discount dedications to
members of the same family, the range of patrons is
is still exceptionally large, and patronage, as
traditionally understood, obviously did not work for
Greene. Instead he placed dedications on the
market, in the sense that he probably hoped for a
cash reward for a dedication rather than expecting
to gain a position or a pension. Sometimes the
characteristics he attributes to a patron go well
beyond courteous exaggeration, extending even to the
complete fabrication of a virtuous personality (e.g.
Margaret, Countess of Derby, wife of Henry Stanley,
to whom he dedicated The Myrrour of Modestie, 1584,
for her renowned virtue, although her reputation
seems to have been rather the opposite). He is
warmly affectionate toward Thomas Burnaby and Roger
Portington, but most of his dedications have a

certain distance about them, which is even more apparent when they are compared with the friendly tone of the later epistles to the reader.

This distant quality of his dedications is exemplified in that to Robert Carey in <u>Greenes Orpharion</u> (1590):

> so hearing your Worship to be endued with such honourable virtues and plausible qualities, as draws men to admire and love such united perfection: I embolden myself to trust upon your Worships courteous acceptance, which if it be such as others have found and I hoped for . . . (XII, pp. 5-6)

Greene must have had some joy from Carey because he then dedicated <u>Greenes Farewell to Folly</u> (1591) to him, but that in no way lessens the strangeness of a dedication quite openly based on hearsay.

Dedications, whatever their financial value, are only a sideline for Greene. As a professional, his main concern is with selling works. The most obvious attempt at this is the advertising of his forthcoming productions. His practice is not basically different from that of his contemporaries in this respect, but he engages in it to a far greater degree and with greater variety of manner. In <u>Mamillia</u> (1580 or 83) it is not known where the vicious Pharicles, forced to leave the country to escape the consequences of his two-timing, intends to stay: 'But as soon as I shall either hear, or learn of his abode, look for news by a speedy Post' (II, p. 135). In the second part of <u>Mamillia</u> (1583) Greene brings the story to what seems a conclusion, rescuing Pharicles from his wicked ways and the danger of false execution, returning him to Padua, and marrying him to Mamillia; yet he interests the reader in a possible sequel: 'Marry whether Pharicles proved as inconstant a husband as a faithless wooer, I know not: but if it be my hap to hear, look for news as speedily as may be'(II, p. 248). In <u>Morando, the Tritameron of Love</u>, part I (1584), he denies knowledge of what happened between two of the characters 'but if I learn, look for news' (III, p. 109). By 1587 he had learned -- and published the second part. In <u>Penelopes Web</u> (1587) the framework for the tales is completed when a messenger announces that Ulysses is in port, which breaks off the discourse:

> but for that fell out after his homecoming, I
> refer you to the Paraphrase, which shortly
> shall be set out upon Homers Odissea: till when
> let us leave Penelope attending the return
> either of her husband, her son, or of both.
> (V, pp. 233-34)

Such a work by Greene seems never to have appeared,
but the market was at least prepared for it. He
closes Perimedes the Blacke-Smith (1588) in the same
fashion: 'If the rest of their discourse happen into
my hands, then Gentlemen look for News'(VII, p. 85);
and in that volume he extends his advertising to the
epistle to the reader: if the work does not please
the reader, he says, 'I vow to make amends in my
Orpharion, which I promise to make you merry with
the next term'(VII, p. 9). The printer, he claims,
delayed the merry-making for a year.

Greene is certain of continuing his Never too
Late (1590). Not wanting to tire the palmer who
narrates the tale, the host and his wife accept his
promise to tell the rest of the story on the next
day:

> and so taking up the candle lighted him to bed,
> where we leave him. And therefore as soon as
> may be Gentlemen, look for Francescos further
> fortunes, and after that my Farewell to follie,
> and then adieu to all amorous Pamphlets. (VIII,
> p. 109)

The reader is led to expect a whole publishing
programme as well as the continuation of the story.
The continuation appeared as Francescos Fortunes in
the same year, but Greene ran out of story early and
had to find additional matter to make up the book.
Even so, he leaves the reader prepared for a third
volume: when the palmer-narrator leaves his hosts
for Venice Greene says, 'what there he did, or how
he lived, when I am advertised (good Gentlemen) I
will send you tidings'(VIII, p. 229).

While Greene's self-advertisement in his early
and middle works is of interest mainly because of
its extent, in the conny-catching works it becomes
part of his art. In The Second Part of Conny-
catching he claims that the first part, A Notable
Discovery, has caused a decline in the conny-
catching trade, and forced the conny-catchers to
seek new methods (X, pp. 88-89). One practitioner
suffered such reduction in his trade that he swears
he will kill Greene (Greene says he would name him,

but that he hopes for his repentance -- X, pp. 90-91). More than announcing forthcoming works, Greene is here offering testimonials for what has already been published, and he mentions a gentleman who says that the first book, if he had had it earlier, would have saved him nine pounds (X, pp. 95-96). In A Disputation betweene a Hee Conny-catcher and a Shee Conny-catcher (1592) the art and the advertising are mixed: the characters he creates to carry on the disputation talk about Robert Greene ('R.G.') and the trouble he has caused the mystical science of conny-catching. Nan says she lives by her ripe wits, 'in despite of that peevish scholar, that thought with his conny-catching books to have crossbit our trade'(X, p. 204), while Lawrence, her antagonist, says:

> I need not describe the laws of villainy, because R. G. hath so amply penned them down in the first part of Conny-catching, that though I be one of the faculty, yet I cannot discover more than he hath laid open. (X, p. 206)

The mock testimony to the efficacy of the conny-catching pamphlets is good advertising, and the confusion of the reality and the fiction -- the creations talking about the creator -- is delightful. Nan will not and need not name her colleagues:

> I fear me R. G. will name them too soon in his black book: a pestilence on him, they say, he hath there set down my husbands pedigree, and yours too Lawrence: if he do it, I fear me your brother in law Bull [the hangman], is like to be troubled with you both. (X, p. 225)

Greene warms his audience's expectation with frequent other allusions to his threatened name-naming black book. Although it is unlikely that he ever intended to produce such a book (his material is more traditional anecdote than contemporary reporting), a promised climax of revelation probably served to maintain the interest of readers.

In The Defence of Conny catching (1592) Greene perfects the publicity techniques used in A Disputation. The testimonials to the effects of the former books are given an aura of greater authenticity because the author is supposedly Cuthbert Cunny-catcher, Licentiate in Whittington College, not Master R. G. himself (STC 5656 has the address

to the reader signed by Cuthbert; that of STC 5655
is the one to A Notable Discovery repeated and
signed 'Robert Greene'). When Cuthbert declares
that the popularity of the three-penny conny-catching books caused him to be arrested in Exeter (XI,
p. 45) it seems like independent evidence. Yet
Greene is still producing publicity for himself
rather than offering a serious testimonial (and,
despite the credulity of some critics, it is
unlikely that his audience was fooled by the
pretence of Cuthbert). Cuthbert sometimes talks
about Greene directly:

> At last I learned that he was a scholar, and a
> Master of Arts, and a Conny-catcher in his
> kind, though not at cards, and one that
> favoured good fellows, so they were not
> palpable offenders in such desperate laws.
> (XI, p. 47)

Even Cuthbert's description of Greene's own conny-
catching (selling the same play twice -- XI, pp. 75-
76) is back-handed praise, showing him to be a man
of practical wit, though less than scrupulous.
Cuthbert concludes The Defence with the traditional
advertisement for forthcoming publications, saying
that all will be right between the conny-catchers
and Greene if he produces The repentance of a
Conny-catcher, discovering the abuses of jailors
(XI, pp. 103-4) -- the 'stripping law' promised in A
Disputation (X, p. 237). The promise would probably
have been kept, had it not been for Greene's death.

* * *

Self-advertisement alone could not ensure a
market; Greene had not only to promise, but also to
give his public what they wanted. His amorous
pamphlets certainly dealt with a catch-penny subject
matter and, like his contemporaries, Greene was not
reluctant to follow a literary fad, as his early
reliance on Euphues shows (he made specific
reference to Euphues in his titles only twice,
however -- Euphues his Censure to Philautus, 1587,
and Menaphon, Camillas Alarum to Slumbering Euphues,
1589). Greene also made a more fundamental adjustment to his audience, adapting his writing to their
class outlook. Unlike Sir Philip Sidney, he had no
deep-rooted ideological position, nor was he a
profound or original thinker. He was trying to
appeal to a wide audience without losing anyone,

which meant appealing to the highest common denominator, gentlemen, without ignoring the interests of middle-class readers. He struck a precarious balance between aristocratic and bourgeois values that was as much the result of commercial sense as personal conviction.

One might suppose that the most successful commercial posture for Greene would have been the classlessness attempted by many modern writers, but that was impossible in Elizabethan society: class was not a matter of conscious choice but of place in the social order; everyone, it was accepted, had a definite place in that order and thus a class position. 'Different views are to be expected from different positions on the Hill' of Fortune, as John F. Danby expresses it; 'literature is addressed by a man from his place to those of his contemporaries (on the same Hill) who are in a position to listen to him'(1). However, unlike Lyly at Court, Greene was given no 'natural' audience; as a professional he could choose from a wider section of the Hill of Fortune. The rhetorical problem of establishing the author as one who shares the world-view of the audience was present as much for Greene as for Lyly, but, unlike Lyly, Greene had some choice in the ideology he would advance. He moved from appealing to a genteel audience to presenting the world-view of the petty bourgeoisie -- from speaking up the Hill to speaking down.

Greene attempted to appeal to a wide audience most obviously through his subject matter. The first works are 'amorous pamphlets', concerned with characters whose primary role is either lover (e.g. Pharicles in Mamillia) or object of passion (as in The Myrrour of Modestie, a re-telling of Susannah and the Elders). Certainly other elements were introduced into the stories -- adventure, correspondence, formal debate -- but love (or lust) is central. Thus Gwydonius has danger and intrigue, but love motivates most of the action and holds the work together. The theme of Arbasto is ostensibly fortune but, again, love is the principal matter and motivation. Greene's love matter is not that of the jest books -- anecdotes of lust; he presents a more courtly, refined love concerned with principles of conduct and genteel gambits rather than witty ways of dubbing knights of the horned order. Even when he had himself turned to jest-book material (as in the conny-catching series), he vigorously denied authorship of The Cobler of Caunterburie (1590), a lewd work yet of sufficient art as not to be unworthy of him (the detractors of the book, he complains in Greene's Vision, 'suspiciously slander me with many hard reproaches, for penning that which never came within the compass of my Quill' -- XII, p. 213).

Greene's love tales are always presented in a moral framework (one reason why he might deny The Cobler of Caunterburie, which does not attempt to moralise its content). In Mamillia, for example, the title claims to show 'how Gentlemen under the perfect substance of pure love, are oft inveighled with the shadow of lewd lust'. The Myrrour of Modestie is presented as 'Showing that the gray heads of doting adulterers shall not go with peace into the grave'. Arbasto offers 'perfect counsel to prevent misfortune' and Morando, The Tritameron of Love shows 'to the wise how to use Love, and to the fond, how to eschew Lust', while Perimedes would teach the reader 'to avoid idleness and wanton scurrility, which divers appoint as the end of their pastimes'. In making such moral claims, and in introducing moral asides throughout the works, Greene is attempting to let his audience both have their cake and eat it; they can read his pamphlets, not for their lascivious content, but in order to eschew lasciviousness:

> They which think there is no God to their Goddess, may here find that wanton loves are the ready paths to prejudice, and that effeminate follies are the efficient causes of dire disparagement. (VIII, p. 116)

An unmoral tale, if loaded with enough moralisation, as Louis B. Wright observes, can be made palatable to a puritanical middle class (2); though Thomas Nashe recognises it as merely a formal posture (see above, p. 101).

Yet Greene's moral balance did not satisfy the entire reading public. If any reliance can be placed on his epistles to readers and dedications, people of sufficient influence thought his moralising did not outweigh his lewd content and that love pamphlets, whatever conclusions the author attempted to draw, were reprehensible. The city fathers had always been worried about immorality and wanton material; Greene felt some pressure to reform and around 1590 began to respond. Between the first part of his Never too Late and the second, Francescos Fortunes (both of 1590), he changed his motto from 'Omne tulit punctum qui miscuit utile dulce' to 'Sero, sed serio'. In Greene's Vision, probably written between the two parts of Never too Late although not published until the year of his death (he says in it that he must finish his Nunquam sera est and tells the reader to look for his Mourning Garment, published 1590 -- XII, p. 274), he back-dated his reformation to include his Never too Late: Gower, conjured up in a vision as the hero of moral literature, says he liked only Greene's Nunquam sera est, and even that not greatly (XII, p. 235). Forced to choose between the literary attitudes of Gower and Chaucer in the Vision, he rejects the witty, jest-book tale assigned to Chaucer -- Kate of Grandchester and Tomkins the wheelwright -- in favour of that of the morally purer Gower. Is not 'a good book as easily penned, as a wanton Pamphlet?' he makes Gower ask (XII, p. 271), accepting the latter's advice to provide moral soundness. He closes by addressing the gentlemen: 'as you had the blossoms of my wanton fancies, so you shall have the fruits of my better labours'(XII, p. 281).

The first fruit of the 'better labours' advertised in the Vision is Greene's Mourning Garment. In it he makes use of the prodigal son theme that supplied the plot of several of his works during this period (it is related simply, with less embroidery, here), and relates the theme to his own situation in the conclusion: 'I hope there will be none so fond as to measure the matter by the man, or to proportion the contents of my Pamphlet, by the former course of my fond life'(IX, p. 220). The Mourning Garment is offered as an earnest of his repentance:

> So I hope, if I have been thought as wanton as Horace, or as full of amours, as Ovid: yet you will vouchsafe of my Mourning Garment, for that it is the first fruits of my new labours, and the last farewell to my fond desires.
> (IX, p. 221)

In Greene's Farewell to Folly (1591), which followed the Mourning Garment, he again stresses his reformation, saying that he is indebted to gentlemen for passing over his superficial subject matter and amorous interests, that these were the follies of youth and now he is getting older (IX, pp. 227-28). Although the framework of the tales of the Farewell is quite clearly moral, the subject matter has not altered; lust again appears as one of the vices

discussed and, naturally, must be embodied in a tale
to make the moral point. The pattern here is the
same as in the earlier works, except that the moral
precedes the story (which is then presented as
illustration) instead of being added as an
afterthought.

The character of the reform is most clearly
illustrated in Greenes Orpharion, written probably
just before his Never too Late in 1590 (the work was
entered in the Stationers' Register on 9th February
1590 but Greene claims the printer had it for year
and the motto is still the old 'Omne tutit
punctum'). Although the full title suggests the
praise of women, the conclusion seems to advocate
abandoning love, in the same reformed spirit as the
fruits of Greene's 'better labours'. When the
shepherd-god, Mercury, makes a highly rhetorical
speech against Venus and the entrapment of love, the
narrator asks him would he not have men love at all:
'Yes, quoth he, so they court Dianas virgins not
Venus wantons'(XII, p. 18). 'Court' gives the game
away: Greene can endlessly admire Diana's virgins,
but if he courts them he has not yet rejected the
ways of Venus. The moral transformation is purely
rhetorical. However much he may have tried to give
a contrary impression, he has undergone no fundamental change and his outlook remains amorous. His
significant reformation, which occurred in the early
1590s, was one of class outlook rather than of
conventional morality.

The attraction of amorous matter was general,
but Greene also tried to appeal to divergent tastes
simultaneously. By adding a strong story-line to
courtly discourse he could hope to hold the interest
of the reader of aristocratic taste with traditional, courtly love material, polite discourse, correspondence, and moral lessons, and at the same time
attract a middle-class audience with a tale. The
attempt to reach Lyly's courtly audience while
attracting a wider bourgeois audience is seen in
Mamillia, his first work, where Euphues both
provides the model and is transformed. Although
style remains of paramount importance -- it is the
chief mark of the work he is imitating -- Greene
makes discourse into story. In Lyly's work euphuism
is really the content, while in Greene's it is only
a style. (In that sense his apology for style in
the dedication is justified, for the reader who
expects to find in Mamillia the sustained balance
and counterpoised wit of Euphues will in some
measure be disappointed.) However, style and story

do not form a unity. Plot frequently becomes entangled in the nets of euphuism and the demands of style often determine the content of discourse. For example, Pharicles tells Mamillia that lovers are not eloquent because they are too full of love to speechify, and then launches into a speech of five pages declaring his love (II, pp. 57ff). (Greene is not yet seeking to discredit Pharicles's love by this; the difficulties of lovers making a rhetorical explanation of the speechlessness of love occurs again in Gwydonius where the lovers are true.) Euphuism, even when it does not obscure argument, reduces individual cases to generalities and formal examples, and thus it is at cross purposes to the tale. However, Greene's very lack of success in combining the two elements shows more clearly what he was trying to achieve than would a completely satisfactory integration of style and story.

In The Myrrour of Modestie and Arbasto, The Anatomie of Fortune, both of 1584, Greene is still unable to make his stories run smoothly in a euphuistic framework. In The Myrrour of Modestie plot is almost brought to a standstill by euphuism. Between introducing the wicked elders and initiating their attack on the virtue of Susannah, Greene spends twenty-two lines on metaphor and euphuistic analogy (III, pp. 11-12). In Arbasto, when Myrania is freeing Arbasto from prison, the sense of the urgency of the event is diminished by the long speeches of the characters. Myrania concludes:

> let us leave therefore these needless protestations, and go to the purpose: delay breeds danger, time tarrieth for no man, speed in necessity is the best spur: let us haste therefore till we get out of France, lest if we be prevented, it breed my mishap, and your fatal misery. (III, pp. 230-31)

Long speeches at a prison-break are amusing in their inappropriateness; but rather than attempting to amuse, Greene is trapped by the need to write euphuistically. In Gwydonius, The Carde of Fancie, also of 1584, he finally finds a proper role for euphuism, using it more as ornament and less as the substance of the work, though he never quite relinquished his attachment to high style and as late as The Second Part of Conny-catching, where style is subordinate to content, he apologises that lack of polish is appropriate to the subject matter (X, p. 71).

With Gwydonius and Arbasto in 1584 Greene found popular and commercial success; they were his first works for which the STC records several editions. While their alteration, or even advance, of style is too slight to account for their increased popularity, in Gwydonius Greene made an important ideological adjustment, appealing simultaneously to opposed values of aristocracy and bourgeoisie, which may well have gained him a wider audience. He deals not only with love and adventure in Gwydonius but explicitly tackles class-based morality. The question of class arises through the problem of love -- which, as one would expect in the sixteenth century, is closely related to social station. Castania, daughter of the duke of Alexandria, feels compelled to reject the suit of Gwydonius (a prince passing as a mere gentleman) because of his inferior status. She has already made clear this principle in rejecting Valericus, one of the Duke's gentlemen-courtiers, shocked by the impudence of his suit and attacking his station, parentage, and patrimony (IV, pp. 51-53). The same principle must be applied to Gwydonius, even though she would like to return his affection:

> Set a beggar on horse back, they say, and he will never alight. Extol one of base stock to any degree of dignity, and who so proud and haughty? I speak of this Gwydonius to thy reproof: is thy stomach alate waxen so queasy, that no diet will down but my Fathers own dish? Will no meaner mate suffice thee, unless thou match with a Prince? . . . Dost though think Gwydonius, that I account so meanly of my person, as to match with a man of thy pitch? Shall I so far crack my credit, as to cumber myself with one of thy calling? Shall I so stain my state, as to stoop to thy lure? No. Where is thy coin to maintain my countenance? Where is thy wealth to uphold my worship? Where is thy patrimony to countervail my personage? (IV, pp. 102-3)

The alliterative pairs that conclude Castania's argument may suggest that it is simply money that Gwydonius lacks, but Greene's euphuism is probably controlling the argument here; the context makes it clear that station is the real issue.

Gwydonius could reveal himself, hinting that his rank is higher than it appears in Alexandria:

> yet thus much I answer in respect of my
> parents, and without arrogancy, thus far I
> stand on my pantuffles, that the credit I have
> in your fathers Court, is not coequal with the
> calling I have in mine own Countrie.
> (IV, p. 104)

Nevertheless, he then pretends that the appearance
is the reality:

> so though want of dignity disgrace me, though
> want of coin discountenance me, though lack of
> wealth impairs my credit, yet Nature hath given
> me such a loyal and loving heart, as I hope in
> the perfection of that, she hath supplied the
> want of all the rest. (IV, p. 105)

Lack of coin is compensated by constancy; of lands,
by loyalty; of wealth, by will to do good --
alliterative pairs again control the argument though
station remains the issue. The point of Gwydonius's
pretence is that he wants to win Castania's love on
his worth as an individual rather than as a
representative of a rank; revelation would alter the
issue and might interfere with the strictly human
success of his love. Rejected once again in a
letter from Castania, he wonders

> whether he should bewray his parents and
> parentage to the Duke and her, or still stand
> to the doubtful chance of Fortune . . . the
> sincerity of his love, would not let him to
> bewray his birth. (IV, p. 117)

He demands success in a specifically individual
love.
Gwydonius writes Castania a farewell letter
arguing that the individual is more important than
the status and citing prominent morganatic relationships, such as those of the Duchess of Malfi and
her servant Ulrico and Venus and Vulcan:

> They madam, respected the man, and not their
> money, their wills, and not their wealth, their
> love, not their livings: their constancy, not
> their coin: their person, not their parentage:
> and the inward virtue, not the outward value.
> (IV, p. 119)

Castania, overcoming the social pressure to distin-
guish reckless fancy from 'lawful' love, accedes to
Gwydonius's suit.

Yet their love must suffer a near disaster
before its final triumph. Valericus, embittered by
his own failure to win Castania, overhears
Gwydonius's unguarded reflection on the obstacles to
the fruition of his love raised by the hostilities
between Alexandria and Metelyne and informs the Duke
Orlanio that Gwydonius was sent from Metelyne to
assassinate him. No questions asked, Gwydonius is
arrested by Castania's brother, Thersandro, who then
releases him for love of Gwydonius's sister,
Lewcippa. Because the slaughter has been so great,
Clerophontes, Duke of Metelyne, and Orlanio agree to
settle the war by single combat. Clerophontes
himself will be champion of Metelyne; Orlanio,
unable to find anyone of equal force, offers his
daughter and the captured Metelyne to anyone who
will be his champion. Thersandro, convinced by
Castania and Gwydonius of the latter's innocence,
agrees to accept Gwydonius's proposal that he be
allowed to enter the single combat disguised as
Thersandro, conveys him to Castania in whose company
he spends the night (Castania now knows his true
rank). Victorious in the single combat, Gwydonius
tells Orlanio that he already has the Dukedom of
Metelyne by inheritance and Castania by love, but he
wishes to have Orlanio's good will as well (IV,
p. 192). True love is victorious.

The man of merit has had his victory over the
disadvantages of fortune. Gwydonius won Castania's
love through constancy and her hand through valour.
The victory would seem entirely that of individualism, since individual qualities have proved more
important than birth and the mere gentlemen has
carried away the princess. But of course that is
not the case, for Gwydonius is no mere gentleman.
Greene is playing both sides. The princess, model
of virtue, loves within the bounds of law and her
speeches on rank are not proved wrong; the man of
merit wins the day and happens also to be a prince.
With such a compromise Greene must have pleased
everybody, even his patron for the work, the Earl of
Oxford, a leader of the old aristocracy. Although
Gwydonius succeeds by his individual qualities and
draws attention to them, they can also be viewed as
his princeliness showing through the disguise.
Greene has found the perfect accommodation of the
professional author to an audience of mixed
outlooks.

Greene achieved a similar dual appeal in other works. Pandosto, Menaphon and Ciceronis Amor all deal with cross-class, or apparently cross-class, marriages. In Pandosto Fawnia, supposed daughter of a shepherd and Dorastus, a prince, succeed in their love, without impropriety since Fawnia turns out to be a long-lost princess. Menaphon has the added complexity of double concealment. Although the royal Samela and Melicertus have a strong mutual attraction, each credits the other's disguise as humble shepherd, and thus cannot yield to a relationship that must span such a social gulf, until they are discovered to be the long-assumed-dead spouses, Sephestia and Maximus. The discrepancy between estates in Ciceronis Amor is actual rather than apparent. The high-born Terentia, required to defend her love for the base-born Cicero before the Senate, cannot give any strong reason 'because love is not circumscript within reasons limits' (VII, p. 216), which effectively justifies individuality over estate by denying the need for justification.

In his use of the ideas of order and nature, Greene also attempts to strike a balance of opposed interests. Throughout his work, as indeed throughout much of the work of the sixteenth century, two opposing views of nature are presented: nature as the inherited order and nature as the individual's organically-generated desires; an abstract order into which the individual must fit irrespective of personal qualities, and the individual's responses to the world extended to general principles. Unabashed individualism is still unacceptable -- Machiavelli taken neat is too strong for the Elizabethan taste -- but it is often acceptable cloaked as natural law. Individualism is regarded as a-social and therefore anti-social, but when voiced as a principle of nature it can be given open approval, and elevated into an abstract force (e.g. fancy termed 'fate') even individual desire is acceptable. The principle need not, in fact, be nature. Since the idea of nature is not derived from the study of the material environment but is a logical extension of social principles to the natural world -- really a metaphor -- other fields such as the pantheon (the gods are an arsenal for every argument) can also provide justification.

While many other writers besides Greene presented opposing views of nature, as would be expected from anyone trained in rhetoric and debate, these views were usually treated simply as no more

than rhetorical occasions; in Greene the opposition
is more fundamental and frequently integral to his
plot. Thus Lyly, for example, uses principles of
nature as elements of the debate so important to the
style; whereas for Greene, in a work such as
Mamillia, the conception of nature is in effect a
principle of the action.

Statements about nature are seldom used
directly by Greene to present the moral of the work;
they provide a perspective within which the action
can be understood. In Arbasto the explicit moral is
Arbasto's conclusion 'that by contemning fortune, I
learn to lead her in triumph'(III, p. 253), but
there is also a nature-order moral that appears at
various points. Arbasto's troubles are caused by
violation of the order of nature. He says he can
accuse neither gods nor fortune because he has
warred against god, fortune and nature: 'in
suffering reason to yield unto appetite, wisdom unto
will, and wit unto affection, thou hast procured
thine own death and thy Soldiers destruction'(III,
p. 219). The problem is presented by Greene as
individual desire; it is Arbasto's succumbing to
fancy which has caused all his troubles. It is
unimportant that the statement of causation is
considerably stronger than the demonstration; as a
general principle (sometimes viewed favourably but
here negatively) it is desire that upsets the world.
Chided by his companion Egerio for placing his
affections on the wrong woman, Arbasto replies that
love is kindled by the eye but engraved on the mind
by destiny. Egerio gives the moral: 'The more pitie
(quoth he) for poor men, and the greater impiety in
the Gods, that in giving love free liberty, they
granted him a lawless privilege'(III, p. 213).

Dorastus and Fawnia, imprisoned by Pandosto in
Bohemia, also blame their troubles on striving
against nature. The prince has eloped with the
supposed shepherdess, against the will of the
parents of both, and when it appears that the whole
affair is about to end in disaster, Fawnia philoso-
phises on the cause:

Ah infortunate Fawnia thou seest to desire
above fortune, is to strive against the Gods,
and Fortune. Who gazeth at the sun weakeneth
his sight: they which stare at the sky, fall
oft into deep pits: haddest thou rested content
to have been a shepherd, thou needest not to
have feared mischance: better had it been for

thee, by sitting low, to have had quiet, than
by climbing high to have fallen into misery.
(IV, p. 308)

Dorastus similarly reflects to himself: 'will not
the Gods plague him with despite that paineth his
father with disobedience?'(IV, p. 309). The moral
is clearly that to strive above one's station is
unnatural -- as it is to upset the paternalistic
hierarchy -- and brings disaster.

It is not that Dorastus and Fawnia simply
discover that their behaviour has been contrary to
the demands of the order of nature; they knew those
demands beforehand and are thus aware of the
violation. Fawnia reflects on her situation, which
joins poverty and aspiration, a dangerous
combination that is likely to lead her into trouble
because it is likely to lead her to violate natural
order:

> No bastard hawk must soar so high as the
> Hobby, no Fowl gaze against the Sun but the
> Eagle: actions wrought against nature reap
> despite, and thoughts above Fortune disdain.
> Fawnia, thou art a shepherd, daughter to
> poor Porrus: if thou rest content with this,
> thou art like to stand, if thou climb thou are
> sure to fall. (IV, p. 279)

Dorastus attempts to justify loving beneath his
station by classical examples but asks himself:
'wilt thou so forget thyself as to suffer affection
to suppress wisdom, and Love to violate thine
honour?'(IV, p. 278). His love for Fawnia is
clearly a wrong love, contrary to nature: 'Subdue
then thy affections, and cease to love her whom thou
couldst not love, unless blinded with too much love'
(IV, p. 278). He does not choose to act in an evil
manner; he is victim of his affections which lead
him knowingly to violate order. The tone is set by
Greene when Dorastus first sees Fawnia and his
delight in her beauty is mixed with foreboding,
'fearing that with Acteon he had seen Diana'(IV,
p. 274).

In Menaphon descending beneath one's station is
explicitly stated to be contrary to nature. Menaphon asks, 'Hath love then respect of circumstance?'
to which Samela replies:

> Else it is not love, but lust; for where the
> parties have no sympathy of Estates, there can

no firm love be fixed; discord is reputed the
mother of division, and in nature this is an
unrefuted principle, that it faulteth which
faileth in uniformity. (VI, p. 61)

Menaphon raises the usual contrary examples and
Samela counters by saying that at least Vulcan was a
god and Sappho rather dishonoured herself with Phaon
(VI, pp. 61-62). The shepherd Menaphon finally
accepts the justice of this order. When he discovers Samela's royal parentage he overcomes his
disappointment, realising such lettuce is too fine
for his lips, and courts within his own class,
marrying his old love Pesana (a name which suggests
her suitability as a mate for a shepherd).

On the domestic level, disregard of filial
piety provides a destruction of order similar to
social over-reaching, and filial piety is a virtue
that Greene is at pains to stress in his exemplary
tales. In the third tale of Perimedes, for example,
the heroine Melissa says that she would rather marry
her father's bad choice and be unhappy than marry
her own choice against her father's will (VII,
p. 79). When it is in actual conflict with the
individual's desires filial piety becomes an issue
of significant moral proportions. Myrania, the
unfortunate daughter of Pelorus in love with
Arbasto, gives full expression to this view:

. . . love to be feared of men, because
honoured of the Gods. Dare reason abide the
brunt, when beauty bids the battle? can wisdom
win the field, when love is Captain? No no,
love is without law, and therefore above all
law, honoured in heaven, feared in earth, and a
very terror to the infernal ghosts.
Bow then unto that Myrania whereunto
lawless necessity doth bend . . . nor strive
not with Sappho against Venus: for love being a
Lord, looks to command by power, and to be
obeyed of force.
Truth Myrania, but what then, to love is
easy, and perhaps good, but to like well is
hard and a doubtful chance: fancy thy fill
(fond fool) so thou bend not thy affection to
thy fathers foe: for to love him who seeks his
life, is to war against nature and fortune. Is
there none worthy to be thy fere but Arbasto,
that cursed enemy to thy country? can none win
thy good will but that bloody wretch, who
seeketh to breed thy fathers bane? can the

eagle and the bird Osiphage build in one tree?
will the falcon and the dove covet to set on
one perch? will the Ape and the Bear be tied in
one tether? will the Fox and the Lamb lie in
one den? no they want reason, and yet nature
suffers them not to live against nature: wilt
thou then be so wilful or witless? as having
reason to guide nature: yet to be more
unnatural than unreasonable creatures? be sure
if thou fall in this thou strivest against the
gods, and in striving with them look for a most
sharp revenge. (III, pp. 197-98)

The gods had their revenge: Myrannia suffered a most
miserable unrequited love.

Castania and Gwydonius are faced with a similar
conflict, although the resolution is a happy one for
them. Castania (before she knows that Gwydonius
will be the Alexandrian champion) is tormented that
an Alexandrian victory in the single combat will
force her to marry someone other than her beloved
Gwydonius, while a victory for Clerophontes means
that her family and friends will be made forever
miserable. She concludes on the basis of her own
desire: 'No, come what come will, let froward
fortune favour whom she please, so I may joy and
safely enjoy my only joy Gwydonius'(IV, p. 182).
Gwydonius, tortured by similar considerations,
arrives at the same individualistic conclusion. But
faced with actually fighting his own father, not his
mortal foe, he falls to doubts again and summarises
the whole problem of individual desire in conflict
with filial obligation:

Alas poor Gwydonius (quoth he) how art thou
cumbered with divers cogitations, what a cruel
conflict dost thou find in thy mind between
love and loyalty, nature and necessity? whoever
was so wilful as willingly to wage battle
against his own father? who so cruel as to
enter combat with his own sire? Alas, duty
persuades me not to practise so monstrous a
mischief: but the devotion I owe to Castania,
drives me to perform the deed, were it thrice
more dangerous or desperate. The honour I owe
to my Father, makes me faint for fear but once
to imagine so brutish a fact: the love I owe to
Castania, constraineth me to defend the combat
if Jupiter himself made the challenge. And is
not (fond fool) necessity above nature, is not
the law of love above King or Kaiser, Father or

> friend, God or the devil? Yes. And so I mean
> to take it: for either I will valiantly win the
> conquest and my Castania, or lose the victory,
> and so by death end my miseries.
> (IV, pp. 190-91)

'Necessity' is above 'nature'. Having elevated the
conflict from a mere choice between father and lover
to principles, Gwydonius is able to follow his
individual desire.

The violations of the order of nature caused by
love are not held to be conscious choices of evil or
the calculated preference of individual desire above
public order -- they are compulsive actions. The
individual does not appear to be a rational agent so
much as the battle ground for forces much greater
than himself. Obviously the individual does, in a
real sense, make the choice, but Greene usually
cushions the force of personal decision in more
general causes.

The first externalisation of individual desire
occurs in Mamillia. When Pharicles considers
whether or not to approach Mamillia when he sees her
with others in a field, his rational answer is 'no'
but his conduct is determined by his desire. He
answers; 'But the law of necessity, saith Plato, is
so hard, that the Gods themselves are not able to
resist it'(II, p. 55). From the first, Greene
elevates desire to a cosmic force. But the necessity that drives Pharicles in this situation is not
the mechanical necessity of a Newtonian universe, it
is the necessity of individual desire. Until the
end of Mamillia (part II), personal desire motivates
Pharicles, even though he challenges himself with
all the arguments of the nature-as-order position.
When his affection turns to Publia, for example, he
berates himself for inconstancy, arguing from the
traditional comparison with animals, that although
they have only sense, they are constant, and
therefore Pharicles, with both sense and reason,
with nurture as well as nature, should be constant
(II, pp. 90-91). But the elevated force of fancy
overcomes the traditional power of order.

In Morando, The Tritameron of Love (Part I,
1584; Part II, 1587) Greene justifies love as a
principle (Morando is a suitable work for this
because it is composed of discourses with slight
action surrounding them rather than actual tales):

> for in truth, he that is an enemy to love, is a
> foe to nature: there is nothing which is either

so requested of men, or desired of brute
beasts, more than mutual society, which neither
the one can gain nor the other attain without
love. (III, p. 92)

The statement is not a justification of individualism; yet, as most of the content of the
individualism in Greene's works is in fact love, it
prepares the reader to accept the idea that the
individualistic lover is acting in accord with
nature. It is a nature different from nature-as-
order, but it too relies on a pseudo-natural history
to justify its principles. A love-motivated
individualism emerges from Morando as acceptable, so
long as it is not directly anti-social; flouting a
code is not the same as acting against the community. In Morando II Greene says, 'he which violateth
friendship, opposeth himself against the common
succour and aid of all men, and as much as in him
lieth, overthroweth human society'(III, p. 156). To
reject the inherited order is not yet breaking the
social contract. There are really two kinds of
individualism here for Greene: what might be
regarded as strictly personal (or desire) motivation
and directly anti-social behaviour. The elders who
attempt Susannah's virtue in The Myrrour of Modestie
are overcome with irresistable fancy in a manner
different from that of Pharicles; they have a
calculating anti-social attitude, which can be seen
in the reflection of one of the elders:

but he that is so scrupulous for the observing
of the law, shall both pass his days without
pleasure, and yet at last be found a sinner. I
mean therefore whatsoever the law wisheth, at
this time to have mine own will. (III, p. 17)

The bold conflict of individual and society shows
the elders to be evil; their lust is not cushioned
as one of the opposing concepts of nature.
At other points' fancy assumes a definite
character as an external force. Pharicles's
decision to resume his pursuit of Publia is not
presented as the vagaries of fancy but as the
working of fate, something outside the control of
those experiencing it. Pharicles attributes to
Aristotle the view that fate never does anything
wrong, and his decision is therefore justified (II,
p. 123). Castania in Gwydonius (a character Greene
presents as fully commendable) reasons in a similar
fashion. Principles dictate that she must reject

Gwydonius as she has rejected Valericus, but fancy demands he be accepted: 'Can I deny that which the destinies have decreed? Is it in my power to pervert that which the Planets have placed? Can I resist that which is stirred up by the stars?'(IV, p. 92 -- this mirrors the words used in Mamillia, II, p. 122). Obviously, she cannot. The will is objectified as destiny or fate or the gods; such cosmic forces cannot be resisted and the person in their grip is forced to do as he or she wishes, even if it contradicts prinicple or the inherited order.

In presenting these two contradictory views of nature -- as order and as the will of the individual -- Greene endows his work with a seriousness that would not be expected in 'amorous pamphlets'. Through a superficially frivolous exploration of the problem of love, he examines the fundmental attitudes of his day -- not abstract philosophical notions but views that served as a basis for action in everyday life.

* * *

In his love tales Greene's social function was to codify an individualistic view that is often taken for granted as part of the Elizabethan period. While much theoretical justification of the established view (that nature equalled order) was offered elsewhere, the opposing individualist view found little advocacy in fiction until Greene; he presents in literary creations the inchoate but deeply felt position of bourgeois individualism. He is not codifying in the fashion of the philosopher or the lawyer but (in a manner probably more socially powerful) gives a concrete expression to individualistic views. He offers to his reader a model of conduct that is in fact a projection of bourgeois ideals. The model is not tied to parti-cular figures -- as in Deloney's champions -- but to a type general enough to include the reader. Greene's greatest appeal was probably to those who took an attitude of individualism without being able to excuse it by pointing to their own material success.

Nevertheless, the mere presentation of a bourgeois-individualistic view is not in itself a justification of that view. Sidney presents such a view in order to attack it. What makes Greene's a justification is that it becomes the perspective in which his tales are written. Events are understood through the eyes of the individualistic heroes. It

is customarily the 'good' that wins in literature
(in fact or essence) and in Greene's fiction a
bourgeois-individualistic view is usually vindicated
by success (Arbasto is an exception). While formal
tribute may also be paid to a traditional view, that
does not diminish the victory of bourgoeis individuality. Arbasto, although he is punished, is given
the attention of a hero on the basis of the very
actions for which he is punished. The situation is
similar to that of Corneille's Le Cid -- a later but
more celebrated case -- where the formal demands of
traditional society are fulfilled but the real
triumph is that of individualism. The traditional
aristocratic view of order is presented by Greene
and other sixteenth-century authors as 'reason' --
understandably, since it is the inherited and
philosophically justified view. Greene gives
'reason' to the individual's desires as a proper
source of action by presenting them as nature (a
nature equal to traditional, ordered nature). In
his fiction Greene has erected what serves as a
philosophy of bourgeois individualism.

Even though Greene accommodates himself to a
bourgeois outlook, he still retains an inherited
aristocratic view that accepts the intrinsic
superiority of the aristocracy (although he may at
other times consciously reject that same view) and
finds tasteful what is aristocratic, distasteful
what is associated with labouring classes. In
Menaphon, the shepherd Menaphon shows Samela (the
noble Sephestia in disguise) his flocks, 'thinking
with the sight of his flocks to inveigle her, whose
mind had rather have chosen any misfortune, than
have dined her eyes on the face and feature of so
low a peasant'(VI, p. 58). Samela says of
Melicertus (her assumed-dead husband whom she does
not recognise but thinks resembles her 'lost'
Maximus):

> May this Melicertus be a shepherd: or can a
> country cottage afford such perfection? doth
> this coast bring forth such excellence? . . .
> but his face is not inchased with any rustic
> proportion, his brows contain the characters of
> nobility, and his looks in shepherds weeds are
> Lordly, his voice pleasing , his wit full of
> gentry . . . (VI, p. 79)

Excellence and the lower classes are assumed to be
incompatible. Menaphon's kinship with Sidney's
Arcadia was strong enough for it to be referred to

127

as 'Greene's Arcadia' (despite the appeal to Euphues in the sub-title), and its aristocratic taste is not therefore surprising. However, in Pandosto, which shows remarkable objectivity in recognising different schemes of class values, such prejudice seems less natural. Greene does not treat the event as strange when Dorastus, disguised as a mere knight, is arrested in Bohemia on suspicion of foul play aroused by his being accompanied by a lady worthy of a prince when he is but a knight; he accepts that beauty belongs to the aristocracy. Nature is stronger than nurture: although Fawnia is raised by shepherds on the coast of Sicily 'she so increased with exquisite perfection both of body and mind, as her natural disposition did bewray that she was born of some high parentage'(IV, p. 269). The people, thinking her to be the shepherd's daughter, are amazed at her beauty and wit. Although birth may be arbitrary, the different estates are marked by innate characteristics.

Despite his reflex acceptance of the view that the aristocracy are naturally superior, Greene manages to express the difference between class image and class actuality with considerable wit. In Pandosto this can be seen particularly in the mocking of pastoral conventions. Fawnia says that she will love the prince Dorastus when he becomes a shepherd. When he complies with her desire by donning rustic apparel, she objects that he has not, in fact, become a shepherd:

> rich clothing make not princes: nor homely attire beggars: shepherds are not called shepherds, because they wear hooks and bags, but that they are born poor, and live to keep sheep; so this attire hath not made Dorastus a shepherd, but to seem like a shepherd.
> (IV, p. 288)

In the host's tale of Francescos Fortunes, Greene offers inverted pastoral. All of her lovers write to Mirimida, but the peasant lover, Mullidor, must first buy paper, adding a touch of realism counter to the pastoral theme: 'although he and a pen were as fit as an ass and a harp; yet he bought him paper, and stealing into the Churchyard under an Apple tree, there in his muses he framed a letter and sent it her'(VIII, p. 204).

Greene's playing with pastoral convention involves distinguishing actual class position from image. A strong sense of actual class reality is developed in <u>Pandosto</u> and the pastoral game is sometimes dispensed with altogether, as when Porrus, her assumed father, speaks of the dangers facing Fawnia:

> I am afraid wife, that my daughter Fawnia hath made herself so fine, that she will buy repentance too dear. I hear news, which if they be true, some will wish they had not proved true. It is told me by my neighbours, that Dorastus the Kings son begins to look at our daughter Fawnia: which if it be so, I will not give her a halfpenny for her honesty at the years end. I tell thee wife, nowadays beauty is a great stale to trap young men, and fair words and sweet promises are two great enemies to a maidens honesty: and thou knowest where poor men entreat, and cannot obtain, there Princes may command, and will obtain. Though Kings sons dance in nets, they may not be seen: but poor mens faults are spied at a little hole: Well, it is a hard case where Kings lusts are laws, and that they should bind poor men to that, which they themselves wilfully break.
> (IV, pp. 292-92)

A remark about his daughter's chastity becomes an eloquent statement about class justice. Porrus's wife, fearing that he may go too far in attempting to stop Dorastus and may lose his own head in trying to save her maidenhead, concludes, 'it is ill jesting with edged tools, and bad sporting with Kings'(IV, p. 293).

Despite his frequent use of the conventional rhetorical notion that poverty is free from care and that trouble affects only aspiring individuals, Greene recognises the uneasy position of the lower classes and is sympathetic to them. Francesco's old beggar-messenger in <u>Never too Late</u> gladly ceases her trade when she is released from want (VIII, p. 49) and such unromantic matter as insecurity of farmers' tenure appears in the tale of Calamus in <u>Penelopes Web</u> (1587 -- V, p. 211). Greene depicts the troubles of the lower classes more particularly than if he were writing only for a gentle audience.

Greene's greatest sensitivity to the humanity of the lower classes appears in the host's tale in <u>Francescos Fortunes</u>. Mullidor, a rustic oaf, courts Mirimida, and Greene presents him in all his oafishness. When his mother tries to discover what ails him, the love-sick Mullidor 'fetched a great

sigh, and with that (being after supper) he brake
wind'(VIII, p. 187). The poor natural -- hunch-
backed, small-witted, with lips 'of the largest size
in folio' (VIII, p. 185) -- is clearly an object of
fun, but Greene's attitude toward him is vastly
different from that of Sir Philip Sidney toward his
comparable creations of Dametas and Mopsa. While
Sidney creates objects of scorn who have no value
other than that of being amusing to their betters,
beings different in kind from the readers and the
other characters of the Arcadia, Greene, although he
laughs at his dim-witted shepherd, still makes
Mullidor of the same race and humanity as reader and
author. He writes from above Mullidor but not as an
Olympian above mortals, as did Sidney with Mopsa and
Dametas; Mullidor is comical but sympathetic and
human.

Mullidor's humanity is in part created by
Greene's placing him in a common and recognisable
context. His mother addresses him:

> for tell me Mullidor, what is she that thou
> lovest and will not love thee? If she be a
> woman as I am, she cannot but fancy thee; for
> mine eye though it be now old (and with that up
> went her apron and she wiped them clear) hath
> been a wanton when it was young, and would
> have chosen at the first glance the properest
> springall in the Parish: and trust me Mullidor,
> but be not proud of it, when I look on thee I
> find thee so lovely, that I count her worse
> than accursed would not choose thee for her
> Paramour. (VIII, pp. 188-89).

This relationship between mother and son is as
charming in its good nature as it is amusing. The
humour is of a M. Hulot variety, whereas Sidney's in
regard to Mopsa is more depersonalised, like Tom and
Jerry bashing each other over the head with spiked
clubs.

Most important in Greene's creation of a human
Mullidor is that he gives him a human dignity.
Mirimida is courted by a gentleman as well as by
Mullidor. The two suitors encounter each other and
Mullidor addresses the gentleman:

> my crook back harboureth more honest
> conditions, can fetch more pence than thy
> silks: for I believe thou makest a sconce of
> the Mercers book: thou hast made such sure
> entrance there, that thou wilt never from

thence till thou beest come out by the ears.
Goodman courtier, though we have backs to bear
your frumps; yet we have queasy stomachs that
will hardly brook them: and therefore fine
fool, be gone with your foul, or I will so
belabour you, as you shall feel my fingers this
fortnight: And with that Mullidor heaved up his
sheephook and bent his brows, so that the
Gentleman giving Mirimida the adieu, he put
spurs to his horse, and went his way.
(VIII, p. 196)

Here we do not have an author addressing gentlemen.
Greene's fool, more than an honest peasant, can also
be seen as a projection of petty-bourgeois sentiments, thrashing the gentry who have nothing but
birth and asserting the dignity of honest conditions. The gentleman is even robbed of his title by
Mullidor who calls him 'Goodman', a style for the
yeomanry, not the gentry. We have to wait another
two years before the upstart courtier is defeated
(in A Quip), but Mullidor sends the faceless
gentleman packing in the meantime. And his
discomfiture is not outrage, but fun. Greene is
turning his back on a gentle audience.

As well as explicitly rejecting gentility,
Greene makes a positive assertion of bourgeois
values. Francesco and Isabell in Never too Late are
gentlefolk but, released from a false imprisonment,
they turn instinctively to work and, with bourgeois
industry, succeed entirely on their own efforts.
While George a Greene cannot be called bourgeois, he
reflects a bourgeoise valuation of the world, saying
that though he has no coat of arms he is a gentleman
and a true poor man is better than a false earl
(3). This is reminiscent of Richard Johnson's
petty-bourgeois appeal of The Nine Worthies of
London, as is George a Greene's refusal of
knighthood. The king gives him lands and would
knight him but George asks to be excused the honour
because there is more credit when men of base degree
(such as himself and his father -- a rather peculiar
tracing of base lineage) do high deeds than when
they are done by men of rank, from whom they are
expected (V, i, 1194ff, p. 216). There is an odd
yet understandable lack of logic here that makes an
interesting comparison with Jack of Newbury's excuse
for refusing a knighthood in Deloney's work, that in
effect he would rather get on with his business and
not waste his substance supporting the estate of
knighthood.

* * *

Greene never became an exponent of petty-bourgeois values in the manner of Deloney in The Gentle Craft, yet he obviously went through some process of disillusionment with gentlemen and the bourgeoisie which became marked towards the end of his career. His Groatsworth displays a bitterness about the plight of scholars unrelieved by the playful invective Nashe excelled in. He puts into the mouth of the dying Gorinius, an unscrupulous usurer, a praise of wealth that amounts to a thorough condemnation of the integrity of his society: 'for to be rich is to be any thing, wise, honest, worshipful, or what not'(XII, p. 106). Greene's, and other scholars', efforts are without honour or reward in a hostile, money-minded age: 'this iron age affords few that esteem of virtue' (XII, p. 131) and the hero, Roberto, is denied his rightful inheritance because of his forthright condemnation of usury. But even if Greene would reject the bourgeoisie, he cannot escape their values, and his social critique, a simplified and outmoded fusion of bourgeois and aristocratic standards, is petty-bourgeois.

A Quip for an Upstart Courtier is the most obviously petty-bourgeois of Greene's social-critical works. It is carefully shaped to appeal to a certain audience, rather than an uncalculated cry from the heart, and the accuracy of his judgement can be seen from the repeated, rapid reissues -- three editions in 1592, or six in the first six months according to Sandra Clark. He begins by attacking the England of his day which offends against both gentle generosity and bourgeois industry, thus insulting the composite sensibility of the petty bourgeoisie. In a dream he sees old men picking the plant thrift and giving it to their children, who destroy it as quickly as their fathers gather it, 'wasting and spoiling it at their pleasure, which their fathers got with labour'(XI, p. 217). Cloth-breeches, the hero, regrets the old days when there was real hospitality and courtiers strove for virtue rather than brave appearance (XI, pp. 234-35) and complains men will not keep their place:

Now every lout must have his son a Courtnell, and those dunghill drudges wax so proud, that they will presume to wear on their feet, what kings have worn on their heads [i.e. velvet]. (XI, p. 238)

Cloth-breeches' complaint is different from Sidney's attack on pretension from a superior station, which seeks to maintain a hierarchy in which he is well placed, and from the upper bourgeoisie's demand of their rights; it is criticism from a lower rung which, accepting hierarchy, objects to being overtaken on the ladder to the top -- a petty-bourgeois protest about forms. Greene explains, in his epistle to the reader, what he objects to:

> not the apparel when 'tis worthily worn, but the unworthy person that wears it, who sprang of a Peasant will use any sinister means to climb to preferment, being then so proud as the fop forgets like the Ass that a mule was his father. (XI, p. 211)

(It would seem that Greene, too, has forgotten his animal if not his social breeding.) The same point is made rather more effectively in The Defence of Conny catching in the anecdote of the tailor who, dressing magnificently on the great sums he extracts from his customers, is delighted that a serving man mistakes him for a gentleman; but when the serving man points out that his worship's man left a needle and thread in his doublet which he should remove lest someone think him a tailor, he flies into a rage. The serving man, immediately aware of his mistake, says that all his caps and knees were done only to the tailor's apparel and bids farewell to the good, honest pricklouse (XI, pp. 97-99).

Pretension, bad in itself, breeds further evils. Velvet-breeches, to maintain his position, must rack the poor and raise his rents, while Cloth-breeches can live modestly. The quarrel between the two regarding their claims to ancient lineage and honour is tried by a jury who give their verdict in favour of Cloth-breeches:

> one that hath been in Diebus illis a companion to kings, an equal with the nobility, a friend to Gentlemen and yeomen, and patron of the poor, a true subject, a good housekeeper, and general as honest as he is ancient, Whereas Velvet-breeches is an upstart come out of Italy, begot of Pride, nursed up by self love,

and brought into this country by his companion Newfangleness: that he is but of late time a raiser of rents, and an enemy to the commonwealth, and one that is not in any way to be preferred in equity before Cloth-breeches. (XI, p. 294)

Greene directs attention to specific injustices in the conny-catching pamphlets. In A Notable Discovery, he stresses how the cosenage practised by colliers (i.e. charcoal merchants) affects the poor especially, those who cannot afford to buy a whole load but must buy it by the sack, thereby facilitating the collier's use of false measure. In The Defense, Cuthbert Conny-catcher explains how most merchants are conny-catchers, using false measures and selling false goods, but he shows sympathy for the small trader, such as the ale-wife forced to cheat simply to meet her obligations:

The Ale-wife unless she nick her Pots and Conny-catch her guests with stone Pots and petty Cans, can hardly pay her Brewer, nay and yet that will not serve, the chalk must walk to set up now and then a shilling or two too much, or else the rent will not be answered at the quarter day. (XI, p. 68)

Greene in all the earlier conny-catching pamphlets shows admiration for the conny-catchers, as fellows of some wit attacking those who, morally or otherwise, invite it. In The Defence this attitude becomes explicit to the extent of saying, more or less, that conny-catching redresses social injustice or effects class justice. Cuthbert says:

for when we meet a country Farmer with a full purse, a miserable miser, that either racks his Tenants rents, or sells his grain in the market at an unreasonable rate: we hold it a devotion to make him a Conny, in that he is a Caterpillar to others, and gets that by pilling and polling of the poor that we strip him of by sleight and agility of wit. (XI, p. 76)

Greene, in the guise of Cuthbert, attacks his earlier pamphlets for being irrelevant -- they expose the small fry while ignoring the big fish in the waters of corruption. In this iron age we live in, says Cuthbert, the conny-catcher like everyone else lives by his wits. Men are now valued according to their wealth rather than their virtues and everything that is found profitable is counted honest and lawful by society. The conny-catcher merely partakes of the generality. The really harmful members of the society are those like usurers, who ruin both rich and poor (XI, pp. 51-52). Cuthbert concludes:

> Thus have I proved to your ma'ships, how there is no estate, trade, occupation, nor mystery, but lives by Conny-catching, and that our shift at cards compared to the rest, is the simplest of all, and yet forsooth, you could bestow the pains to write two whole Pamphlets against us poor conny-catchers. (XI, p. 103)

In The Defence Greene has perhaps at last undergone the reformation he so long talked about. His sympathy for the downtrodden has finally turned into explicit social criticism. From pamphlets attacking superficial or even mock evils, heavily indebted for incident to the older work of Harman, he has turned to significant disorders of his society. He now unashamedly views the world from the standpoint of artisans, serving men and petty bourgeoisie -- perhaps because that is where his best market lies.

* * *

Greene's developing realism can also be seen as a movement away from a genteel audience. His content increasingly reflected ordinary life, and the detailed representation was a flattering attention to the middle class which at the same time helped to maintain the confusion between 'story' and 'history' that made a 'useful' lesson out of poet's lies. 'Historical' realism was a common sixteenth-century technique, often used effectively by Greene in such devices as inventing an 'objective' source for the story. In Perimedes the Blacke-Smith the source is Egyptian annals -- 'There dwelled, as the Annual records of Egypt makes mention, in the City of Memphis, a poor man called Perimedes'(VII, p. 11) -- and Greene further explains how it came about that the discourse of Perimedes and his wife was overheard and recorded in the annals (VII, p. 13). In Menaphon, which emphasises the device with the running title 'The reports of the Shepheards', the behaviour of Samela's child Pleusidippus is 'histor-icised' -- 'I refer it to the Annals of the

Arcadians that dilate not a little of this ingenious argument'(VI, p. 91) -- and his omissions are exused by reference to the annals: 'Much other circumstance of prattle passed between them, which the Arcadian Records do not show, nor I remember'(VI, p. 116). 'The Anatomie of Lovers Flatteries' (attached to the second part of Mamillia) is presented as a letter from Mamillia to Modesta that chanced to fall into Greene's hands (II, p. 252) -- a device borrowed from Lyly. He uses 'historical record' in Ciceronis Amor, but improves upon it, justifying an anecdote he tells of Cicero by saying that Cornelius Nepos forgets it in the telling of Tully's life (VII, p. 138). Offering a love letter that Tully writes to Terentia as coming from Lentulus he explains at length why it has not hitherto been discovered and differs in style from the better-known works of Cicero:

> where by the way gentlemen, I am to crave you to think that Terentia kept the copy secret, so that neither it can be found amongst Lentulus loose papers, nor in the familiar epistles of Cicero. If the phrase differ from his other excellent form of writing, imagine he sought to cover his style, and in his pen rather to play the blunt soldier, than the curious Orator, neither using those verborum fulmina, that Papyrius objects, nor that sweet and musical cadence of words, which he wrote to Atticus: but howsoever or whatsoever, thus it was.
> (VII, pp. 148-49)

Greene is clearly not attempting a hoax; he is only facilitating the readers' indulgence in the fiction with an artificial realism.

Greene's readers do not need much encouragement to 'suspend disbelief'; they need only to be presented with the opportunity. At the end of the last story of Perimedes there is a letter from William Bubb to his friend the author, saying that sonnets he found in Greene's study, feigned to be written by the Chaldees, should be included in the work (VII, p. 86). Although Greene is reluctant to discover his verses for the public, since he is thus conjured by his friend, he says, 'I dare not but rather hazard my credit on your courtesies than lose for so small a trifle' such a good friend (VII, p. 87), and asks the reader to pardon the poems if he does not like them. Despite the prefaced apology, and a second which follows them, Greene

pretends that the poems are Chaldean, kept by Delia
(Mrs. Perimedes) in her casket, adding that, since
the poet is not named, 'I know not whose invention
it was'(VII, p. 90). If this device was at all
successful, the readers must have delighted in the
fiction of authenticity.

Greene's realism of detail can be seen in his
development of character. Even when Lyly served as
his model, Greene made advances on Lyly's construction of character. Euphues is made to fall in love
with Lucilla at their first meeting and even though
his emotional change is stated, no process is
described -- suddenly Euphues is in love. Greene,
in contrast has Mamillia weigh the matter at length
before her affection turns solidly to Pharicles. In
Philomela, Greene constructs a figure of obsessive
and increasing jealousy, Phillippo, similar to
Valdracko of the earlier Planetomachia; but whereas
Valdracko's character is static, determined by
celestial bodies (the influence of Saturn),
Phillippo's jealously is presented in the process of
its pathological development. Even with minor
characters Greene adds detail that makes them
unusually realistic for Elizabethan fiction.
Clerophontes, in Gwydonius, for example, is given
internal complication that makes him more than a
stock father-character. Unable to manage his son,
he must bid Gwydonius leave the kingdom so that he
may be either cured of his licentiousness or killed;
yet at the same time he has great paternal affection
and retires to his chamber in order not to show his
sorrow at his son's departure (IV, p. 23).

The realism of the scene-setting in Greenes
Never too Late is important because the fiction he
presents is in itself much more realistic, a mock
history that could be true rather than an exemplary
tale:

> I will first rehearse you an English History
> acted and evented in my Country of England: but
> for that the Gentleman is yet living I will
> shadow his name, although I manifest his
> follies. (VIII, p. 33)

As in Lyly's Fidus among his bees in Euphues and his
England, the English palmer's tale and the Italian
setting are integrated in a convincing fashion: 'The
Palmer had scarce named Italy, but we were come to
my house (VIII, p. 32); and, like Munday's Zelauto,
difference of languages is recognised: 'The Palmer
that had learned a little broken Italian . . .'(part

two, Francescos Fortunes, VIII, p. 124). The detail
of the framework makes the tale credible. Greene
sometimes develops the realism of the framework for
its own sake. A Disputation betweene a Hee
Conny-catcher, and a Shee Conny-catcher, because it
is a debate, a dialogue, requires no realism of
setting; yet he cannot resist turning even a
discourse into fiction. The dialogue is interrupted
by a noise: 'who is that Lawrence comes in to hear
our talk? Oh 'tis the boy, Nan, that tells us
supper is ready'(X, pp. 234-35). Realism becomes
convention. But it is used also as a bourgeois
perspective to deflate courtly or pastoral
convention. In Menaphon both Samela and Melicertus
follow pastoral convention but recognise it as
convention. When Melicertus makes a rhetorical
speech Samela replies in kind:

> Samela made this reply, because she heard him
> so superfine, as if Ephaebus had learned him to
> refine his mother tongue, wherefore though he
> had done it of an inkhorn desire to be
> eloquent; and Melicertus thinking that Samela
> had learned with Lucilla in Athens to anatomize
> wit, and speak none but Similes, imagined she
> smoothed her talk to be thought like Sappho,
> Phaos Paramour. (VI, p. 82)

Conventions of this sort may have had a reality for
the Court, like the rules of a game played seriously, but for the bourgeoisie, as for Greene, they
were merely conventions, having no function beyond
suggesting courtliness.

Sometimes Greene achieves a realism within the
pastoral convention of shepherds who cite the
classics by making their acquaintance with the
classics second-hand. In the Mourning Garment a
shepherd encountered by the hero says, 'for we
Shepherds have heard tell, that one Darius a great
king, being dry, was glad to swink his fill of a
Shepherds bottle' (IX, p. 145). The innovation is
small but it is a successful accommodation of
pastoral convention and realism. (However, in
Pandosto and Menaphon there is some acceptance of
pastoral convention: the country-reared Fawnia talks
about the courtly ditties and the tastes of ladies
-- IV, p. 282 -- and the shepherd Menaphon makes
classical allusions without any explanation of his
knowledge -- VI, pp. 49, 51, 58.) Greene's audience
(perhaps like that of Munday, who used the same
device in Zelauto) was interested in matter as well

as style and were not so willing as the Court to accept pure literary convention.

Greene's realism of details is defective, however, just because it is a realism of details -- fragmentary. By focusing on the parts he fails to visualise the whole. Arbasto has a first-person narration, which makes the events more dramatic, but Greene gets himself into unavoidable awkwardness when Arbasto has to describe the thoughts of other people. In Never too Late Greene switches person, beginning the narration in the first person but ending in the third, and he confuses even place in A Quip -- the narrator falls asleep in a field and wakes in his bed. Occasionally such carelessness is more seriously destructive of the very effects he is trying to achieve. In The Blacke Bookes Messenger, for example, the supposedly unrepentant villain turns to a pious repentance that destroys his character in unintended comedy.

Greene's fragmentary realism, the failure to present a world in which causal relations extend consistently through all the elements, may give rise to the criticism that he relied on fortune as a substitute for character-based plot. Even though almost all of his characters may be rationally motivated, in his middle works their rationality often has little influence on the outcome of events. Thus fortune, causing the boat in which the infant Fawnia is set adrift to land in Sicily, commences the main plot in Pandosto and, blowing the ship on which Fawnia and Dorastus elope off course to Bohemia, provides for its resolution. Fortune is responsible for the balance of circumstances that bring Gwydonius to fight his father Clerophontes in Gwydonius, and the dispersal and reunion of the family of the first tale in Perimedes is entirely the result of fortune and chance. Fortune is employed as a general cause, in what Wolff regarded as a hellenistic manner (4), that allows plot difficulties to be resolved by improbabilities. Separate incidents are usually presented by Greene as character-determined but, in arranging the broad course of events, he often makes fortune work overtime.

* * *

Greene's relationship with his audience alters significantly in his later works. He still adjusts his writing to their outlook but adds a personal quality not seen in the early and middle works.

Until his late works, except for the conventional
asides and personal reflections common to the
fiction of the sixteenth century (for example, 'my
young youth Gwydonius' -- IV, p. 104; Cloth-breeches
'wisheth me humbly to bid you farewell' -- XI,
p. 212; and the introduction of a sonnet in Greene's
own person: 'but Gentlemen, since we have talked of
Love so long, you shall give me leave to show my
opinion of that foolish fancy thus' -- VI, p. 140),
Greene's personality remains hidden behind the
fiction. The sense of audience is clear, but
exactly who is exercising it is not revealed. From
1590 the relationship becomes more obvious; the
works no longer have an independent existence but
they are clearly Greene's creations. About half the
works outside the conny-catching series are titled
'Greenes' something or other (Greene had used his
name in the subtitle of Alcida in 1588, but only in
the subtitle), and although this is in part an
indication of his commercial success -- that by
making his name prominent he can expect to sell more
copies -- it also accompanies a change in
relationship.

Greene becomes to some degree the subject of
his writing. On the simplest level, his late
fiction is the illustration of his 'reform'; he
becomes the actual subject of his 'prodigal son'
works because of their autobiographical nature.
Greenes Mourning Garment, Greenes Never too Late
(including the second part, Francescos Fortunes),
and Greenes Groatsworth of witte all tell basically
the same story: the Mourning Garment is a fairly
straight retelling of the prodigal son story, Never
too Late brings the prodigality nearer home to
London, and the Groatsworth, toward the end of the
story, becomes confessed autobiography:

> Here (Gentlemen) break I off Robertos speech;
> whose life in most parts agreeing with mine,
> found one self punishment as I have done.
> Hereafter suppose me the said Roberto, and I
> will go on with that he promised: Greene will
> send you now his groatsworth of wit, that never
> showed a mitesworth in his life: and though no
> man now be by, to do me good, yet ere I die, I
> will by my repentance endeavour to do all men
> good. (XII, p. 137)

It is not really important whether or not the life
presented in the Groatsworth is the real Greene;
probably there are some experiences in it that

accord with his own life and a number of attitudes that can be accepted as genuine rather than commercial (Roberto's disinheritance because of his honest attack on usury -- XII, pp. 106-7 -- may suggest that Greene would like to attribute his own lack of financial success to intellectual honesty). Repentance, sometimes a commercial posture for Greene, may be serious in the Groatsworth; when he unmasked Roberto he might really have been too ill to hope to cash in on it.

Greene enters his work directly also in the conny-catching pamphlets where he is sometimes the subject. Instead of a fiction based on the real Greene, we are presented with a supposedly real Greene which is in fact fictional. He creates both a personality for himself and a realism in the series by stressing the personal danger he puts himself in through the exercise of his public duty ('nascimur pro patria' is now his motto). In A Notable Discovery he says he would reveal names even though he might have his hand cut off for it, but he hopes for the amendment of the characters (X, p. 12). In the Second Part he mentions that the conny-catchers have threatened him but, 'I live still, and I live to display their villainies, which, gentlemen you shall see set down in most ample manner in this small treatise' (X, pp. 70-71). In A Disputation he says that a bunch of whores tried to kill him because of the book, but he will continue to do his country good -- so look for The blacke Booke soon, which will name names (X, pp. 236-37). When Greene stresses the danger to himself he is not only building up an image; he is creating a realism that makes for good fiction. After the second or third pamphlet it is impossible that anyone inside the London literary scene would have taken the work seriously; but they could enjoy the wit of his posture.

Part of the wit is the image of himself he creates through his characters -- e.g. in A Disputation he figures prominently in the discussion of Nan and Lawrence. In The Defence he expands his use of self-image with a delightful irony. Cuthbert Conny-catcher addresses most of his remarks to Greene:

> I cannot but wonder master R. G. what Poetical fury made you so fantastic, to write against Conny-catchers? Was your brain so barren that you had no other subject? or your wits so dried with dreaming of love Pamphlets,

that you had no other humour left, but
satirically with Diogenes, to snarl at all mens
manners: You never found in Tully nor
Aristotle, what a setter or a verser was.
   It had been the part of a scholar, to have
written seriously of some grave subject, either
Philosophically to have shown how you were
proficient in Cambridge, or divinely to have
manifested your religion to the world.   Such
trivial trinkets and threadbare trash, had
better seemed T. D. [Thomas Deloney] whose
brains beaten to the yarking up of Ballads,
might more lawfully have glanced at the quaint
conceits of conny-catching and cross-biting.
(XI, pp. 49-50)

'Cuthbert's' criticism has a certain force: Greene
is at times writing beneath himself in the conny-
catching series.   He pretends seriousness for an
audience, part of which may not be very sophisticated, which is of a different composition from the
gentlemen of the early works -- 'Young Gentlemen,
merchants, citizens, apprentices, yeomen, and plain
country farmers'(X, p. 69).   His tone is unques-
tionably warm --'kind friends' and 'loving Countrymen'(X, p. 197) -- and the reader is given the
courtesy of 'gentle' reader, but despite this Greene
is condescending.   He is a man of experience
talking to the wide-eyed country cousin:

   I can decipher their qualities, though I
   utterly mislike of their practices.   To be
   brief Gentlemen, I have seen the world and
   rounded it, though not with travel, yet with
   experience. (X, p. 6)

Fortunately, everyone (almost) could enjoy Greene's
conny-catching series: the literary gentlemen,
although not directly addressed, could relish
the posturing and wit and the country cousin could
enjoy the 'danger' and the tales.   Greene's posture
of service to his country enables the moralistic
contemner of poesy to read the tales without guilt,
for whereas a jest book was mere entertainment, the
jest material and style of the conny-catching
pamphlets is justified (as in the early 'moral'
works), by the sheepskin of 'utile' (or 'pro
patria') which covers the wolf of 'dulce'.
   In the conny-catching pamphlets Greene is warm
and personal, yet lacking that sense of equality
which marks the earlier works; there is no longer

the feeling he might be part of the group he addresses. He is presenting himself as the show -- Greene as the creation of his own wit -- and his audience becomes abstract. As with Nashe, the performance that bound him to the audience at the same time separated him from them. Greene moved from an elegant literature for gentlemen to a petty-bourgeois, even artisan, literature as the commercial possibilities became more apparent. Even so, he did not offer them a mindless simplification of reality as did Richard Johnson; commercial as he was, he fulfilled a genuine artistic need for the petty bourgeoisie without pandering to a debased idea of dignity, offering works that could support their individuality and strengthen their consciousness. Almost all of Greene's work is entertainment, but his enduring contribution was to provide an embodiment in the novel of a new world view, a coherent alternative model by which readers could interpret the world.

NOTES

1. John F. Danby, Elizabethan and Jacobean Poets (London, 1964), p. 16.

2. Louis B. Wright, Middle-class Culture in Elizabethan England (Chapel Hill, 1935), pp. 384-85.

3. George a Greene, the Pinner of Wakefield in Plays and Poems of Robert Greene, ed., J. Churton Collins (Oxford, 1905), vol. II, p. 196, Act II, sc. iii, 450, 473-74.

4. Samuel Lee Wolff, The Greek Romances in Elizabethan Prose Fiction (New York, 1961). See the chapter on Greene.

8 THOMAS DELONEY

Writing for a readership that never was or could have been a present audience, Thomas Deloney, sometime ballad maker, transposed his oral-traditional skills to print. His novels are impersonal, but their perspective is obvious. Formerly a silk weaver, he portrays artisan attitudes sympathetically and in detail, and advances the consciously-held values of the class of which the readers form a part without having to argue them. Directing Jack of Newbury not to gentlemen but to English clothiers, 'for whose sake I take pains to compile it' (Lawlis ed., p. 3), Deloney 'sought his inspiration as well as well as his patronage in the ranks of a newly rising, newly proud and even boisterously vocal economic class' (1). He is a bourgeois propagandist.

It is easy to overlook Deloney's role as a propagandist because he presents his values as valid, not for one class alone, but for society as a whole. Moreover, today, when the attitudes he celebrates have largely been incorporated in the accepted outlook of Western industrial society, and when most narrative is impersonal in character, his writing may appear simply 'natural' (as a number of critics have found it). He displays none of the artifice of Lyly or Sidney or Nashe, and avoids even Greene's literary quality. But his attitudes are no more natural than Sir Philip Sidney's and his excursions into history, no less than Sidney's chivalry, are value-laden. In such figures as John Winchcomb Deloney 'discovers' bourgeois values in the past. Although he appears to voice the feelings and aspirations of the entire middle class, he speaks especially for the industrial bourgeoisie, such as cloth manufacturers.

Although it is sometimes convenient to use the term 'middle class' to refer to the population between the gentry and the labouring poor, there was no single stratum such as the term would imply. Sidney and Lyly obviously are concerned with an entirely different section of the population as is, to a lesser extent, Nashe. Greene although concerned with the middle social strata, is not so focused in his attention as Deloney, and it is only with Deloney that the term 'middle class', so heavily employed in discussion of the period, becomes over-burdened. Deloney's work presents as a unity sections of the population between which there was much class conflict; and Deloney may feel he speaks for the whole middle class, for it is likely that the industrial bourgeoisie believed the special conditions of their own advancement to be those for the whole society. Merchants, an organised body of traders outside craft organisation (and therefore distinguished from capitalist employers who originated inside the craft guild itself), differentiated themselves from craftsmen as a separate class. Harrison, in his four 'sorts' of the population, distinguished clearly between citizens or burgesses and artificers or labourers (with whom he included landless retailers). Merchants took pride in the fact that those who engaged in commerce (not petty trading) performed no manual labour and their social prestige can be seen in the recruitment of younger sons of the gentry to the class. The lawyer in Thomas Wilson's A Discourse Upon Usury went so far as to say that the merchant was the fellow of a lord in dignity.

The division between the craft-master and his employees is less immediately obvious but of comparable importance. L. B. Wright (who exemplifies the popular prejudice among critics of an Elizabethan social harmony) said that, with the exception of a few areas such as cloth manufacture, 'throughout the period the skilled craftsman could expect, provided he was industrious and thrifty, to become a manufacturer employing assistants to increase his output, and marketing directly his own handiwork' (Middle-class Culture in Elizabethan England, p. 8). That was not, in fact, the case. Even though there may have been little difference between master and workman in terms of dignity or social outlook, their class positions were different. By the end of the century journeyman had changed from a transitional status (between apprentice and mastership) to a permanent one from

which most individuals had little hope of ever
rising. The increasing time and money required for
the production of the masterpiece prevented many
journeymen from becoming masters themselves while
enabling their masters to keep them as wage-earners
(2).

Even though the industrial bourgeoisie may not
have been highly developed as a class (and hence
less obviously marked off from their workers), there
was a clear distinction between master and man,
which Deloney himself indicates. Although he
presents the master-worker relationship as symbiotic
and cordial (he suggests serious conflict only in
Thomas of Reading, pp. 337-38), he writes from the
point of view of the master-employer.

The upper reaches of the audience Deloney
addresses, and whose ideology he expounds, were
already confirmed in their principles by material
success and did not need to have them proved. Their
self-assurance, reflected in Deloney's confident
presentation of bourgeois attitudes, is more
apparent when compared with Robert Greene's cautious
assertion of middle-class values. Pandosto,
Ciceronis Amor, and Menaphon suggest an audience
who, caught between opposed ideologies, still need
their values justified. Since Deloney does not feel
it necessary either to demonstrate the possibility
of holding a bourgeois view or to make it acceptable, we can assume that his readers are secure in
their way of life and certain of their own worth.
What Deloney provides is a flattering mirror; he
offers the bourgeoisie the satisfaction of con-
templating their image and seeing their values
rehearsed in fiction.

Deloney is outside the range of polite writers
and has no pretension to conventional patronage.
Abel Chevalley comments that, like nine-tenths of
writers at any period, Deloney wrote to earn a
living; 'Everybody cannot write for his sister, like
Sir Philip Sidney', he adds (3). His audience,
although some of them may be materially successful,
lack refinement and he writes on their level. Jack
of Newbury is written 'in a plain and humble manner,
that it may be the better understood' by the
clothiers for whom he writes (p. 3). The Gentle
Craft, Part I, is addressed to shoemakers. In Part
II he again defends his homely style:

> Gentle Reader, you that vouchsafe to cast
> courteous looks into this rude Pamphlet: expect
> not herein to find any matter of light value,

> curiously penned with picked words, or choice
> phrases, but a quaint and plain discourse, best
> fitting matters of merriment, seeing we have
> herein no cause to talk of Courtiers or
> Scholars. (p. 174)

Although decorum is the principle here -- the
unrefined style is appropriate to the subject -- his
defence also asserts the worthiness of the humble
style, a solid simplicity in contrast to the empty
affectation of the Court. Deloney shows a complex
awareness of what his audience wants -- in the
jest-book material he presents, anecdotes rather
than fully developed fictions, and the absence of
polite literary conventions -- but also in the
ironic tone that undermines the traditional view of
the superiority of courtiers.

The social level to which Deloney addressed his
novels rose. Jack of Newbury (probably 1597) and
The Gentle Craft, Part I (probably 1597) are
dedicated to clothiers and shoemakers respectively,
but The Gentle Craft, Part II (probably 1598) found
a higher social mark in its dedication to the Master
and Wardens of the Cordwainers' Company (even though
no particular officers are named, cordwainers -- and
the company of cordwainers -- are a considerable
step above cobblers). By The Gentle Craft (II) and
Thomas of Reading (probably 1600) the reader he
addresses has become a gentleman. As his social
pretension grew, so did his literary pretension.
Thomas of Reading is not another story of commercial
success, with characters who are embodiments of
moral qualities, but shows an interest in the fates
of the characters as human beings; and, in the
discovery of Cole's murder, for example, Deloney
reveals considerable literary skill by showing a
single event from several perspectives (4). Yet,
with a conception of art inevitably shaped by polite
literature, Deloney sometimes attempts high style
and gets out of his depth. In Jack of Newbury, for
example, he makes a classical allusion which shows
no understanding either of the incident itself or of
the complexity of the relations it could suggest:
'As Mars and Venus danced naked together in a net,
so I doubt, you and some knave have played naked
together in a bed' (p. 65). Besides the learned
associations, Deloney gets no more from the allusion
than a reference to sex. Greene, even in a popular
context, Porrus the shepherd's comments on class
justice, found the net a much richer image (see
above, p. 129).

Deloney wished to entertain his audience, as his title pages indicate in standard fashion, and they are unlikely to have been discouraged by failed essays at high style so long as the anecdotes remained good. Nevertheless pure entertainment cannot alone account for Deloney's popularity (Lawlis says his works were so popular that the early editions 'were read completely out of existence' -- p. xi -- and Sterg O'Dell lists fourteen editions between 1597 and 1640 in A Chronological List of Prose Fiction, which is fewer than for Greene but enough to suggest very considerable popularity). It is probably the outlook that organises and informs his anecdotes as much as the tales themselves that entertain the readers.

Deloney's heroes are images of virtue, but virtue of a new kind. The eponymous hero of Jack of Newbury is not merely an individual of excellent qualities; he is a bourgeois hero. Richard Johnson's Nine Worthies presented citizen heroes, but their heroic qualities were not particularly bourgeois; Jack of Newbury is the embodiment of bourgeois virtue, at once an individual and the representative of a class.

Deloney details Jack's virtues at the beginning of the work. He is hard-working yet sociable, open-handed yet thrifty. He cannot be enticed away from overseeing his mistress's looms during the week, but on Sunday afternoons and holidays he drinks with his mates (p. 6). He is well beloved of both rich and poor 'especially because in every place where he came he would spend his money with the best, and was not at any time found a churl of his purse' (p. 5). Nevertheless he is careful about money: Jack allows twelve pence for his weekly drinking, calculating that twelve pence a Sunday comes to fifty-two shillings a year, which is enough for a craftsman to spend (p. 6). Thus, Deloney depicts Jack as a moral type as well as individual.

The creation of characters with a moral value is seen clearly in his drawing of minor characters, his walk-on parts. Without depicting a complete individual, in a few strokes he indicates to the reader the important moral qualities. The qualities of the tailor-suitor of the widow Jack eventually marries are briefly indicated in his reaction to her rejection of his suit: when he hears her sour words, 'shaking up himself in his new russet Jerkin, and setting his hat on one side, he began to speak thus' (p. 18). The russet is plain and suggests a yeoman quality, while the newness of the jerkin conveys the idea that he is hard-working and thrifty. Deloney uses items not in themselves moral to create a moral value for the character.

Jack gains the reader's attention, Walter Davis points out, not through wit 'but by his harmonious relation with his society (Idea and Act, p. 239). The virtues Deloney depicts are more than those of an individual; like social harmony, they are the virtues of a community or a way of life. Community is stressed in his dedication to shoemakers in The Gentle Craft (I): many shoemakers have been famous in feats of valour, he says, but adds that they are a peaceable lot who live in harmony with their neighbours (p. 91). Throughout his work the sense of community of shoemakers and of clothiers, as much as the virtues of individual practitioners, is emphasised. Even in Thomas of Reading, where he is concerned with individual psychology, the quality of a group is evident.

The importance Deloney places on sense of community and peaceable, harmonious living is clearer when it is recognised that these virtues are not yet the fashionable ones of the society. It was such an outlook that Nashe attacked when describing a tradesman's purchased coat of arms -- a lion without teeth or claws because the tradesman is a man of peace who must not keep quarrelsome beasts to annoy his neighbours. Deloney's clothier heroes have too much sense of their own worth to purchase arms, and they perceive as a virtue that which Nashe can only scorn.

The worthiness of the hero depends largely on his role in society rather than on purely personal qualities such as courage. The clothiers, as a group, have a heroic role because of their great benefit to the kingdom, which Deloney makes clear at the beginning of Thomas of Reading, explaining at length that they keep half the population in employment:

> And it was verily thought, that the one half of the people in the land lived in those days thereby, and in such good sort, that in the Commonwealth there was few or no beggars at all: poor people, whom God lightly blesseth with most children, did by means of this occupation so order them, that by the time that they were come to be six or seven years of age, they were able to get their own bread: Idleness

was then banished our coast, so that it was a
rare thing to hear of a thief in those days.
(p. 267).

Though modern readers might find ironic the
attribution of great social benefit to an industry
that keeps children of six and seven in full-time
employment (and for 'bread' instead of the earlier
general term 'meat'), Deloney's praise is sincere.
More important than its specific content is that he
is altering the standards of social value. Even to
raise the question of social value is in many ways
contrary to the traditionally accepted criterion for
social evaluation. The traditional view holds that
all degrees are important and one has social value
simply by fulfilling the demands of the appropriate
degree. Deloney's explicit concern for social value
implies that traditional degree is irrelevant and
that the worth of each individual or occupation is
related to its benefit to the country. It is not
station, but active contribution to social good,
that is Deloney's measure of worth. Obviously the
most visible contribution to the country's welfare
is that made by work (as Deloney has Henry I
recognise when he sees the endless trains of
cloth-laden wagons coming from the West -- pp.
270-71). He does not attempt to prove the
fundamental value of work -- he assumes it -- and
the lengthy presentation of clothiers' benefit to
the realm is designed to show the value, not of work
in general, but of the specific work of the
clothiers.
    The enemy of work (and also of the realm
therefore) is idleness. This is demonstrated in
Jack's morality of the ants and butterflies played
before the king. Jack, as Prince of the ants, is
protecting his hard-working subjects from the
parasites that prey on them. The grasshopper and
the caterpillar have already been banished from the
kingdom because they live idly on the labours of
other men. The present problem is the butterfly:
'the Butterfly was very much misliked, but few durst
say anything to him because of his golden apparel'
(p. 37). The moral is completely clear: parasitic
courtiers and idle gentlemen are a menace to a
kingdom whose welfare is based on work. Altering
the traditional standards, Deloney says that
learning a trade is good while genteel idleness is
bad (5). The same attitude is taken in The Gentle
Craft (II), in a slightly different form, where
lusty Peachey, the shoemaker of Fleet Street, has to

defend himself against Stuteley and Strangwidge --
notorious swaggerers but captains and therefore
gentlemen -- who object to his show of bravery in
appearing in London with forty liveried men.
Deloney is not at all ambiguous: Peachey is a pillar
of the commonwealth; Stutely and Strangwidge,
parasites and disrupters of honest labour.   When
they behave in an insulting manner in his shop, the
swaggerers are told by Peachey that they have
forgotten their manners, and he adds, 'I would you
well knew I keep forty good fellows in my house,
that in respect of their manhood may seem to be your
equals' (p. 216).   Stuteley and Strangwidge, unable
to stand the comparison, offer a challenge and are
defeated in equal combat.   The ants prove better men
than the butterflies.

Since work is what is of value for Deloney,
gentility defined as mere degree is meaningless for
him.   Jack is of sufficient substance to be a
gentleman (he dresses his men in costly livery to
fight against the Scots) but disclaims the
conventional attributes of gentility:

> Most gracious Queen quoth he, Gentleman I am
> none, nor the son of a Gentleman, but a poor
> Clothier, whose lands are his Looms, having no
> other Rents but what I get from the backs of
> little sheep, nor can I claim any cognisance
> but a wooden shuttle. (p. 31)

Although he 'will bear the port, charge and
countenance of a gentleman', he will not 'live
idly and without manual labour' -- and therefore he
is no gentleman.   Nevertheless the Queen replies to
his disclaimer, saying 'though a Clothier by trade,
yet a Gentleman by condition . . . and would to God
the King had many such Clothiers'(p. 32).   Aside
from the ideological importance of thus disposing of
the conventional idea of gentility, Deloney produces
a most charming picture of the bourgeois's ironic
self-effacement; Jack's 'a poor Clothier' and
'little sheep' suggest a humble position at odds
with that presented shortly before of a master of
more than a thousand workers.   In denying gentility
Jack expresses a tremendous sense of his own worth.
He is similar to Shaw's Undershaft, belittling
himself according to polite standards while at the
same time exhibiting total confidence in the
correctness (if not righteousness) of his own
position, and thereby denying the importance and
appropriateness of polite standards.

Jack's refusal of a knighthood shows again that he values solid productive activity above mere title:

> I beseech your Grace let me live a poor Clothier among my people, in whose maintenance I take more felicity, than in all the vain titles of Gentility: for these are the labouring Ants whom I seek to defend, and these be the Bees which I keep: who labour in this life, not for ourselves, but for the glory of God, and to do service to our dread Sovereign. (p. 49)

The honest clothier prefers substantial bourgeois achievement to empty gentility. Jack's refusal appears more significant in comparison with the refusal of Greene's George a Green (described above -- see p. 131), who rejects knighthood on the frivolous ground that there is more credit for men of base degree in performing high deeds than for men of exalted position. George declines the one honour in order to increase his honour in another way; Jack's refusal places industrial success above vain title.

Deloney's gentility of production, unlike that of mere degree, involves responsibility. In his rejection of knighthood Jack indicated his responsibility for the maintenance of workers and Deloney expresses the same idea clearly elsewhere. Mistress Frank, the bad gossip, is shown to be vicious in persuading Mistress Winchcomb to reduce the quality of the servants' food; Jack, however, demands that his workpeople be fed properly, as befits a good master (pp. 72-73). A full statement of the responsibility of the master towards his servants is offered in Thomas of Reading when Tom Dove, one of the six worthy yeomen of the West, falls into bankruptcy:

> Now when his wicked servants saw him in this disgrace with the world, they on the other side began to disdain him. Notwithstanding that he (to his great cost) had long time brought them up, yet did they nothing regard it. (p. 337)

Tom Dove presents himself as the bourgeois benefactor to his servants:

> where from paltry boys, I brought you up to mans estate, and have, to my great cost, taught

> you a trade, whereby you may live like men.
> And in requital of all my courtesy, cost and
> good will, will you now on a sudden forsake me?
> (p. 338)

Like Jack, the clothier Tom Dove would seem to
employ workmen out of altruism, without regard for
his own profit. The clothier's labours, as Deloney
usually presents them, are a public service done by
a man who puts the welfare of the country above
other considerations: to be a clothier is to
exercise a charity. Yet, to his credit, Deloney
allows the departing servants to present their own
position: 'If you taught us our trade, and brought
us up from boys to men, you had our service for it,
whereby you made no small benefit, if you had as
well used it, as we got it' (p. 338).

Drone-like gentility, as well as being
subjected to serious attack (as in Jack and the
butterflies), is reduced with mockery. In The
Gentle Craft (II) Tom Drum, a shoemaker, travels
with Harry Nevelle, a gentleman fleeing his family's
displeasure. Promising to anoint Tom a gentleman if
Tom makes him into a shoemaker, Harry Nevelle cuts
his finger and smears Tom's face with blood. Tom's
response is 'he might by that means as well anoint
him a Joiner, as a Gentleman'(p. 223). The incident
shows again the meaningless character of gentility
of degree -- a gentleman, unless, like Jack, he be
gentleman by condition, is nothing.

Despite his dislike of the aristocracy, Deloney
has a genuine reverence for the King in his role as
protector. The mere presence of the King, said
Jack, put to flight the butterflies he fought in his
role of the Prince of the ants. Throughout his
works Deloney presents royalty as the fountainhead
of justice and magnanimity, and royalty also
receives great respect from the honest bourgeoisie
on every occasion. (Richard Casteller, for example,
takes elaborate pains to outfit his man, Round
Robin, and his fellows to sing before the King.) It
is for his attachment to the King that Jack is
disliked, he indicates in another venture into
allegory: the monster envy attacked him, not because
he first attacked the monster, but because he was so
eager to serve his prince and country (p. 32).

Work is more than a moral foundation in
Deloney's writing. Its importance from him is such
that it serves as an artistic organising principle.
In Jack of Newbury, for example, Jack's factory is
described at length (pp. 26-28), while the banquet

he provides for the King and Queen is disposed of in
a few words: 'the description whereof were too long
for me to write, and you to read' (p. 39). Lyly
uses a similar formulation (e.g. he will not repeat
material the reader already knows, 'which will both
offend your ears which I seek to delight and trouble
my hand which I covet to ease' -- II, p. 159), but
whereas Lyly is calling attention to himself,
Deloney here is in effect making a value judgement.
The ceremony and display, which often attract the
attention of other authors, are of little concern to
Deloney; he devotes his literary energy to matters
of more practical interest.

For all his bourgeois spirit, Deloney still
retains a prejudice toward gentility (which was
probably inescapable in the sixteenth century). In
The Gentle Craft (I) he spends much time seeking
gentle associations for shoemaking and the title
itself, the gentle craft, looks approvingly toward
superior degree. The tales of St. Hugh and Crispine
and Crispianus give shoemaking no value other than
as a retreat for nobles (see Davis, Idea and Act,
p. 256) and the whole orientation of the work seems
to be the justification of shoemkaing through its
noble connections. Even in the second part of The
Gentle Craft, so much more democratic in character,
the gentle associations are subtly carried on by Tom
Drum when he explains his trade: 'I am a Goldsmith
that makes rings for womens heels . . . I am (quoth
Tom) of the Gentle Craft, vulgarly called a
Shoemaker' (p. 221). There is an ironic wit here,
but Deloney still feels it necessary to elevate
Tom's trade by association with one of greater
status.

Similarly, The Gentle Craft (I) shows that
Deloney has not eradicated his belief in the
inherent virtue of the aristocracy -- a prejudice
more appropriate to Greene's work. Crispine,
employed as a shoemaker, reveals his royal origins
to the Princess Ursula with whom he is in love:

> The which when fair Ursula with great wonder
> heard, giving him an earnest of her love, with
> a sweet kiss; she said, My dear Love, and most
> gentle Prince, ever did I think, that more than
> a common man was shrowded in these poor
> habiliments, which made me the bolder to impart
> my mind unto thee. (pp. 123-24)

It seems that even for Deloney, the superior man
must be a prince in disguise. Workmen, and Deloney,

have not yet become accustomed to assuming superiority in their own persons. In Thomas of Reading the mistress laments the departure of her servant Margaret (the daughter of the Earl of Shrewsbury, unknown to the mistress): 'O Meg, wert thou here again, I would never chide thee more: but I was an unworthy dame for such a servant' (p. 333). It is natural that she lament the departure of a good and trusted servant, but the sentiment that the mistress is unworthy of the servant is something imported into the work by Deloney's unconscious prejudice.

Whatever residual aristocratic views may lurk in Deloney's unconscious, his moral is very clearly that of the triumphant bourgeoisie. Jack exhorts his servants to hard and honest work with the portraits of fifteen men who have risen from baseness to great honour:

> there is none of you so poorly born, but that men of baser birth have come to great honours: the idle hand shall ever go in a ragged garment, and the slothful live in reproach: but such as do lead a virtuous life, and govern themselves discreetly, shall of the best be esteemed, and spend their days in credit. (p. 55)

Credit and estimation are the least rewards promised for a life of virtuous labour, although the portraits and Jack's speech together suggest a much richer fulfilment.

Hard work and material success are not temporal objectives set apart from spiritual concerns; in the spirt of a protestant ethic the two become confused. Work and spiritual virtue, if the rewards of labour are well used (and all Deloney's successful men lead charitable lives), are in practice the same, and God watches over the fortunes of the bourgeoisie. Thus it is God's will that Simon Eyre, through a dubious transaction, should change from shoemaker to substantial merchant. His wife, the instigator of the deal, says that if Simon becomes Lord Mayor he will have her to thank; he says he will have God to thank (p. 149). The sentiment is not the casual 'thank God' of today, but the Calvinist idea of virtue shown through reward on earth. Jack, advanced from foreman to master, expressed a similar attitude in addressing his former equals:

> My masters muse not at all: for although by
> Gods providence and your Dames favour, I am
> preferred from being your fellow to be your
> Master, I am not thereby so much puffed up in
> pride, that any way I will forget my former
> estate: Notwithstanding, seeing I am now to
> hold the place of a Master, it shall be wisdom
> in you to forget what I was, and to take me as
> I am; and in doing your diligence, you shall
> have no cause to repent that God made me your
> master. (p. 21)

The mistress's favour enables his advancement, but
the cause is stated to be God's will. Deloney
comforts the bourgeoisie by showing their earthly
endeavours blessed by the Almighty.

* * *

Deloney serves a real function for his audience
in providing a reassurance that material success
itself cannot offer: he reaffirms their belief that
material success is good, and assures them that it
deserves pride and honour. The merchant offered the
dignity and collective lordship of the London livery
companies enjoyed a prestige yet denied the industrial bourgeoisie. He took pride in performing no
manual labour, often moved (and sometimes married)
in the circle of the gentry, and might be able to
retire as a gentleman to lands in the country. Thus
Deloney offered less to the London merchant than to
the hopeful artisan or the provincial industrialist.
The middle class's liking for pseudo-historical
novels, Margaret Schlauch observes, 'reflects the
desire of a newly risen social group to establish
bases and precedents for its recently achieved
status and prestige' (p. 235). Although the
industrialist had less status and prestige than the
great merchant, he too could be comforted by the
sense of historical roots offered in Deloney's
works. The works are all set in the past, although
not a very distant past, and the clothier or shoemaker reading them could feel secure that his own
ambitions had a sound traditional basis. Furthermore, at a time when fewer and fewer journeymen had
the hope of ever becoming masters, Deloney provided
reassurance for apprentices, conveying the feeling
that any able apprentice, if he works hard and
honestly, may hope some day himself to reap the
benefits of material success. It is perhaps ironic

that both Jack of Newbury (in marrying a wealthy widow) and Simon Eyre (in exceeding honest business practice) have 'providence' rather than diligent labour to thank for their success.

Chevalley concludes his study of Deloney by saying he was a good worker at the novel and a good novelist of work:

Un bon travailleur du roman.
Un bon romancier du travail. (pp. 249-50)

He was English literature's first propagandist for a modern bourgeoisie.

NOTES

1. Margaret Schlauch, Antecedents of the English Novel 1400-1600 (from Chaucer to Deloney) (Warsaw and London, 1963), p. 247.

2. Ephraim Lipson, The Economic History of England, vol. I, 12th ed. (London, 1959), pp. 434, 408-10. William Harrison, An Historicall Description of the Islande of Britayne, with a briefe rehearsall of the nature and qualities of the people of England, and of all such commodities as are to be founde in the same (London, 1577), sigs. N6, Olv. George Unwin, Industrial Organization in the Sixteenth and Seventeenth Centuries (Oxford, 1904), p. 79, and The Gilds and Companies of London (London, 1908), pp. 265-66. W. G. Hoskins, 'The Elizabethan Merchants of Exeter' in Elizabethan Government and Society: Essays Presented to Sir John Neale, ed. S. T. Bindoff et al. (London, 1961), p. 168. Thomas Wilson, A Discourse upon Usury, ed. R. H. Tawney (London, 1962); first ed., 1925), p. 203.

3. Abel Chevalley, Thomas Deloney: Le roman des metiers au temps de Shakespeare (Paris, 1926), p. 238.

4. Walter R. Davis, Idea and Act in Elizabethan Fiction (Princeton, 1969), pp. 273, 279-80.

5. Schlauch, op. cit., p. 239.

9 CONCLUSION

The disintegration of the orderly feudal universe
was reflected in the literature of the late
sixteenth century. The increasing importance of the
nouveaux riches and merchants and artisans in
Elizabethan social life, and the consequent strain
on a hierarchical view of the world, can be seen in
the evolution of fiction toward the novel. Fiction,
in its content, presents more of the experiences of
ordinary individuals and the concerns of everyday
life and, in its organisation, more frequently takes
a middle-class view of the world. The use of print
as the medium for fiction also meant expansion and
change of audience to a dispersed readership which,
however sociable its reading habits, lacked the
collective character of the Court or Great House.
This change is reflected in the objectification of
literary works. What initially had been the
reflection of direct social relations in literature,
little more than their transfer from life to
literature, ossified to become literary conventions,
and even those finally dropped from fiction; the
fiction became impersonal.

Lyly did not have to form an audience out of
an anonymous public, nor did Sidney; the Court
and the Great House were audiences already in
existence to which the author from that circle had
only to address himself. Lyly, even though he had
printed Euphues, clearly addressed his writing to
the Court and Sidney initially wrote to amuse his
sister's coterie. They both display in their
fiction a relationship with the reader that
maintains, even in work designed for print, the
character of a direct relationship. Lyly, using
writing to exhibit his worth to a group within which
he aspired to improve his position, kept his
personality in evidence, for his ends would be

little served unless his audience were constantly aware that their enjoyment of his witty constructions was owed to Lyly's wit. In the Old <u>Arcadia</u> Sidney addressed his sister's friends as if he were present, and the fiction depends on a narrator who is often in evidence. In the New <u>Arcadia</u>, entertaining a more general audience, he removed the obviously personal qualities, and part of the seriousness of the revision is that it no longer appears a projection of the author's outlook but explores 'objectively' the values of his aristocratic audience. Despite the objectification of the fiction, it is so controlled, so obviously controlled, that it appears artificial and retains a personal quality.

Nashe, switching his attention between Great House and printing house, speaks often to an audience which he invents, the 'studio' audience within the work, and readers witness his personality without it being directed to them. Like Mrs. Gradgrind, they know that there is a relationship somewhere but cannot say they are a part of it. Nashe uses the formal elements employed by Lyly and Sidney (of the Old <u>Arcadia</u>) without having their situation or content of relationship.

Greene and Deloney create a relationship with their audience entirely through print, and the author's personality has little or no role in the fiction -- social outlook provides the bond with readers. Greene in his fiction reorganised reality in a petty-bourgeois perspective without having to make explicit comment. Deloney, providing encouragement for a growing industrial class, like Lyly offers his readers a flattering mirror, but his flattery is based on an inversion of the values which Lyly presents. Greene, using a more conventional material than Deloney's (until his last works), evaluated the fundamental conflicts between the established order and individuality faced by the middle classes. Countering a traditional view of society while using traditional forms, he could not rely on an established outlook but had to create attitudes from a new construction of reality; it was necessary for him to create a fiction that embodied, and proved, the attitudes he wished to convey. Deloney's task was an easier one because he could simply dispense praise and blame on the basis of what, for a section of the population, had become an established outlook. He deals with the certainties which Greene, dealing also with his readers' fears and doubts, had laboured successfully to establish.

159

In social terms, the increased objectivity of fiction meant the possibility of presenting a different perspective in literature. Freed from the confining tact of patronage, the commercial author could exercise an independence of choice in the audience he addressed (unlike Lyly who was tied to the Court), the material he used and the point of view he took. He could be not only the celebrator of a patron's virtue and social outlook but he could offer an imaginative challenge to the status quo. Peter Burke says 'Another important shift in popular attitudes between 1500 and 1800 may be described as the "politicisation" of popular culture, or the spread of political consciousness'(1). The dissemination of literature through print and the objectification of fiction allowed the novel a real political role.

It is not hyperbolic to speak of a political role for fiction (as distinct from mere political comment), for Deloney's bourgeois heroes or Greene's resolutions of value conflicts provided models of behaviour, significant because they organised coherently and memorably important elements of the lives of the readers. And the readers are not the single readers in isolation that we assume as usual today but ones who read aloud in groups, who became thereby an audience. But even for private readers, authors speak to them as a collective, organise matter for them as if they are a group. Thus the diffusion of attitudes through print could be seen as a class experience: individual experience could be generalised through print to become class experience. Battles of ideas are not fought on the field of formal logic, but in the minds of people. Print gave the Elizabethan novel a class value and a hegemonic force.

Certainly Elizabethan fiction was not even predominantly oppositional (although genteel doubts about the associations of print probably made fiction more oppositional than other literature). Much popular novelistic work elaborated adventure broadly within received ideology, either explicity, as in the Arcadia, or in simplistic and often contradictory assumptions about social order, as in The Seven Champions of Christendom. Nevertheless, there was a substantial body of novels that produced a detailed representation of reality evaluated according to a different scheme of values. In the work of Greene and Deloney, in particular, the fictional world is made increasingly close to a recognisable social reality and increasingly coherent within a clear perspective.

Whatever importance it had in its own day, Elizabethan fiction is largely disregarded in literary study today. If attended to, it is often distorted by being forced into the mould of works regarded as more central to Eng. Lit. For example, Deloney is blunted when read through The Shoemakers' Holiday, and Dekker's idea of a general social harmony of all classes -- merchants, artisans, nobles and royalty -- obscures Deloney's pointed differentiation of values and attitudes. Greene is misunderstood and unappreciated when read through The Winter's Tale; the centrality of conflicting social values and even the class wit of Pandosto are missed if the work enters discussion as a source for Shakespeare, and it is found lacking in Shakespeare's 'universal' concerns, such as spiritual/natural harmony, forgiveness and redemption. The 'aesthetic' qualities that constitute mainstream literature (e.g., development of individual character and psychology, polished description, the mot just, 'universal' reflections, consistency and complication of plot that can be mastered only through studious examination) are not maximized in Elizabethan fiction. It was constructed for a different context. Its public character and residue of oral tradition (such as linear construction and attention to immediate effect rather than textual richness) conflict with current notions of excellence. Fiction for the Elizabethans was not the mode of enduring literary art. Poetry is the vehicle for permanence, as Nashe makes clear: 'in some elaborate polished Poem, which I will leave to the world when I am dead, to be a living Image to all ages . . .'(I, p. 195).

But that is not to say that the Elizabethan novel or alternative fiction are to be valued only for historical study or as sociology. They are imaginative constructions that gain whatever force they have, not from a simple mirroring of the world around them, but from an aesthetic transformation of it; as image and metaphor that have an inherent judgement without explicitly confronting the immediate material world. As Robert Weimann says, in the Elizabethan period 'the language of metaphor fulfilled many of the functions that were soon to be taken over by conceptual modes of expression'(2). Arguments about material reality conducted in metaphor were no less effective for being imagistic rather than logical, and no less artistic for being tendentious.

The tendency in literary education to separate the aesthetic from other areas of living, and (despite notions of personal moral improvement to be gained through literature), to regard social statement and exercise of taste as opposed activities, make it difficult to understand literature in terms of the life of a community. The Elizabethan novel in its own time was subject to no such view, and representations of the world were recognised as having no less moral (or political) value for being poesy. Fiction was recognised as one means of inculcating social values, and almost all Elizabethan authors, even the most purely formal such as Lyly, propose to their readers priorities of being. Readers of The Adventures of Lady Egeria or the Arcadia or Pandosto or A Quip for an Upstart Courtier or The Gentle Craft probably sought entertainment rather than instruction; but unavoidably the pastime presented a way of comprehending the world they lived in. Thus there was no contradiction between life and art; the art of Elizabeth fiction was about life.

Recent controversy around the idea of the canon of English literature and the increased interest in popular culture and alternative literature of different periods (especially of working-class writing of the last hundred years) have probably destroyed in theory the notion of the 'universality' of received 'great works' (the blast has been blown even if Jericho is not yet crumbling) and shown them to be bound to specific historical conditions; and the canon has been seen to represent the ideas of the dominant class rather than simply abstract excellence. It is to be hoped that it will now become possible to read Elizabethan fiction so as to appreciate both its relation to the historical conditions of the Elizabethan age and the delight in significant metaphor its original readers found so satisfying.

NOTES

1. Peter Burke, Popular Culture in Early Modern Europe, p. 259.

2. Robert Weimann, Structure and Society in Literary History: Studies in the History and Theory of Historical Criticism (London, 1977), p. 230.

BIBLIOGRAPHY

For convenience I have divided the bibliography into
two sections:

I -- full titles of works of Elizabethan fiction (or
translations of fiction) and of other works
treated as fiction in the text, and some verse
works by primarily fiction writers. When the
edition used has not been the original, it has
been indicated beneath the date of the
original. Where a modern edition has been used
the title has been corrected from an earlier or
the original edition whenever possible.
Punctuation and capitalisation in titles have
been reproduced but distinctions of type face
have been ignored. To facilitate reading long
titles, I have not followed in this section the
customary practice of underlining them.

II -- non-fiction works cited in the text and a
selection of critical, social and other works
found useful in its preparation.

I

Breton, Nicholas. The Miseries of Mauillia. The
     most unfortunate Ladie, that ever lived.
     1599.
     The Works in Verse and Prose of Nicholas
     Breton. Ed. Alexander B. Grosart. Blackburn,
     Lancs., 1879. Vol. II.

_____. The Strange Fortvnes of Two Excellent
     Princes: In Their liues and loues, to their
     equall Ladies in all the titles of true honour.
     1600.

C., W. The Aduentures of Ladie Egeria. Containing
     her miserable bannishment by Duke Lampanus her
     husbande, through the inducement of Ladie
     Eldorna the harlot, and Lord Andromus the
     Flatterer: who for his periurie and false
     insinuation, was by a wonderfull iudgement
     vtterly subuerted and deuoured. The Combat
     fought by Lord Trauenna, (with Necto the Slaue
     insteade of Andromus the Flatterer) obtayning
     the victorie, was afterwardes Bannished. The
     graue Letters, wise and sentencious Orations,
     of the Counsaile, Iudges and others. The
     bannishment of the Dukes two children. Lastly,
     the Duke himselfe bannished, by Pasifer the
     Flatterer, and Eldorna the harlot: the bloudy
     murther of Eldorna, by her owne bastarde sonne
     Rastophel, who through their meanes vsurped the
     gouernement: with a wonderfull description of
     other Flatterers, and insolent persons: with
     many other memorable accidents; contayning
     wisedome, discretion and pollicie; no lesse
     renowmed then profitable.
     1585?

Chettle, Henry. Kind-Harts Dreame. Conteining fiue
     Apparitions, with their Inuectiues against
     abuses raigning. Deliuered by seuerall Ghosts
     vnto him to be publisht, after Piers Penilesse
     Post had refused the carriage.
     1592.

_____. Piers Plainnes seauen yeres Prentiship.
     1595.

BIBLIOGRAPHY

The Cobler of Caunterburie, Or An Inuectiue against
    Tarltons Newes out of Purgatorie. A merrier
    Iest then a Clownes Iigge, and fitter for
    Gentlemens humors.
    1590.

Deloney, Thomas. The Pleasant History of Iohn
    Winchcomb, in his younger yeares called Iack of
    Newberie, the famous and worthy Clothier of
    England: declaring his life and loue, together
    with his charitable deeds and great
    hospitality: And how hee set continually fiue
    hundred poore people at worke, to the great
    benefit of the Common-wealth: worthy to be read
    and regarded.
    1597? (Title from 1619 ed.)
    The Novels of Thomas Deloney. Ed. Merritt E.
    Lawlis.
    Bloomington, Indiana, 1961.

_____. The Gentle Craft. A Discovrse Containing
    Many Matters of Delight, Very pleasant to be
    read: shewing what famous men haue beene
    Shoomakers in time past in this Land, with
    their worthy deeds and great Hospitality.
    Declaring The Cavse Why it is called the Gentle
    Craft: and also how the Prouerbe first grew; A
    Shoomakers sonne is a Prince borne.
    1597? (Title from 1627 ed.)
    Lawlis ed.

_____. The Gentile Craft. The second Part. Being
    a most merrie and pleasant Historie, not
    altogether vnprofitable nor any way hurtfull:
    verie fit to passe away the tediousnesse of the
    long winter evenings.
    1598? (Title from 1639 ed.)
    Lawlis ed.

_____. Thomas of Reading. Or, The sixe worthy
    yeomen of the West.
    1600? (Title from 1612 ed.)
    Lawlis ed.

Dickenson, John. Arisbas, Euphues amidst his
    slumbers: Or Cupids Iourney to Hell.
    Decyphering A Myrror of Constancie, a
    Touch-stone of tried affection, begun in chaste
    desires, ended in choise delights: And

emblasoning Beauties glorie, adorned by Natures
bountie. With the Trivmph of Trve Loue, in the
foyle of false Fortune.
1594.

_____. The Shepheardes Complajnt. A passionate
Eclogue, written in English Hexameters:
Wherevnto are annexed other conceits, brieflie
expressing the effects of Loues impressions,
and the iust punishment of aspiring beautie.
1596.
Prose and Verse by John Dickenson.   Ed.
Alexander B. Grosart.
Blackburn, Lancs. 1878.

_____. Greene in Conceipt. New raised from his
graue to write the Tragique Historie of faire
Valeria of London. Wherein is Trvly Discovered
the rare and lamentable issue of a Husbands
dotage, a wiues leudnesse, & childrens
disobedience.
1598.
Grosart ed.

Fenton, Geoffrey. Certaine Tragicall Discourses
written oute of Frenche and Latin, by Geffraie
Fenton, no lesse profitable then pleasaunt, and
of like necessitye to al degrees that take
pleasure in antiquityes or forreine reapportes.
1567.

Forde, Emanuel. The Most Pleasant History of
Ornatvs and Artesia. Wherein is contayned the
vniust Raigne of Thaeon King of Phrygia. Who
with his Sonne Lenon intending Ornatvs his
Death, right Heyre to the Crowne, was
afterwards slaine by his owne Servants; and
Ornatvs, after many extreame miseries Crowned
King.
1595?
1634 ed.

_____. Parismus, The Renovmed Prince of Bohemia.
His most famous, delectable, and pleasant
Historie. Conteining His Noble Battailes
fought against the Persians. His loue to
Laurana, the Kings Daughter of Thessaly. And
his straunge Aduentures in the Desolate Iland.
With the miseries and miserable imprisonment,
Laurana endured in the Iland of Rockes. And a

description of the Chiualrie of the Phrygian
Knight, Pollipus: and his constant loue to
Violetta.
1598.

_____. Parismenos: The Second Part of the most
famous, delectable, and pleasant Historie of
Parismus, the renowned Prince of Bohemia. The
aduenturous trauels and Noble Chiualrie of
Parismenos, the Knight of Fame, in diuers
countries.
1599.

_____. The Famous History of Montelion Knight of
the Oracle. Son to the true Mirrour of
Princes, the most Renowned King Persicles of
Assyria. Shewing His strange Birth,
Unfortunate Love, Perilous Adventures in Armes;
And how he came to the Knowledge of his
Parents. Interlaced with much variety of
pleasant and delightful Discourse.
? soon after Parismenos?
1633 ed.

Gascoigne, George. A discourse of the aduentures
passed by Master F. I.
in A Hundreth sundrie Flowres bounde vp in one
small Poesie. Gathered partely (by
translation) in the fyne outlandish Gardins of
Euripides, Ouid, Petrarke, Ariosto, and others:
and partly by inuention, out of our owne
fruitefull Orchardes in Englande: Yelding
sundrie sweete sauours of Tragical, Comical,
and Morall Discourses, bothe pleasaunt and
profitable to the well smellyng noses of
learned Readers.
1573.
George Gascoigne's A Hundreth Sundrie Flowres.
Ed. C. T. Prouty.
Columbia, Missouri, 1942.

Gosson, Stephen. The Ephemerides of Phialo, deuided
into three Bookes. The first, a method which
he ought to follow that desireth to rebuke his
friend, when he seeth him swarue: without
kindling his choler, or hurting himselfe. The
second, A Canuazado to Courtiers in foure
pointes. The third, The defence of a Curtezan
ouerthrowen. And a short Apologie of the

Schoole of Abuse, against Poets, Pipers,
Players, & their Excusers.
1579.

Grange, John. The Golden Aphroditis: A pleasant
    discourse, penned by Iohn Grange Gentleman,
    Student in the Common Lawe of Englande.
    Wherevnto be annexed by the same Authour aswell
    certayne Metres vpon sundry poyntes, as also
    diuers Pamphlets in prose, which he entituleth
    His Garden: pleasant to the eare, and
    delightful to the Reader, if he abuse not the
    scente of the floures.
    1577.

Greene, Robert. Mamillia: A Mirrour or
    Looking-glasse for the Ladies of Englande.
    Wherein is deciphered, howe Gentlemen vnder the
    perfect substaunce of pure loue, are oft
    inueigled with the shadowe of lewde luste: and
    their firme faith, brought asleepe by fading
    fancie: vntil wit ioyned with wisdome, doth
    awake it by the helpe of reason.
    1580? (Title from 1583 ed.)
    The Life and Complete Works in Prose and Verse
    of Robert Greene, M.A. Ed. Alexander B.
    Grosart. Blackburn, Lancs., 1881-86. Vol. II.

_____. Mamillia: The second part of the triumph of
    Pallas: Wherein with perpetval fame the
    constancie of Gentlewomen is canonised, and the
    vniust blasphemies of womens supposed
    ficklenesse (breathed out by diuerse iniurious
    persons) by manifest examples clearely
    infringed.
    1583. (Title from 1593 ed.)
    Grosart ed. Vol. II.

_____. The Myrrovr of Modestie, wherein appeareth
    as in a perfect Glasse howe the Lorde
    deliuereth the innocent from all imminent
    perils, and plagueth the bloudthirstie
    hypocrites with deserued punishments. Shewing
    that the graie heades of dooting adulterers
    shall not go with peace into the graue, neither
    shall the righteous be forsaken in the daie of
    trouble.
    1584.
    Grosart ed. Vol. III.

_____. Gwydonivs. The Carde of Fancie Wherein the Folly of those Carpet Knights is decyphered, which guyding their course by the compasse of Cupid, either dash their ship against most daungerous Rocks, or els attaine the hauen with paine and perill. Wherein also is described in the person of Gwydonius, a cruell Combat betweene Nature and necessitie.
1584.
Grosart ed. Vol. IV.

_____. Arbasto, The Anatomie of Fortune. Wherin is discouered by a pithie and pleasant Discourse, that the highest state of prosperitie, is oftimes the first step to mishap, and that to stay vpon Fortunes lotte, is to treade on brittle Glasse. Wherin also Gentlemen may finde pleasaunte conceytes to purge Melancholy, and perfite counsell to preuent misfortune.
1584.
Grosart ed. Vol. III.

_____. Planetomachia: Or the first parte of the generall opposition of the seuen Planets: wherein is Astronomically described their essence, nature, and influence. Diuersly discouering in their pleasaunt and Tragicall histories, the inward affections of the mindes, and painting them out in such perfect Colours, as youth may perceiue what fond fancies their florishing yeares doe foster: and age clerely see what doting desires their withered heares doe affoorde. Conteyning also a briefe Apologie of the sacred and misticall Science of Astronomie:
1585.
Grosart ed. Vol. V.
Jupiter's tale from Robert Greene's Planetomachia and the text of the third tragedy, ed. D. F. Bratchell (Amersham, 1979).

_____. Morando The Tritameron of Loue: The first and second part. Wherein certaine pleasant conceites, vttered by diuers worthie personages, are perfectly discoursed, and three doubtfull questions of Loue, most pithely and pleasantly discussed: shewing to the wise how to vse Loue, and to the fond, how to eschew Lust: and yeelding to all both pleasure and profit.

1587 (first part, 1584)
Grosart ed., Vol. III.

_____. Penelopes Web: Wherein a Christall Myrror of faeminine perfection represents to the viewe of euery one those vertues and graces, which more curiously beautifies the mynd of women, then eyther sumptuous Apparell, or Iewels of inestimable valew: the one buying fame with honour, the other breeding a kynd of delight, but with repentance. In three seuerall discourses also are three especiall vertues, necessary to be incident in euery vertuous woman, pithely discussed: namely Obedience, Chastitie, and Sylence: Interlaced with three seuerall and Comicall Histories.
1587.
Grosart ed. Vol. V.

_____. Euphues his censure to Philautus, Wherein is presented a philosophicall combat betweene Hector and Achylles, discouering in foure discourses, interlaced with diuerse delightfull Tragedies, The vertues necessary to be incident in euery gentleman: had in question at the siege of Troy betwixt sondry Grecian and Troian Lords: especially debated to discouer the perfection of a souldier. Containing mirth to purge melancholy, holsome precepts to profit maners, neither vnsauerie to youth for delight, nor offensiue to age for scurrilitie.
1587.
Grosart ed. Vol. VI.

_____. Pandosto. The Triumph of Time. Wherein is Discouered by a pleasant Historie, that although by the meanes of sinister fortune Truth may be concealed, yet by Time in spight of fortune it is most manifestly reuealed. Pleasant for age to auoyde drowsie thoughtes, profitable for youth to eschue other wanton pastimes, and bringing to both a desired content.
1588.
Grosart ed. Vol. IV.

_____. Perimedes The Blacke-Smith, A golden methode, how to vse the minde in pleasant and profitable exercise: Wherein is contained speciall principles fit for the highest to imitate, and the meanest to .put in practise,

how best to spend the wearie winters nights, or
the longest summers Euenings, in honest and
delightfull recreation: Wherein we may learne
to auoide idlenesse and wanton scurrilitie,
which diuers appoint as the end of their
pastimes. Heerein are interlaced three merrie
and necessarie discourses fit for our time:
with certaine pleasant Histories and tragicall
tales, which may breed delight to all, and
offence to none.
1588.
Grosart ed. Vol. VII.

_____. Alcida Greenes Metamorphosis, Wherein is
discouered, a pleasant transformation of bodies
into sundrie shapes, shewing that as vertues
beautifie the mind, so vanities giue greater
staines, than the perfection of any quality can
rase out: The Discourse confirmed with diuerse
merry and delightfull Histories; full of graue
Principles to content Age, and sawsed with
pleasant parlees, and witty answeres, to
satisfie youth: profitable for both, and not
offensiue to any.
1588. (Title from 1617 ed.)
Grosart ed. Vol. IX.

_____. Ciceronis Amor. Tullies Loue. Wherein is
discoursed the prime of Ciceroes youth, setting
out in liuely portratures how young Gentlemen
that ayme at honour should leuell the end of
their affections, holding the loue of countrie
and friends in more esteeme then those fading
blossomes of beautie, that onely feede the
curious suruey of the eye. A worke full of
pleasure as following Ciceroes vaine, who was
as conceipted in his youth as graue in his age,
profitable as conteining precepts worthie so
famous an Orator.
1589.
Grosart ed. Vol. VII.

_____. Menaphon Camillas Alarum to slumbering
Euphues, in his melancholie Cell at Silexedra.
Wherein are deciphered the variable effects of
Fortune, the wonders of Loue, the triumphes of
inconstant Time. Displaying in sundrie
conceipted passions (figured in a continuate
Historie) the Trophees that Vertue carrieth
triumphant, maugre the wrath of Enuie, or the
resolution of Fortune. A worke worthie the

youngest eares for pleasure, or the grauest
censures for principles.
1589.
Grosart ed. Vol. VI.

_____. The Spanish Masquerado. Wherein vnder a
pleasant deuise, is discouered effectuallie, in
certaine breefe sentences and Mottos, the pride
and insolencie of the Spanish estate: with the
disgrace conceiued by their losse, and the
dismaied confusion of their troubled thoughtes.
Whereunto by the Author, for the better
vnderstanding of his deuice, is added a breefe
glosse.
1589.
Grosart ed. Vol. V.

_____. Greenes Orpharion. Wherin is discouered a
musicalll concorde of pleasant Histories, many
sweet moodes graced with such harmoniuous
discords, as agreeing in a delightfull closse,
they sound both pleasure and profit to the
eare. Heerein also as in a Diateheron, the
branches of Vertue, ascending and descending by
degrees: are covnited in the glorious praise of
women-kind. With Diuers Tragicall and Comicall
Histories presented by Orpheus and Arion,
beeing as full of profit as of pleasure.
1590. (Title from 1599 ed.)
Grosart ed. Vol. XII.

_____. Greenes Neuer too late. Or, A Powder of
Experience: Sent to all youthfull Gentlemen: to
roote out the infectious follies, that
ouer-reaching conceits foster in the spring
time of their youth. Decyphering in a true
English historie, those particular vanities,
that with their frostie vapours nip the
blossoms of euerie ripe braine, from atteining
to his intended perfection. As pleasant, as
profitable, being a right pumice stone, apt to
race out idlenesse with delight, and follie
with admonition.
1590.
Grosart ed. Vol. VIII.

_____. Francescos Fortunes: Or, The second part of
Greenes Neuer too late. Wherein is discoursed
the fall of Loue, the bitter fruites of Follies

pleasure, and the repentant sorowes of a
reformed man.
1590.
Grosart ed. Vol. VIII.

_____. The Royal Exchange. Contayning sundry
Aphorismes of Phylosophie, and golden
principles of Morrall and naturall
Quadruplicities. Vnder pleasant and effectuall
sentences, dyscouering such strange
definitions, decisions, and distinctions of
vertue and vice, as may please the grauest
Cittizens, or the youngest Courtiers. Fyrst
written in Italian and dedicated to the
Signorie of Venice, noew translated into
English, and offered to the Cittie of London.
1590.
Grosart ed. Vol. IX.

_____. Greenes Mourning Garment: Given Him By
Repentance at the Funerals of Love; Which he
presents for a fauour to all young Gentlemen,
that wish to weane themselues from wanton
desires. Both Pleasant and Profitable.
1590. (Title from 1616 ed.)
Grosart ed. Vol. IX.

_____. Greenes farewell to Folly: Sent to Covrtiers
and Schollers as a president to warne them from
the vaine delights that drawes youth on to
repentance.
1591.
Grosart ed. Vol. IX.

_____. A Notable Discouery of Coosnage Now daily
practised by sundry lewd persons, called
Connie-catchers, and Crosse-biters. Plainely
laying open those pernitious sleights that hath
brought many ignorant men to confusion.
Written for the general benefit of all
Gentlemen, Citizens, Aprentises, Countrey
Farmers and yeomen, that may hap to fall into
the company of such coosening companions. With
a delightfull discourse on the coosnage of
Colliers.
1591.
Grosart ed. Vol. X.

_____. The Second part of conny-catching.
Contayning the discouery of certaine wondrous
Coosenages, either superficiallie past ouer, or

vtterlie vntoucht in the first. As the nature
of The blacke Art, Picking of lockes, The
Vincents Law, Coosenage at Bowls. The Prigging
Law, Horse stealing. The Courbing Law, Hooking
at windows. The Lifting Law, Stealing of
parcels. The Foist, The Picke picket. The
Nippe, The cut purse. With sundrie pithy and
pleasant Tales worthy the reading of all
estates, that are ennemies to such base and
dishonest practises.
1591.
Grosart ed. Vol. X.

_____. The Thirde and last Part of Conny-Catching.
With the New Devised knauish Art of
Foole-taking. The like Cosenages and Villenies
neuer before discouered.
1592.
Grosart ed. Vol. X.

_____. A Dispvtation Betweene a Hee Conny-catcher,
and a Shee Conny-catcher, whether a Theefe or a
Whoore, is most hurtfull in Cousonage, to the
Common-wealth Discovering the Secret Villanies
of alluring Strumpets. With the Conuersion of
an English Courtizen, reformed this present
yeare. 1592.
1592.
Grosart ed. Vol. X.

_____. The Blacke Bookes Messenger. Laying open
the Life and Death of Ned Browne one of the
most notable Cutpurses, Crosbiters, and
Conny-catchers, that euer lived in England.
Heerein hee telleth verie pleasantly, in his
own person such strange prancks and monstrous
villanies by him and his Consorte performed, as
the like was yet neuer heard of in any of the
former bookes of Conny-catching.
1592.
Grosart ed. Vol. XI.

_____. The Defence of Conny catching. Or A
Confvtation of those two iniurious Pamphlets
published by R. G. against the practitioners of
many Nimble-witted and mysticall Sciences.
By Cuthbert Cunny-catcher, Licentiate in
Whittington Colledge.
1592.
Grosart ed. Vol. XI.

_____. Greenes Vision: Written at the instant of
his death. Conteyning a penitent passion for
the folly of his Pen.
1592.
Grosart ed. Vol. XII.

_____. Philomela. The Lady Fitzwaters Nightingale.
1592.
Grosart ed. Vol. XI.

_____. A Qvip for an Vpstart Courtier: Or, A quaint
dispute between Veluet breeches and
Cloth-breeches. Wherein is plainely set downe
the disorders in all Estates and Trades.
1592.
Grosart ed. Vol. XI.

_____. Greenes, Groats-worth of witte, bought with
a million of Repentance. Describing the follie
of youth, the falshood of makeshifte
flatterers, the miserie of the negligent, and
mischiefes of deceiuing Courtezans. Written
before his death and published at his dyeing
request.
1592.
Grosart ed. Vol. XII.

_____. The Repentance of Robert Greene Maister of
Artes. Wherein by himselfe is laid open his
loose life, with the manner of his death.
1592.
Grosart ed. Vol. XII.

Harington, John. A New Discovrse of a Stale
Svbiect, called the Metamorphosis of Aiax.
Written by Misacmos to his friend and cosin
Philostilpnos.
1596.

Johnson, Richard. The nine Worthies of London
Explayning the honourable exercise of Armes,
the vertues of the valiant, and the memorable
attempts of magnanimious minds. Pleasant for
Gentlemen, not vnseemely for Magistrates, and
most profitable for Prentises.
1592.

_____. The Most Famovs History of the seuen
Champions of Christendome: Saint George of
England, Saint Denis of Fraunce, Saint Iames of
Spayne, Saint Anthony of Italie, Saint Andrew

of Scotland, Saint Patricke of Ireland, and
Saint Dauid of Wales; Shewing their Honorable
battailes by Sea and Land: their Tilts, Iousts
and Turnaments for Ladies: their Combats with
Giants, Monsters, and Dragons: their aduentures
in forraine Nations: their inchauntments in the
holy Land: their Knighthoods, Prowesse and
Chiualtry, in Europe, Affrica, and Asia, with
their victories against the enemies of Christ.
1596.
1608 ed.

_____. The second Part of the famous History of the
seauen Champions of Christendome. Likewise
shewing the Princely prowesse of Saint Georges
three Sonnes, the liuely Sparke of Nobilitie.
With many other memoriall atchiuements worthy
the golden spurres of Knighthood.
1597.

_____. The Most Pleasant History of Tom A Lincoln
That Ever Renowned Souldier The Red-Rose Knight
Who for his Valour and Chivalry, was Sirnamed
the Boast of England. Shewing his Honourable
Victories in Forrain Countries, with his
strange Fortunes in the Fayrie-Land: and how he
married the Faire Anglitora, Daughter to
Prester John, that renowned Monark of the
World. Together with the Lives and Deaths of
his two famous Sons, the Black Knight, and the
Fairy Knight, with divers other memorable
accidents, full of delight.
1599.
1655 ed.

_____. The Pleasant Conceites of Old Hobson the
merry Londoner, full of humorous discourses,
and witty meriments. Whereat the quickest
wittes may laugh, and the Wiser sort take
pleasure.
1607.

The Life and Pranks of Long Meg of Westminster.
1590?
Mid-seventeenth-century ed., sophisticated to
appear 1582.

Lodge, Thomas. [A Reply to Stephen Gosson's Schoole
of Abuse In Defence of Poetry Musick and Stage
Plays]
1580?

The Complete Works of Thomas Lodge. Ed. Edmund
W. Gosse.
Glasgow, 1883. 4 volumes. Vol. I.

_____. An Alarum against Vsurers. Containing tryed
experiences against worldly abuses. Wherein
Gentlemen may finde good counselles to confirme
them, and pleasant Histories to delight them:
and euery thing so interlaced with varietie: as
the curious may be satisfied with rarenesse,
and the curteous with pleasure. Heerevnto are
annexed the delectable historie of Forbonius
and Prisceria: with the lamentable Complaint of
Truth ouer England.
1584.
Hunterian ed. Vol. I.

_____. Rosalynde. Euphues golden Legacie, found
after his death in his Cell at Silexedra.
Beqveathed to Philavtvs Sonnes noursed vp with
their Father in England.
1590.
1592 ed.

_____. Catharos Diogenes in his Singularitie.
wherein is comprehended his merrie baighting
fit for all mens benefits: Christened by him, A
Nettle for Nice Noses.
1591.
Hunterian ed. Vol. II.

_____. The Famous, true and historicall life of
Robert second Duke of Normandy, surnamed for
his monstrous birth and behauiour, Robin the
Diuell. Wherein is contained his dissolute
life in his youth, his deuout reconcilement and
vertues in his age: Interlaced with many
straunge and miraculous aduentures. Wherein
are both causes of profite, and manie conceits
of pleasure.
1591.
Hunterian ed. Vol. II.

_____. Evphves Shadow, The Battaile of the Sences.
Wherein youthfull folly is set downe in his
right figure, and vaine fancies are prooued to
produce many offences. Hereunto is annexed the
Deafe mans Dialogue, contaying Philamis
Athanatos: fit for all sortes to peruse, and
the better sorte to practise.

1592.
Hunterian ed.   Vol. II.

_____.   The Life and Death of william Long beard,
the most famous and witty English Traitor,
borne in the Citty of London.   Accompanied with
manye other most pleasant and prettie
histories.
1593.
Hunterian ed.   Vol II.

_____.   A fig for Momus: Containing Pleasant
varietie, included in Satyres, Eclogues, and
Epistles.
1595.
Hunterian ed.   Vol. III.

_____.   A Margarite of America.
1596.
Hunterian ed.   Vol. III

_____.   The Divel coniured.
1596.
Hunterian ed.   Vol. III.

_____.   Wits Miserie, and the Worlds Madnesse:
Discouering the Deuils Incarnat of this Age.
1596.
Hunterian ed.   Vol. IV.

_____.   Prosopopeia Containing The Teares Of The
holy, blessed, and sanctified Marie, the Mother
of God.
1596.
Hunterian ed.   Vol. III.
Lyly, John.   Evphves.   The Anatomy of Wyt.   Very
pleasant for all Gentlemen to reade, and most
necessary to remember: wherin are contained the
delights that Wyt followeth in his youth by the
pleasauntnesse of Loue, and the happynesse he
reapeth in age, by the perfectnesse of
Wisedome.
1578.
The Complete Works of John Lyly.   Ed. R.
Warwick Bond.
Oxford, 1902.   3 volumes.   Vol. I.

_____.   Euphues and his England.   Containing his
voyage and aduentures, myxed with sundry pretie
discourses of honest Loue, the discription of
the countrey, the Court, and the manners of

that Isle. Delightfvl to be read, and nothing
hurtfull to be regarded: wher-in there is small
offence by lightnesse giuen to the wise, and
lesse occasion of loosenes proffered to the
wanton.
1580.
Bond ed. Vol. II.

M., C. The first part of the nature of a Woman.
Fitly described in a Florentine Historie
composed by C. M.
1596.

_____. The Second Part of The Historie, Called The
Natvre of A Woman: Contayning the end of the
strife betwixt Perseus and Theseus.
1596.

Melbancke, Brian. Philotimus. The Warre betwixt
Nature and Fortune.
1583.

Middleton, Christopher. The Famous Historie of
Chinon of England, with his strange aduentures
for the loue of Celestina daughter to Lewis
King of Fraunce. With the worthy Atchiuement
of Sir Lancelot du Lake, and Sir Tristram du
Lions for faire Laura, daughter to Cador Earle
of Cornewall, beeing all Knights of King
Arthurs round Table.
1597.

Munday, Anthony. Zelavto. The Fovntaine of Fame.
Erected in an Orcharde of Amorous Aduentures.
Containing A Delicate Disputation, gallantly
discoursed betweene two noble Gentlemen of
Italye. Giuen for a freendly entertainment to
Euphues, at his late ariuall into England.
1580.
Zelauto, The Fountaine of Fame. Ed. Jack
Stillinger. Carbondale, Illinois, 1963.

Nashe, Thomas. The Anatomie of Absurditie:
Contayning a breefe confutation of the slender
imputed prayses to feminine perfection, with a
short description of the seuerall practises of
youth, and sundry follies of our licentious
times. No lesse pleasant to be read, then
profitable to be remembred, espécially of
those, who liue more licentiously, or addicted
to a more nyce stoycall austeritie.

1589.
The Works of Thomas Nashe. Ed. Ronald B.
McKerrow. 1904-10. Reprinted with corrections
and supplementary notes ed. F. P. Wilson.
Oxford, 1966. 5 volumes. Vol. I

_____. Pierce Penilesse his Supplication to the
Diuell. Describing the ouer-spreading of Vice,
and suppression of Vertue. Pleasantly
interlac'd with variable delights: and
pathetically intermixt with conceipted
reproofes.
1592.
McKerrow ed. Vol. I.

_____. Strange Newes, Of the intercepting certaine
Letters, and a Conuoy of Verses, as they were
going Priuilie to victuall the Low Countries.
1592.
McKerrow ed. Vol. I.

_____. Christs Teares Over Ierusalem. Wherunto is
annexed, a comparatiue admonition to London.
1593.
McKerrow ed. Vol. II.

_____. The Terrors of the night Or, A Discourse of
Apparitions.
1594.
McKerrow ed. Vol. I.

_____. The Vnfortvnate Traveller. Or, The life of
Iacke Wilton.
1594.
McKerrow ed. Vol. II.

_____. Haue with you to Saffron-walden. Or,
Gabriell Harueys Hunt is vp. Containing a full
Answere to the eldest sonne of the
Halter-maker. Or, Nashe his Confutation of the
sinfull Doctor.
1596.
McKerrow ed. Vol. III.

_____. Nashes Lenten Stuffe, Containing, The
Description and first Procreation and Increase
of the towne of Great Yarmouth in Norffolke:
With a new Play neuer played before, of the
praise of the Red Herring. Fitte of all
Clearkes of Noblemens Kitchins to be read: and

not vnnecessary by all Seruing men that haue
short boord-wages, to be remembred.
1599.
McKerrow ed. Vol. III.

Painter, William. The Palace of Pleasure
Beautified, adorned and well furnished, with
Pleasaunt Histories and excellent Nouelles,
selected out of diuers good and commendable
Authors.
1566.
The Palace pof Pleasure. Ed. Joseph Jacobs.
London, 1890. 3 volumes. Vols. I and II.

_____. The second Tome of the Palace of Pleasure,
conteyning store of goodly Histories, Tragicall
matters, and other Morall arguments, a very
requisite for delighte and profit. Chosen or
selected out of diuers good and commendable
Authors.
1567.
Jacobs ed. Vols. II and III.

Parry, Robert. [Moderatus, or The Adventures of the
Black Knight].
1595.

Pettie, George. A petite Pallace of Pettie his
pleasure: Contaynyng many pretie Hystories by
him set foorth in comely colours, and most
delightfully discoursed.
1576.
A Petite Pallace of Pettie His Pleasure. Ed.
Herbert Hartman. London, 1938.

Rich, Barnaby. Riche his Farewell to Militarie
profession: conteinyng verie pleasaunt
discourses fit for a peaceable tyme: Gathered
together for the onely delight of the courteous
Gentlewomen, bothe of Englande and Irelande,
for whose onely pleasure thei were collected
together, And vnto whom thei are directed and
dedicated by Barnabe Riche Gentleman.
1581.
Rich's Farewell to Military Profession 1581.
Ed. Thomas Mabry Cranfill. Austin, Texas,
1959.

_____. The straunge and wonderfull aduentures of
Do[n] Simonides, a gentilman Spaniarde:
Conteinyng verie pleasaunte discourse: Gathered

for the recreation aswell of our noble yong
gentilmen, as our honourable courtly Ladies.

_____. The Second Tome of the Trauailes and
aduentures of Don Simonides, enterlaced with
varietie of Historie, wherein the curteous and
not curious Reader, maie finde matters so
leueled, as maie suffice to please all humours.
For malancholie men, they shall not neede to
saile to Anticera, for here they shall finde
pleasaunt expulsiues. For merrie myndes, sober
discourses to preuent excesse. For deuoute,
wholesome lessons to confirme their
contemplatio[n]. For al sortes, such delightes
as neither alow of daliaunce, nor discommende
honest pleasure.
1584.

_____. R[ich?]., B[arnaby?]. Greenes Newes both
from Heauen and Hell.
1593.
Reprinted from 1593 ed. Ed. R. B. McKerrow.
London, 1911.

Robarts, Henry. A Defiance to Fortune. Proclaimed
by Andrugio, noble Duke of Saxony, declaring
his miseries, and continually crossed with
vnconstant Fortune, the banishment of himselfe,
his wife and children. Whereunto is adioyned
the honorable Warres of Galastino, Duke of
Millaine in reuenge of his wrongs vpon the
trayterous Saxons. Wherin is noted a myrrour
of noble patience, a most rare example of
modest chastity, and the perfect patterne of
true friendship. Verie delectable and ful of
varietie.
1590.

_____. Pheander, The Mayden Knight; Describing His
Honovrable Trauailes and hautie attempts in
Armes, with his successe in loue. Enterlaced
with many pleasant discourses, wherein the
grauer may take delight, and the valiant
youthfull, be encouraged by honourable and
worthie aduenturing, to gaine Fame.
1595.

_____. Honovrs Conquest. Wherin is conteined the
famous Hystorie of Edward of Lancaster:
recounting his honourable trauailes to
Ierusalem, his hardie aduentures and honours,

in sundrie Countries gained: his resolutions
and attempts in Armes. With the famous
victories performed by the knight, of the
vnconquered Castel, a gallant English Knight,
his admirable forces, and sundrie conquests
obtained, with his passions and successe in
loue: full of pleasant discourses, and much
varietie.
1598.

Saker, Austen. Narbonvs. The Laberynth of
Libertie. Very pleasant for young Gentlemen to
peruse, and passing profitable for them to
prosecute. Wherein is contained the
discommodities that insue, by following the
lust of a mans will, in youth: and the
goodnesse he after gayneth, being beaten with
his owne rod, and pricked with the peeuishnesse
of his owne conscience, in age.
1580.

_____. Narbonvs. The seconde parte, of the Lust of
Libertie. Wherin is conteyned, the hap of
Narbonus, beeing a Souldioure: his returne out
of Spayne, and the successe of his loue
betweene him and Fidelia. And lastly, his life
at the Emperoures Court, with other actions
which happened to his freend Phemocles.
1580.

Sidney, Sir Philip. The Covntesse of Pembrokes
Arcadia.
1590.
The Prose Works of Sir Philip Sidney. Ed.
Albert Feuillerat.
1912; rpt. Cambridge, 1969. Vol. I.

The Countess of Pembroke's Arcadia: Being the
Original Version.
Ed. Feuillerat. 1926; rpt. Cambridge, 1967.
Vol. IV.

The Countess of Pembroke's Arcadia (The Old
Arcadia), ed., with introduction, Jean
Robertson. Oxford, 1973.

Tarltons newes out of Purgatorie. Onely such a iest
as his Iigge, fit for Gentlemen to laugh at an
houre, & c.
1590.

Warner, William. Pan his Syrinx, Or Pipe, Compact
    of seuen Reedes: including in one, seuen
    Tragical and Comicall Arguments, with their
    diuers Notes not impertinent: Whereby, in
    effect, of all thinges is touched, in few,
    something of the vayne, wanton, proud, and
    inconstant course of the World. Neither
    herein, to some-what praise-worthie, is prayse
    wanting.
    1584.

_____. The First and Second parts of Albions
    England. The former reuised and corrected, and
    the latter newly continued and added.
    Containing an Historicall Map of the same
    Island: prosecuted from the liues, Actes, and
    Labors, of Saturne, Iupiter, Hercules, and
    AEneas: Originalles of the Brutons, and
    Englishmen, and Occasion of the Brutons their
    first ariuall in Albion, Prosecuting the same
    Historie vnto the Tribute to the Romaines,
    Entrie of the Saxones, Inuasion by the Danes,
    Conquest by the Normaines, Restauration of the
    Royall English blood, Discention and vnion of
    the two Linages Lancaster and Yorke. With
    Historicalll Intermixtures, Inuention, and
    Varietie: profitably, briefly, and pleasantly
    performed in Verse and Prose by William Warner.
    1589.

Whetstone, George. The Rocke of Regard, diuided
    into foure parts. The first, the Castle of
    delight: Wherin is reported, the wretched end
    of wanton and dissolute liuing. The second,
    the Garden of Vnthriftinesse: Wherein are many
    sweet flowers, (or rather fancies) of honest
    loue. The thirde, the Arbour of Vertue:
    Wherein slaunder is highly punished, and
    vertuous Ladies and Gentlewomen, worthily
    commended. The fourth, the Ortchard of
    Repentance: Wherein are discoursed, the
    miseries that followe dicing, the mischiefes of
    quareling, the fall of prodigalitie: and the
    souden ouerthrowe of foure notable cousners,
    with diuers other morall, natural, & tragical
    discourses: documents and admonitions: being
    all the inuention, collection and translation
    of George Whetstons Gent.
    1576.

_____. An Heptameron of Ciuill Discourses.
Containing: The Christmasse Exercise of sundrie
well Courted Gentlemen and Gentlewomen. In
whose behauiours, the better sort, may see, a
represe[n]tation of their own Vertues: And the
Inferiour, may learne such Rules of Ciuil
Gouernme[n]t, as wil rase out the Blemish of
their basenesse: wherin, is Renowned, the
Vertues, of a most Honourable and braue mynded
Gentleman. And herein, also, (as it were in a
Mirrour) the Vnmaried may see the Defectes
whiche Eclipse the Glorie of Mariage: and the
wel Maried, as in a Table of Housholde Lawes,
may cull out needefull Preceptes to establysh
their good Fortune. A Worke, intercoursed with
Ciuyll Pleasure, to reaue tediousness from the
Reader: and garnished with Morall Noates to
make it profitable, to the Regarder.
1582.

Altman, Joel B. The Tudor Play of Mind: Rhetorical
     Inquiry and the Development of Elizabethan
     Drama. Berkeley, 1978.
Awdeley, John. The Fraternitye of Vacabondes. Ed.
     Edward Viles and F. J. Furnivall from the 1575
     edition. London, 1937.
Aydelotte, Frank. Elizabethan Rogues and Vagabonds.
     Oxford, 1913.
Baker, Ernest A., ed. The Countesse of Pembroke's
     Arcadia. London, 1907.
_____. The History of the English Novel. Vol. II:
     The Elizabethan Age and After. 1936; rpt. New
     York, 1963.
Barish, Jonas A. 'The Prose Style of John Lyly' in
     ELH, Vol. 23 (1956), pp. 14-35.
Bennett, H. S. English Books & Readers 1475 to
     1557: Being a Study in the History of the Book
     Trade from Caxton to the Incorporation of the
     Stationers' Company. 2nd ed.; Cambridge, 1969.
_____. English Books & Readers 1558 to 1603: Being
     a Study in the History of the Book Trade in the
     Reign of Elizabeth I. Cambridge, 1965.
Boas, Frederick S. Sir Philip Sidney:
     Representative Elizabethan: His Life and
     Writings. London, 1955.
Bratchell, D. F.. Robert Greene's Planetomachia and
     the text of the third tragedy: A
     bibliographical explanation and a new edition
     of the text. Amersham, 1979.
Burke, Peter. Popular Culture in Early Modern
     Europe. London, 1978.
Buxton, John. Elizabethan Taste. London, 1966.
_____. Sir Philip Sidney and the English
     Renaissance. 1954; rpt. London, 1964.
Byrne, Muriel St. Clare. The Elizabethan Home:
     Discovered in Two Dialogues by Claudius
     Hollyband and Peter Erondell. London, 1925.
Camp, Charles W. The Artisan in Elizabethan
     Literature. New York, 1923.
Caspari, Fritz. Humanism and the Social Order in
     Tudor England. Chicago, 1954.
Chevalley, Abel. Thomas Deloney: Le roman des
     metiers au temps de Shakespeare. Paris, 1926.

Cholakian, Patricia Francis and Rouben Charles
    Cholakian, eds. The Early French Novella.
    Albany, 1972.

Clark, Sandra. The Elizabethan Pamphleteers:
    Popular Moralistic Pamphlets 1580-1640.
    London, 1983.

Crane, Ronald S. The Vogue of Medieval Chivalric
    Romance During the English Renaissance.
    Menasha, Wisconsin, 1919.

Crane, William G. Wit and Rhetoric in the
    Renaissance: The Formal Basis of Elizabethan
    Prose Style. New York, 1937.

Croll, Morris William. 'The Sources of the
    Euphuistic Rhetoric', introduction to Euphues:
    The Anatomy of Wit and Euphues and His
    England. Ed. Morris William Cross and Harry
    Clemons. 1916; rpt. New York, 1964.

Dahl, Torsten. Linguistic Studies in Some
    Elizabethan Writings I: An Inquiry into Aspects
    of the Language of Thomas Deloney. Copenhagen,
    1951. Acta Jutlandica XXIII.

Danby, John F. Elizabethan and Jacobean Poets:
    Studies in Sidney, Shakespeare, Beaumont &
    Fletcher. First published as Poets on
    Fortune's Hill, 1952; rpt. London, 1964.

_____. Shakespeare's Doctrine of Nature: A Study of
    King Lear.
    1948; rpt. London, 1972.

Davis, Walter R. Idea and Act in Elizabethan
    Fiction. Princeton, 1969.

_____. A Map of Arcadia: Sidney's Romance in Its
    Tradition. New Haven, 1965. Yale Studies in
    English Vol. 158.

_____. 'Thematic Unity in the New Arcadia' in
    Studies in Philology, Vol. 57 (1960), pp.
    123-43.

Dent, Robert W. 'Greene's Gwydonius: A Study in
    Elizabethan Plagiarism' in The Huntington
    Library Quarterly, Vol. 24 (1960-61),
    pp. 151-162.

Dobb, Maurice. Studies in the Development of
    Capitalism. 1946; rpt. London, 1967.

Doran, Madeleine. 'On Elizabethan "Credulity": with
    some questions concerning the use of the
    marvelous in literature' in The Journal of the
    History of Ideas, Vol. I (1940), pp. 151-76.

Drummond, Sir Jack Cecil and Anne Wilbraham. The
    Englishman's Food: A History of Five Centuries
    of English Diet. Revised by Dorothy
    Hollingsworth. London, 1957.

Eisenstein, Elizabeth L.   The Printing Press as an
    Agent of Change: Communications and Cultural
    Transformations in Early-modern Europe.
    Cambridge, 1979.
Elyot, Sir Thomas. The Book named the Governor
    (1531). London, 1962.
Feuillerat, Albert. John Lyly: Contribution a
    l'histoire de la renaissance en Angleterre.
    Cambridge, 1910.
Gascoigne, George. The Whole woorkes of George
    Gascoigne Esquyre. London, 1587.
Gibbons, Brian. Jacobean City Comedy. 2nd ed.
    London, 1980.
Goldman, Marcus Selden. Sir Philip Sidney and the
    Arcadia. Urbana, Illinois, 1934.
Greene, Robert. The Plays and Poems of Robert
    Greene. Ed. J. Churton Collins. Oxford, 1905.
Greg, W. W. Some Aspects and Problems of London
    Publishing Between 1550 and 1650. Oxford,
    1956.
Greville, Fulke. Life of Sir Philip Sidney (1652).
    Ed. Nowell Smith. Oxford, 1907.
Hall, Hubert. Society in the Elizabethan Age.
    London, 1901.
Hanford, James Holly and Sara Ruth Watson.
    'Personal Allegory in the Arcadia: Philisides
    and Lelius' in Modern Philology, Vol. 32
    (1934), pp. 1-10.
Harbison, E. Harris. The Christian Scholar in the
    Age of the Reformation. New York, 1956.
Harman, Edward George. The Countesse of Pembrokes
    Arcadia. London, 1924.
Harman, Thomas. A Caueat or Warening, For Commen
    cvrsetors vulgarely called Vagabones. London,
    1567/8.
Harner, James L. English Renaissance Prose Fiction,
    1500-1660. London, 1978.
Harrison, William. An Historicall Description of
    the Islande of Britayne, with a briefe
    rehearsall of the nature and qualities of the
    people of Englande, and of all such commodities
    as are to be founde in the same in Raphael
    Holinshed's the Firste Volume of the Chronicles
    of England, Scotlande, and Irelande. London,
    1577 and 1587/8.
Haydn, Hiram. The Counter-Renaissance. New York,
    1950.
Hexter, J. H. Reappraisals in History. London,
    1961.
Hibbard, G. R. Thomas Nashe: A Critical
    Introduction. London, 1962.

Hill, Christopher. Reformation to Industrial
    Revolution. The Pelican Economic History of
    Britain, Vol. II: 1530-1780. Harmondsworth,
    1969.
Hook, Frank S., ed. The French Bandello: A
    Selection: The Original Text of Four of
    Belleforest's Histoires Tragiques translated by
    Geoffrey Fenton and William Painter 1567.
    Columbia, Missouri, 1948.
Hoskins, W. G. ' The Elizabethan Merchants of
    Exeter' in Elizabethan Government and Society:
    Essays Presented to Sir John Neale. Ed. S. T.
    Bindoff, J. Hurstfield, and C. H. Williams.
    London,, 1961.
Howarth, R. G. Two Elizabethan Writers of Fiction:
    Thomas Nashe and Thomas Deloney. Cape Town,
    1956.
Howell, Roger. Sir Philip Sidney: The Shepherd
    Knight. London, 1968.
Hunter, G. K. John Lyly: The Humanist as Courtier.
    London, 1962.
Hurstfield, Joel. 'The Historical and Social
    Background' in A New Companion to Shakespeare
    Studies. Ed. Kenneth Muir and S. Schoenbaum.
    Cambridge, 1971.
Jenkins, Harold. 'On the Authenticity of Greene's
    Groatsworth of Wit and The Repentance of Robert
    Greene in The Review of English Studies, Vol.
    11 (1935), pp. 28-41.
Jordan, John Clark. Robert Greene. New York, 1915.
Kelso, Ruth. The Doctrine of the English Gentleman
    in the Sixteenth Century. Urbana, Illinois,
    1929. University of Illinois Studies in
    Language and Literature, Vol XIV.
    _____. Doctrine for the Lady of the Renaissance.
    Urbana, Illinois. 1956.
Knight, G. Wilson. 'Lyly' in The Review of English
    Studies, Vol. 15 (1939), pp. 146-63.
Lanham, Richard A. The Old Arcadia. New Haven,
    1965. Yale Studies in English, Vol. 158.
Lawlis, Merritt E. Apology for the Middle Class:
    The Dramatic Novels of Thomas Deloney.
    Bloomington, Indiana, 1960.
Leavis, Queenie D. Fiction and the Reading Public.
    1932; rpt. London, 1965.
Lewis, C. S. English Literature in the Sixteenth
    Century excluding Drama. The Oxford History of
    English Literature, Vol. III. 1954; rpt.
    Oxford, 1968.
Lipson, Ephraim. The Economic History of England.
    Vol. I, The Middle Ages. 12th ed.; London,

1959. Vol. II, The Age of Mercantilism. 6th
ed.; London, 1956.

Maclean, Ian. The Renaissance Notion of Women: A
Study in the Fortunes of Scholasticism and
Medical Science in European Intellectual Life.
Cambridge, 1980.

Marx, Karl. The Eighteenth Brumaire of Louis
Bonaparte. Moscow, n.d.
_____. Pre-Capitalist Economic Formations. Ed.
with an introduction by Eric J. Hobsbawm.
Trans. Jack Cohen. New York, 1966.

McGinn, Donald J. 'Nashe's Share in the Marprelate
Controversy' in PMLA 59 (1944), pp. 952-84.

Miller, Edwin Haviland. The Professional Writer in
Elizabethan England: A Study of Nondramatic
Literature. Cambridge, Mass., 1959.

Muir, Kenneth. Sir Philip Sidney. Writers and
their work, no. 120. London, 1960.

Myrick, Kenneth Orne. Sir Philip Sidney as a
Literary Craftsman. Cambridge, Mass., 1935.

Neale, J. E. The Elizabethan Political Scene. The
Proceedings of the British Academy, Vol. XXXIV
(1948).
_____. Essays in Elizabethan History. London,
1958.

Nef, John U. The Conquest of the Material World:
Essays on the Coming of Industrialism.
Cleveland, 1967.

Nelson, William. 'From "Listen Lordings" to "Dear
Reader"' in University of Toronto Quarterly,
vol. 46, no. 2 (1976-77), pp. 111-24.

Nicholl, Charles. A Cup of News: The Life of Thomas
Nashe. London, 1984.

O'Dell, Sterg. A Chronological List of Prose
Fiction in English Printed in England and Other
Countries, 1475-1640. Cambridge, Mass., 1954.

Ong, Walter J. Orality and Literacy: The
Technologizing of the Word. London, 1982.

Paradise, N. Burton. Thomas Lodge: The History of
an Elizabethan. New Haven, 1931.

Plant, Marjorie. The English Book Trade: An
Economic History of the Making and Sale of
Books. 2nd ed.; London, 1965.

Pollard, A. F. The History of England from the
Accession of Edward VI to the Death of
Elizabeth (1547-1603). 1910; rpt. London,
1929.

Prouty, C. T. George Gascoigne's A Hundreth Sundrie
Flowres. Columbia, Missouri, 1942. University
of Missouri Studies, Vol. XVII.

Pruvost, Rene. <u>Matteo Bandello and Elizabethan Fiction</u>. Paris, 1937.

_____. <u>Robert Greene et ses romans -- 1558-1592: Contribution a l'histoire de la renaissance en Angleterre</u>. Paris, 1938.

Ramsey, Peter. <u>Tudor Economic Problems</u>. London. 1963.

Read, Conyers. <u>The Government of England under Elizabeth</u>. Washington, D. C., 1960.

_____. <u>Social and Political Forces in the English Reformation</u>. Houston, Texas, 1953.

Rhodes, Neil. <u>Elizabethan Grotesque</u>. London, 1980.

Ringler, William. 'The Immediate Source of Euphuism' in <u>PMLA</u>, Vol. 53 (1938), pp. 678-86.

_____. ed. with introduction, <u>The Poems of Sir Philip Sidney</u>. Oxford, 1962.

Rollins, Hyder E. 'Deloney's Sources for Euphuistic Learning' in <u>PMLA</u>, Vol. 51 (1936), pp. 399-406.

_____. 'Thomas Deloney's Euphuistic Learning and The Forest' in <u>PMLA</u>, Vol. 50 (1935), pp. 679-86.

Rosenberg, Eleanor. <u>Leicester, Patron of Letters</u>. New York, 1955.

Rowse, A. L. <u>The England of Elizabeth: The Structure of Society</u>. 1950; rpt. London, 1964.

Salingar, L. G. 'The Social Setting' in <u>The Age of Shakespeare. The Pelican Guide to English Literature</u>, Vol. II. Harmondsworth, 1964.

Saunders, J. W. <u>The Profession of English Letters</u>. London, 1964.

_____. 'The Stigma of Print. A Note on the Social Bases of Tudor Poetry' in <u>Essays in Criticism</u>, Vol. 1 (1951), pp. 139-64.

Schlauch, Margaret. <u>Antecedents of the English Novel 1400-1600 (from Chaucer to Deloney)</u>. Warsaw and London, 1963.

Schrickx, W. <u>Shakespeare's Early Contemporaries: The Background of the Harvey-Nashe Polemic and Love's Labour's Lost</u>. Antwerp, 1956.

Sheavyn, Phoebe. <u>The Literary Profession in the Elizabethan Age</u>. 2nd ed., revised by J. W. Saunders. Manchester, 1967.

Sidney, Philip. <u>A Defence of Poesie</u> in <u>Miscellaneous Prose of Sir Philip Sidney</u>, ed. Katherine Duncan-Jones and Jan van Dorsten. Oxford, 1973.

Siegel, Paul N. 'English Humanism and the New Tudor Aristocracy' in <u>The Journal of the History of Ideas</u>, Vol. 13 (1952), pp. 450-68.

_____. <u>Shakespearean Tragedy and the Elizabethan Compromise</u>. New York, 1957.

Sisson, Charles J., ed. Thomas Lodge and Other
    Elizabethans. 1933; rpt. London, 1966.
Spufford, Margaret. Small Books and Pleasant
    Histories: Popular Fiction and Its Readership
    in Seventeenth-Century England. London, 1981.
Stephenson, Henry Thew. The Elizabethan People.
    New York, 1910.
Stone, Lawrence. The Crisis of the Aristocracy:
    1558-1641. Oxford, 1965.
    _____. The Family, Sex and Marriage in England
    1500-1800. London, 1977.
Stow, John. A Survay of London. London, 1598. A
    Survey of the Cities of London and Westminster.
    Ed. John Strype. London, 1720.
Tawney, R. H. The Agrarian Problem in the Sixteenth
    Century. London, 1912.
    _____. Religion and the Rise of Capitalism. 1926;
    rpt. Harmondsworth, 1961.
    _____. Social History and Literature. London,
    1950.
Tayler, Edward William. Nature and Art in
    Renaissance Literature. New York, 1964.
Tenney, Edward Andrews. Thomas Lodge. Ithaca, New
    York, 1935.
Thomson, Patricia. 'The Literature of Patronage,
    1580-1630' in Essays in Criticism, Vol. 2
    (1952), pp. 267-84.
Tieje, Arthur Jerrold. The Theory of
    Characterization in Prose Fiction Prior to
    1740. Minneapolis, 1916.
Tillyard, E. M. W. The Elizabethan World Picture.
    London, 1943.
Unwin, George. The Gilds and Companies of London.
    London, 1908.
    _____. Industrial Organization in the Sixteenth and
    Seventeenth Centuries. Oxford, 1904.
    _____. Studies in Economic History: The Collected
    Papers of George Unwin. Ed. R. H. Tawney.
    London, 1927.
Vasari, Giorgio. The Lives of the Artists. Trans.
    George Bull. Harmondsworth, 1965.
Walker, Alice. 'The Life of Thomas Lodge' in The
    Review of English Studies: Part I, Vol. 9
    (1933), pp. 410-32; Part II, Vol. 10 (1934),
    pp. 46-54.
    _____. 'The Reading of an Elizabethan: Some Sources
    of the Prose Pamphlets of Thomas Lodge' in The
    Review of English Studies, Vol. 8 (1932),
    pp. 264-81.
Wallace, Malcolm William. The Life of Sir Philip
    Sidney. Cambridge, 1915.

Weimann, Robert. Structure and Society in Literary History: Studies in the History and Theory of Historical Criticism. London, 1977.

Wilson, F. P. Elizabethan and Jacobean. Oxford, 1945.

_____. The Plague in Shakespeare's London. Oxford, 1927.

Wilson, Mona. Sir Philip Sidney. London, 1931.

Wilson, Thomas. The Arte of Rhetorique, for the vse of all suche as are studious of Eloquence. London, 1553.

_____. A Discourse upon Usury by way of dialogue and orations, for the better variety and more delight of all those that shall read this treatise (1572). Ed. with an introduction by R. H. Tawney. 1925; rpt. London, 1962.

Wolff, Samuel Lee. The Greek Romances in Elizabethan Prose Fiction. 1912; rpt. New York, 1961.

_____. 'The Humanist as Man of Letters: John Lyly' in The Sewanee Review, Vol. 31 (1923), pp. 8-35.

_____. 'Robert Greene and the Italian Renaissance' in Englische Studien, Vol. 37 (1907), pp. 321-74.

Wright, Louis B. Middle-class Culture in Elizabethan England. Chapel Hill, 1935.

Zandvoort, R. W. Sidney's Arcadia: A Comparison Between the Two Versions. Amsterdam, 1929.

INDEX